THE FACE OF

O'Connor related ... approached the door and once again directed his attention to this seemingly innocuous older man with the blank stare and unassuming manner. This man could hardly be anyone's candidate for the role of a brutal slayer, not someone capable of committing the type of crime being described by O'Connor.

O'Connor spoke of the bloody scene at the Busacca home: blood on the walls, floor, and ceiling of the porch, blood in the trunk of the car, and even grislier evidence—things that Walker recoiled from, his eyes closed, trying to paint a picture in his mind of this gruesome scene.

"And," O'Connor went on, "he claims he left his wife ALIVE after all this was done . . ."

ROGER W. WALKER, a former Army Counter Intelligence Corpsman, was a Nassau County Police Detective for twenty years and was among the investigators of the Busacca murder case. The overwhelming evidence Mr. Walker helped gather in that case secured the first murder conviction without the *corpus delecti* in New York State—only the second in the U.S. Mr. Walker is the divorced father of three, living in East Hampton, New York, where he is completing his second book, a novel.

SILENT TESTIMONY

A True Story

ROGER W. WALKER

ST. MARTIN'S PAPERBACKS

Published by arrangement with Carriage House Press, Inc.

SILENT TESTIMONY

Copyright © 1984 by Roger Walker.

Library of Congress Catalog Card Number: 88-91220

ISBN: 0-312-92141-1

Printed in the United States of America

Previously published by Carriage House Press
St. Martin's Paperbacks edition/October 1990

10 9 8 7 6 5 4 3 2 1

This book is dedicated to my mother, Evelyn B. Walker, who is ninety-four years young as this book goes to press.

God bless you, Mom!

ACKNOWLEDGMENTS

My sincere thanks to Joanne Franzen from whose typewriter this book began to materialize and take shape; to Barbara Olsen and Mary Taylor for their help in editing my manuscript.

My thanks to the police departments of Nassau and Suffolk Counties, their detectives and uniformed officers who spent countless hours and long nights in the search for Florence Busacca; to Nassau's Crime Prevention Unit whose members walked miles of highways and parkways in the two counties; to Barry Grennan and Abby Boklan of Nassau's District Attorney's office.

Last but most important, my thanks to Geraldine and Larry Busacca for their courage and strength and their testimony during the trial of their father; to them a special salute.

IT BEGINS

August 29, 1976
10:15:58 P.M.

911 Operator:	"Police emergency 189"
Unknown	"Yes,—is this the police station?"

911 Operator: "Yes, it is."

Unknown: "Yes, I'd like to report . . . a . . . missing person—ah—the name is Florence Busacca, ah, ah, I came into the house . . . to find blood on the floor . . . and . . . the teeth and the keys . . . and I think we . . . we could use a squad car here."

911 Operator: "Hold a minute. Now where's the address?"

Unknown: "The address is—ah—1442 Circle Drive West."

911 Operator: "Circle?"

Unknown: "Circle Drive West."

911 Operator: "Yeah . . . what town?"

Unknown: "Baldwin."

10:16:58 P.M.

911 Operator: "What is your name?"

Unknown: "My name is Mrs. Newman. It's in relation to the Busacca Family—B-U-S-A-C-C-A."

911 Operator:	"Well, this is . . . Mrs. . . . You're Mrs. Newman now?"
Mrs. Newman:	"Yeah."
911 Operator:	"And 1442 Circle Drive West?"
Mrs. Newman:	"That's right."
911 Operator:	"Baldwin?"
Mrs. Newman:	"That's right. That's her home."
911 Operator:	"You said that when you got there, you said there was blood on the floor?"
Mrs. Newman:	"There's blood on the mats . . . her teeth were on the floor . . . her keys on the floor . . . and, ah, there's blood all over the newspapers and, ah, ah, there's a problem here."

10:17:17 P.M.

911 Operator:	"Okay. You stay there. . . . we'll send a car right out."
Mrs. Newman:	"I'll be right here."
911 Operator:	"Okay."
Mrs. Newman:	"Thank you very much."

Chapter One

IT HAD BEEN a grueling tour of duty for police officers Paul Ennis, Fred Swain and Roger Caltobianco, all assigned to Nassau County's First Precinct. The three officers were looking forward to catching up with their paper work and escaping from the hectic pace the day had wrought. But at 10:22 P.M. the officers received a "missing persons" report and were told to respond to 1442 Circle Drive West, Baldwin. Ennis and Swain, together in one police cruiser, and Caltobianco, in the second cruiser, arrived at the location at 10:35 P.M. They were greeted on the front lawn of the residence by a hysterical older woman, an equally distraught young woman and an excited young man in his teens.

The officers were able to determine that both parents of the children, Geraldine and Larry Busacca, were not at home. The children had returned home, after having been away all day, only to find blood splashed all over the mud room of the house and the family car gone from the driveway. The officers' attention was then directed toward the driveway and the back porch area of the house.

Ennis walked up the driveway, flashlight in hand,

and to his astonishment, followed a trail of blood that led up the driveway toward the back door of the house. The four-year rookie was a bit apprehensive as to what the three might find. He instructed the two children and the hysterical woman to wait in the front yard for the moment. He then opened the back door leading into a mud room and kitchen of the house. The lights were on in both rooms. Large drops of blood painted the steps, apparently having dripped down from the door sill. Enough blood was collected in a puddle to flow down the steps to the driveway. Ennis suddenly became gelid, and his knees weakened as he looked down and realized he was about to step into a very large pool of blood just inside the mud room, near the door sill. All four walls were spattered with blood up to a height of six feet. He looked around incredulously at the gruesome sight. His eyes then became fixed upon a reddish, meaty-looking object beneath a chair adjacent to the kitchen door. He did not want to think what it might be, but his most apparent conjecture was a correct one: A piece of flesh. He gagged and turned in the direction of the rear door where his associates were looking on in horror. Ennis motioned them back and joined them in the driveway.

"What the hell is all that?" Swain asked the shaken officer whose face had turned ashen white.

"Beats the hell out of me," said Ennis. "But we've got to go through this house and see who or what we'll find! That room is worse than a butcher shop!"

Caltobianco suggested he would start calling hospitals to see if they had received any emergency cases that were results of beatings.

Swain, Ennis and Lawrence Busacca, the young son of the missing parents, searched throughout the house, the upstairs, the basement and the yard. Nothing. The neighbors were questioned and although they had not seen anything, some had heard what they thought was either children shouting or their next door neighbors' television. At 11:00 P.M. Ennis called his desk officer, Lieutenant Charles Steuer. Steuer notified the precinct detective squad and asked that they dispatch someone to the scene.

Fred Swain went to the kitchen door and looked into the mud room. Under a bench that abutted the front wall was a rolled-up scatter rug that was soaked with a crimson red color. A newspaper on the bench had been spattered with blood. In his three years on the job he had never been witness to such a puzzling, grotesque scene.

It was 12:32 A.M. when the first detective, Jack Marjoribanks, arrived at 1442 Circle Drive West. He was met by Sergeant Hanley and Officer Terry who had arrived just ahead of him. Detective Marjoribanks was shown the blood trail in the driveway, the blood stains on the steps, the pool of blood on the porch and the spattered blood on the walls. A kite hanging on one of the walls had not escaped the spray of gore.

Marjoribanks then went into the living room where he was introduced to Margaret Newman, a family friend, Lawrence and Geraldine Busacca, and Nancy Leviton who had returned to the house with Gerri, as

Geraldine preferred to be called. Larry handed Detective Marjoribanks a partial denture and a gold clasp that had been found on the floor of the mud room. It took Jack by surprise, and he gingerly accepted the items, placing them in a small evidence envelope and placing the envelope and contents into his jacket pocket. He spoke to each of them briefly and telephoned Lieutenant Charles Steuer, the Frist Precinct desk officer, and requested that a notification be broadcast to all units describing the missing couple and the family car. He asked Steuer to request that the Crime Scene Unit respond to the location. He himself then made a cursory inspection of the house. When he had completed the inspection he decided to request the whole "nine yards."

A short time later Geraldine jumped from her window seat, startling everyone. She looked out of the window, and recognized the sound of her father's car and, peering out into the night, she watched in disbelief as it drove slowly past the house. She ran to the front door and out into the yard, followed closely by her brother, Jack Marjoribanks and the other police officers. The car was nowhere in sight.

"That was my father's car," she protested loudly. "Do something!"

"You can't be sure," suggested the detective.

"It was him, damn it! I'd know that motor anywhere. There's not another car in the world that sounds like it," she explained, livid at the apparent scepticism of the officers.

They returned to the house. Geraldine looking over

her shoulder questioningly. She WASN'T wrong. That WAS her father's car.

Marjoribanks then decided that they would wait. If it had been Thomas Busacca's car that had passed the house, he would return. Jack instructed the officers to move their cars from the street and away from the house.

At 3:10 A.M. the sound that Gerri knew so well had returned once again.

"There he goes!" she screamed. "There's my father's car." Marjoribanks and Terry were out of the front door as though catapulted by the force of Geraldine's voice. It had broken an unsettling silence that had pervaded the house since the earlier incident. The car made a U turn and crept slowly back toward the Busacca house. Terry was instructed to go to his car in the event a pursuit followed. The big black Oldsmobile moved slowly now toward the house. Even more slowly, it turned into the driveway, almost reluctantly. Geraldine and Larry were requested to go back into the house. Jack Marjoribanks did not know what might happen next. He did not know what to expect from Tom Busacca at this point in time.

Slowly the driver's door opened. It was on the opposite side of where Marjoribanks and Terry stood, and Jack did not have a clear view of the figure that emerged from the car. He turned his flashlight beam in the direction of the man who was now walking toward the rear of the car where the officers were waiting.

"Where's Mrs. Busacca?" Jack asked quickly. An unintelligible grunt was the only answer he received.

Marjoribanks put the flashlight in his left hand and slowly moved his right hand toward his weapon. He released the strap from the safety position and eased the weapon halfway out of the holster. The man looked frenzied, agitated. Jack trained his light on the small, impish man who stood before him.

Glancing down at the bumper, Marjoribanks saw a sight that made his heart pound and his flesh crawl. Blood was dripping from the trunk lip onto the bumper. He stepped back, his hand firmly placed on his weapon.

"Mr. Busacca, open the trunk!" Marjoribanks ordered.

Timidly fumbling for his keys, the man turned to the car, hesitated and placed the key in the lock. Marjoribanks and Terry leaned forward, straining—and bracing for what might be found there. The latch popped and Tom slowly lifted the lid. Marjoribanks shone the beam of light into the trunk. What he saw was indescribable. Blood appeared everywhere within the confines of the trunk. It was not difficult to surmise what had happened to Mrs. Busacca, but now the questions were: To what extent was she injured and where had he left her?

Jack, himself a married man with two young children, a girl, eleven and a boy, thirteen, felt anger and resentment that this man, for whatever insane reasons, had apparently savagely beaten his wife to death. His own wife was battling for her life, a victim of stomach lupus erythematosis or SLE.

Marjoribanks turned the light directly into the face of the figure before him and saw scratches on the left side of the man's face extending from the area of the cheekbone down toward the chin.

"Cuff him!" Marjoribanks said firmly as he turned to Officer Terry. He then recited the prisoner's rights to Busacca, against self-incrimination. The three then went into the house. Marjoribanks had called for a back-up detective and a police officer earlier, and at 3:20 A.M. Detective Michael O'Connor and Officer Frank McDonald arrived on the scene. Marjoribanks explained what had occurred and showed O'Connor and McDonald the mud room, the dentures and the clasp.

"Mike, I would like you and McDonald to take this guy back to the precinct. I've got to wait for Crime Scene and take statements from the kids, so I need somebody to transport this character," quipped Jack.

"Sure! . . . You say you've notified Homicide already?" O'Connor asked.

"Yeah. Roger Walker is on call, and I've asked the Main Office to call Gene Dolan."

The two detectives talked briefly and contemplated their next move. Marjoribanks had called for everyone. He didn't want to get caught short and he wasn't certain of what he had. An assault? A murder? Attempted murder? He wasn't sure.

O'Connor and McDonald left the house with Tom Busacca in tow and returned to the First Precinct stationhouse.

Once back in the squad room, O'Connor took off his coat, loosened his tie and sat the defendant down in a chair in a small office and instructed Officer Frank

McDonald to stay with him. Busacca's left wrist was cuffed to the chair; his right arm remained free.

O'Connor was a thirteen year veteran with the department and had a reputation of being a thorough investigator, unpretentious and low-keyed. He had been a member of the force since 1963 and was assigned to the detective division in 1967. He received a degree in Criminal Justice Administration from SUNY. Married, he was the father of four boys ranging in age from four years to fifteen years.

After signing Busacca's name in the blotter, Mike returned to the defendant and read him his rights from a card which is required to be carried by all officers. After reading them, he asked Busacca if he understood them. The defendant answered in the affirmative and the card was dated and initialed by Busacca and O'Connor. O'Connor then sat down and faced the defendant.

"Mr. Busacca, where is your wife Florence?" he began.

"I don't know. I haven't seen her since early in the day," he replied.

"That's now what you told the other officer," O'Connor countered. "Now, again, where is your wife Florence?"

Busacca looked away and then up at the ceiling. There was a long pause before he finally answered. "I left her near a motel in Suffolk County . . . on Sunrise Highway. . . . in Holbrook. . . . at about ten o'clock or ten thirty last night."

"What happened before then?" O'Connor asked.

"My wife and I had an argument regarding financial problems in the home," he said meekly. "I told her when the first of the month rolled around, which would be several days in the future, that we were going to be three months behind in our mortgage payments and there was a chance that the house would be foreclosed on us."

"Go on!" encouraged O'Connor, now that the man apparently was ready to talk.

"I made a proposal to my wife that my father and mother move in with us and take over the mortgage payments," he continued. "My wife became infuriated and we got into a heated argument."

"What happened next?"

"We both calmed down a bit and she told me she was going out for a while. I asked her to mail a couple of letters for me but when I couldn't find them and I went back to tell her . . ." Tom hesitated then continued. "She was out in the yard and I saw her embracing someone in the driveway, at which time I ran out yelling and screaming and this . . . this . . . person . . . ran from the side of the house, through the yard."

O'Connor looked at Thomas Busacca disbelievingly. But he let the man go on, because Tom had suddenly developed diarrhea of the mouth and if he questioned Busacca's story, the man might simply clam up.

Busacca looked at O'Connor who gestured with his head for Tom to go on.

"I grabbed my wife. . . . slapped her several times and pushed her back into the mud room." Busacca stared down at the floor as though the reality of the incident had him mesmerized. "I picked up an object," his voice trembled and squeaked. "I don't remember what it was. A stick, or bat, or shovel. I don't know." Another pause. His breathing became labored. ". . . . I struck her. . . . several times in the head. She began to bleed from the head. I lifted her up and took her outside. . . . I opened the trunk of the car. . . . I put her in the trunk." Busacca began to perspire. He wiped at his face with his free hand.

"What were you going to do with her?" O'Connor asked quickly, not wanting to disrupt the communication.

"I was going to dump her in Lindenhurst Bay," replied Busacca, matter-of-factly. "I started driving in that direction. Then I was sure I heard her yelling and kicking in the trunk and I became panicky. I wanted then to go to a hospital but became confused as to exactly where I was, and I wound up driving east on Sunrise Highway in Suffolk County."

Busacca appeared now to be more at ease as O'Connor listened intently, hanging on to every word.

"Somewhere along the road I stopped to pick up a young girl who was hitchhiking," he continued. "I was going to have sex with her to spite my wife. . . . but then I noticed that she was sitting with both feet on a bloody rag that was on the floor. I was also afraid that she would hear my wife yelling and screaming. So, after a few minutes I. . . . let her out of the car. I then drove a few more miles and after passing a gas station, I turned around and pulled over to the side of the road near some model homes. I went to the trunk and pulled my wife's legs out first, and they angled over the rear bumper. I found it difficult to grab her upper body so I wrapped something around her shoulders and pulled her out the rest of the way. As I was pulling her out, I saw blood flowing from her ears. I asked her if there was anything I could do for her and she said, 'Fuck you. I'll get home by myself!' I propped her up against a rail fence and left her." Tom paused, seemingly to reflect on what he had just related to O'Connor. His face was drawn and pale. "I got back into the car," he continued, "and drove a short distance down the road, stopped for gas at a Sunoco station, and then I went home."

The first bit of corroborative information finally fell upon O'Connor's ears. Marjoribanks had, in fact, given Mike a gas receipt which showed that Busacca had purchased $7.00 worth of gas at a Sunoco station on Sunrise Highway in Holbrook. He had used a Sun Oil Company credit card. The receipt was dated 08–29–76. If even half of what Busacca had told him was true, O'Connor thought it was an incredible story. But now his thoughts wandered to Suffolk County and the condition of Florence Busacca. Where might she be and was she dead or alive? He would now have to wait for the arrival of Homicide Detective Roger Walker. In the meantime he would alert Suffolk County.

Chapter Two

THE PIERCING RING of the telephone cut into the deep sleep like a buzz saw attempting to halve a piece of granite. The room was dark, with only a street light's probing beam penetrating the night past the drawn window shades. It had to be early, very early, and there would be only one reason the phone would be ringing at that ungodly hour. Walker knew only too well what it meant.

He tried to clear the cobwebs from his head as the persistent ringing shrieked louder. He found his way to the hallway and fumbled for the phone without trying to find the light switch in the dark. He yanked the receiver from the cradle.

"Hello!"

"Hello, Roger? Gene Dolan! . . . You're squealing tonight, right?"

"Yeah, right!" Why was Gene Dolan calling, Walker wondered. The calls usually came from the main office. "What's up, Loo?" Walker asked hoarsely, using the vernacular for lieutenant.

"I'm at a house in Baldwin. We have a situation here where a woman is missing and her husband came home a little while ago while the cops were here, and they found blood in the trunk of his car. Marjoribanks is here with me, and O'Connor has taken the husband down to the First Squad, and I want you to head down there, and he'll fill you in on the story. I'll stay here."

"Okay! What's the address where you are now?"

"Fourteen forty-two Circle Drive West. Mike has the number. As soon as you get there, give me a call."

"Right. I'm on my way."

Walker hung up the phone and looked at his watch—3:25 A.M. He made his way into the bathroom and flipped on the light. A cold shower would put him on track. There wouldn't be time for coffee; the ride from Westchester would take about forty-five minutes at that hour of the morning. There certainly wouldn't be that many people on the parkways going to work that early.

The night was clear, the air refreshing as he left the house, wondering if he had everything—weapon, badge, wallet, house keys, car keys. He took a quick mental inventory as he climbed behind the wheel and eased the car towards the New York Thruway.

It was 4:30 A.M.; Walker parked in the rear yard of the First Precinct. The upstairs squad room appeared deserted. He had for some reason expected a little more activity, but then again, the squads are not staffed with many men on the midnight-to-eight tour.

He sprinted up the stairs, two steps at a time, to the squad room where he was met by Detective Mike O'Connor.

"Good morning, Mike! What's up?" Walker glanced

into the next office where, seated next to a desk with one of his wrists handcuffed to the chair, his every move observed by a uniformed officer, sat a balding, submissive, disheveled, rather frail-looking man of about fifty or sixty. His trance-like stare was directed toward the floor, his shoulders drooped, his free hand pinching nervously at his chin.

"Gene fill you in?" O'Connor interrupted Walker's inquisitive gaze. "That's Thomas Busacca."

"Just the very basics."

O'Connor related the story as Walker walked over to the door and once again directed his attention to this seemingly innocuous older man with the blank stare and unassuming manner. He would hardly be anyone's candidate to fill the role of a brutal slayer, not someone who would be capable of committing the type of crime being described by O'Connor. But then Walker had been with the police force long enough to appreciate the fact that more often than not, killers or assassins neither ascribed to a particular profile, nor came from a particular walk of life or age group.

Mike had spoken of the bloody scene: blood in the trunk of Busacca's car; blood on the walls, floor and ceiling of the porch, dentures, pieces of flesh, and what appeared to be a piece of bone. Hearing this alone made Walker recoil, his eyes closed, trying to paint a picture in his mind of this apparently gruesome scene.

"And he claims he left his wife 'ALIVE' in Suffolk County?" Walker asked in response to O'Connor's comment indicating that to be the case.

"Yeah, propped up against a fence post. I'll call

Suffolk County and get him to send someone in that area and have a look. Meanwhile, you talk to that sick bastard and see if you can get any more from him." Mike turned away and then glanced over his shoulder at Walker. "Jack and I both gave him his rights. He says he'll talk to us."

"Maybe I can convince him to take us to Suffolk . . . to the place where he says he dumped his wife." Walker turned and walked into the room where Tom Busacca was cuffed to his chair, and sat down at the desk next to him.

"Tom, I'm Detective Walker of the Homicide Squad. You say your wife is still alive somewhere in Suffolk County?"

Busacca didn't answer. He looked at Walker, an odd expression on his face. He glanced away and then back to Walker.

"Well, what happened?" queried Walker, leaning forward in his chair, his face within a few intimidating inches of Tom's.

Walker noticed some long scratch marks running diagonally down the left side of Busacca's face from the upper right temple area toward the forward part of his lower jaw.

"How'd that happen?" snapped Walker, showing his annoyance at the man's unresponsiveness.

"I don't know," Tom replied, his voice weak and hesitant.

"Ah ha. . . . you can talk!" Walker quipped, disdainfully moving back in his chair, staring at Busacca. "Was it during the fight with your wife? Maybe it was when you were dumping the body."

"No. . . . no, I don't know," his voice apprehensive, his behavior becoming fidgety and restless, his hands trembling, and his brow beginning to perspire.

"Time . . . !" Walker stood up in front of Busacca's chair and leaned forward, his hand on Tom's shoulder, his voice almost a whisper. "Listen, Tom, if your wife is alive, she needs medical help. It may not be too late to save her if you just tell us where she is so that we can get help to her."

Busacca didn't answer, his retreating stare now directed at the ceiling. Walker didn't know whether Tom was thinking or simply trying to take his mind off whatever occurred that night. The man was perhaps trying to crawl into a little shell away from the torment and pain that pounded in his subconscious. We were prying into an area he wanted to forget and did not want to relive again.

"Tom, take us to where you left your wife. You can save her life if you just tell us where she is. Why get yourself into deeper trouble, which is what will happen if your wife dies?" There was pleading in Walker's voice and frustration toward Busacca as questions were now going unanswered.

O'Connor came into the room. It was a welcomed entrance for Walker; it helped ease the tension that was beginning to build.

Busacca's expression suddenly changed and he pawed at his chest and leaned forward in the chair.

"What's the matter, Tom?" Mike asked. "You don't feel well?"

"No. . . . I . . . I have some pains in my chest," he murmured.

"My ass!" shot back Walker, turning to O'Connor. "Better take the cuff off this wrist!"

O'Connor took his handcuff key out and unlocked the one cuff that was on Busacca's left wrist. He then stepped around Busacca and looked him straight in the eyes. "What kind of pain is it, Tom? . . . Do you think you need a doctor?"

"Not as badly as his wife needs one," said Walker sarcastically. "He's complaining of pain and his wife is probably dying of a beating he gave her. Where the hell is his sense of remorse?" Walker asked rhetorically, nodding his head in bewilderment.

It was 4:45 A.M. Mike got on the phone to the desk officer and requested an emergency medical technician (EMT) to check out Tom's chest pains. EMT Gavin who was assigned to the Special Services Bureau, but stationed at the Seventh Precinct, responded to the squad room.

"Let's take him downstairs to the ambulance, and I'll hook him up to the EKG," suggested Gavin. "That'll give us some idea of a problem, if there is one."

Walker, O'Connor and the EMT walked downstairs to the ambulance with Busacca. The early morning darkness made a beautiful stage for the brilliant display of stars that shone unobscured by clouds or washed out by the fading light of a quarter moon which was waning in the western sky.

They had reached the ambulance that was fully equipped with an EKG monitor which was hooked into the Nassau County Medical Center in East Meadow. Gavin ushered Busacca into the back of the

vehicle and made a few preparations before starting
the test. O'Connor and Walker looked on and mar-
velled at the progress made by the department's ac-
quiring ambulances with such sophisticated
equipment and having them manned around the clock
at strategic locations within the county. Response time
to the scenes of automobile accidents or other emergency situations was reduced to about three or four
minutes.

Gavin motioned to Walker and O'Connor. The test
indicated that there was a problem sufficient enough
to warrant being checked out by a doctor at the Medical Center.

"I don't want to make a judgment here," said
Gavin. "I don't think it is serious or much of a problem, but let's leave that to a doctor. From what you
tell me, it may only be tension."

"Okay, let me get to Dolan and let him know what's
going on." O'Connor started back into the precinct.
"I'll find out what he wants to do after that."

Walker looked back at Busacca. He couldn't believe
that this man was remaining so absolutely calm, composed and undisturbed. It did not make sense. There
was perhaps a mental problem; maybe the guy was a
psycho. There was no time to probe into his background at that moment; that would come later.

O'Connor returned to the ambulance. It was decided that he would drive the ambulance, and Gavin
would ride in the back with Busacca where he could
continue to monitor the EKG. Walker would follow
in the squad car. Fifteen minutes had transpired since
Busacca's complaint of chest pains.

At 5:24 A.M. Busacca was wheeled into a treatment room on a trundle. He was asked to disrobe and was given a hospital gown to wear. Dr. Samuels of the hospital staff introduced himself to Walker and O'Connor and was briefed on the matters leading up to Busacca's complaint of chest pains. Busacca was wheeled into an examining room and followed in by Dr. Samuels. The detectives waited outside the room.

"What do you think?" asked Walker, turning to O'Connor.

"I think he's full of shit and just stalling. He knows what he did with her, and I think we're going to have to drive him to Suffolk and see if we can jog his memory a little."

"I agree," said Walker. "God knows what we'll find out there. I hardly think she's alive as he claims. He knows that himself. That's why he's stalling.

"Dolan should be back in the squad when we get back there. He says the porch and the trunk of Busacca's car are unbelievable sights."

"Those scratches on the side of his face are probably from her when they fought." Walker scratched his head; he was searching his mind for some answers.

Dr. Samuels came out of the examining room and motioned to the two detectives. They walked over to him, hoping the news wasn't bad. They needed this man healthy; a lot of work had to be done; a woman had to be found, and it didn't appear that Tom was going to make it easy for them.

"He doesn't seem to have any heart problems," stated Dr. Samuels. "But he does have a slightly high blood pressure reading that poses no serious concern at this time. I would say the condition is consistent with his agitated and nervous state at the moment."

"It won't present a problem, then, if he assists us in trying to locate his wife?" inquired O'Connor, confident Tom was well enough.

"None at all," answered Samuels. "There is no problem with the heart at all."

O'Connor picked up a copy of the hospital release form signed by the doctor. It was a record which was now going to be a part of a file jacket on Thomas Busacca. It was now 5:50 A.M.

While Tom was seated on the examining table in his hospital gown, Walker and O'Connor reentered the room. Sheets had been removed, exposing his legs as they hung limply over the side of the table. O'Connor reached over and touched Walker's elbow. He was trying to call Walker's attention to something on Tom's legs. Smudges of a dark reddish-brown color were evident on both ankles and calves of each leg. O'Connor and Walker stood silent for a long moment, their attention drawn to the smudges, then to each other. Their instinct and past experiences told them what it was, and it did not appear that Tom had any injuries in those areas.

"Tom, what's that?" O'Connor asked, directing Busacca's attention to the smears. "Where'd that come from?"

Busacca recoiled without answering, panic etched in his face. He began to fidget with the gown and tried looking away from the two detectives.

O'Connor moved closer to Tom, the expression on

his face telling Busacca that he was waiting for an answer; he wanted an answer now.

Busacca looked back at O'Connor. His lips moved but the sound was barely audible.

"Where'd this come from, Tom?" There was a little more urgency in O'Connor's voice.

"I don't know. . . . I can't remember!" Busacca was obviously upset. He must have time to think. He had not been aware there was blood on his legs.

"Make sure we get pictures of those smears and the scratches on his face later on," Walker interjected. "Right now, we'd better get a move on to Suffolk."

Time was becoming more important now. If Florence Busacca was alive but badly beaten, she would bleed to death within a short time. Maybe Tom knows that she's already dead.

The ride back to the squad seemed much faster. Return trips always do for some reason. The shift from dawn to daybreak had gone without much notice. The rays of the warm, advancing morning sun streaked through a pale blue sky. Whimsical streaks of velvety, high-altitude cirrus clouds added an artist's touch to nature's morning ritual. The world was awakening; early morning commuters were beginning to clog the parkways.

Lieutenant Gene Dolan and Inspector Wayne Seay were in the squad room when they returned. Lieutenant Dolan was the commanding officer of the Homicide Squad; it was his telephone call that had put Walker into motion. Inspector Seay was the duty officer for the night. A young, ambitious, and sincere officer, he was well respected by the rank and file. His unpretentious manner, his knowledge of the needs of the department were pluses for this young inspector.

O'Connor approached Dolan. "Hello, Loo! We're just getting back from the emergency room and there's no problem with Tom's ticker."

"You got a release, I hope?" Dolan asked, a stickler for thoroughness, too much sometimes of the trivial kind.

"Of course. This is the First Squad. We do things right down here," Mike quipped.

"Roger, did you get a chance to talk to this guy at all?" Dolan asked, walking over to Busacca.

"Yeah, he told me the same story he told Jack Marjoribanks and Mike. He claims he left his wife 'alive' in Suffolk, and he has agreed to take us out to the spot."

"Well, the Inspector and I want to talk to him for a minute. Check with Suffolk and see what they have come up with. Let them know you'll be on your way out there very shortly." Dolan and Inspector Seay went into the next office with Busacca.

"Mike, I'll gas the car while we have time, and we won't have to worry about that." The pumps were in the precinct parking lot and Walker took a lesson from his flight training days when he was going for his private pilot's license. You never leave on a trip without "topping off" the tanks.

Mike notified Suffolk County. So far, their man had come up with nothing, but now with the daylight hours they could be more thorough.

Chapter Three

IT WAS 5:30 on the morning of August 30th when Police Officers Larry Gilbert and Robert Horan of the Crime Scene Unit arrived on the scene met by Detective Marjoribanks. Jack explained the sequence of events to the young officers and told them what he wanted in the way of photographs and samplings. He also gave Horan the partial denture and gold clasp that was then put into an evidence envelope and sealed. Now Horan and Gilbert would begin the grim task of processing the scene and gathering and photographing evidence.

The blood spatterings were tested using a field kit designed to indicate the presence of blood, but it was not capable of differentiating between human or animal. A newspaper stained with blood was photographed and tagged. An ortho-toloidine test was performed on it, as it would be on all suspected blood stains that morning by Horan, and a positive reading was taken. The blood-soaked carpet that was rolled up under the bench was examined. Wet puddles of thick coagulated blood were found under the door saddle that had been removed by Horan, and he observed swirls of blood stains on the mud room floor that gave the indication that an attempt had been made to wipe up the blood. Horan could not determine the original size of the puddle of blood but was able to define the point of origin, a five by six foot area with a blood coagulation trace line which had been extended to a point of six by seven feet as a result of the wiping action. Horan drew a diagram of the area, taking measurements and photographing as he went along. Some blood spatterings were photographed one-on-one to represent the actual size of the stains and show the direction of travel of the blood as it came in contact with the walls. Individual swabbings were taken from random stains and sealed in glass vials to be further tested by the Scientific Investigation Bureau.

Horan then directed his attention and examination of the scene to the driveway. The early morning light cast its faint rays on the area and presented a more grisly reminder of what had taken place that portentous day and evening past. The blood trail in the driveway that extended from the porch to approximately half the length of the seventy-four foot driveway, became more vivid as the early dawn intensified the crimson glow against the blacktop driveway. Detective Horan made two more disturbing discoveries: The first was a piece of cartilage with what appeared to be human hair attached to it. The second appeared to be a piece of bone that he found in the blood-drenched trunk. Florence Busacca had taken a merciless beating and couldn't possibly be alive, despite Mr. Busacca's utterances to the contrary.

After Horan had finished an extensive examination of the scene, Marjoribanks ordered the police tow truck to tow the vehicle to Police Headquarters in Mineola where the Scientific Investigation Bureau guys could start their tests and examinations. Blood typing had to be made in addition to what already had been accomplished by Robert Horan. The car had to be dusted for fingerprints and photographed in the daylight. Hair samples from the trunk had to be taken and examined for later comparison to known samples of Florence Busacca's if she could be found.

After Thomas Busacca's car had been towed to the police parking field at Headquarters in Mineola, Detective James Granelle was assigned by SIB's Commanding Officer Lt. Carl Moeller to give the automobile a thorough going over. His task was a monumental one, for the vehicle was filled with camping equipment, fishing rods and dozens of other items. There was hardly an item in the trunk that did not wear a trace of blood. Where possible the blood would have to be examined and carefully typed with the RH factor determined. To accomplish this, Granelle conducted three important tests: a hemochromagen test to confirm the presence of blood, an absorption elution test, and a lattes crust test to determine which of the blood groups the stains were from. With the benefit of full sunlight, he directed that photographs be taken of the interior of the trunk and the exterior and interior of the vehicle showing everything in place before he began his examination.

In the trunk of the car, Granelle found a heavily blood-stained pocketbook with hair fragments adhering to it. In the pocketbook he found credit cards, a driver's license, a wallet, a checkbook, an automobile registration, and three dollars and sixty-six cents.

Granelle's lab tests showed the blood to be AB negative, and it was determined that only one half of one percent of the people in the United States have AB negative blood.

The hair samples were turned over to Detective Charles Fraas of S.I.B., an expert in the field of hair identification as well as examination and analysis of blood.

The eventual testimony of these expert witnesses would be crucial in a case of this nature—in the event Florence Busacca were never found. It would be a case based upon circumstantial evidence making the S.I.B. examinations in conjunction with the Medical Examiner's reports a matter of critical importance.

It was 7:50 A.M. when Walker and O'Connor arrived in Holbrook and Tom pointed out the Sunoco gas station where he had bought gas the night before. He directed them to go just a little farther east. There he pointed out two buildings, on the north side of Sunrise Highway, that at one time served as model homes, but now were used for office space. It was just a few hundred feet east of the Sunoco station. Walker made a turn across the median that separated the east and west-bound lanes of the high way. He drove back to the two houses which were situated on either side of a very short dead end street, Jersey Avenue.

"Right over there near that rail fence," Busacca volunteered.

Anticipation flowed through Walker's body. Tom

had mentioned he propped his wife up against a fence near two model homes. There was the fence; there were the model homes; but where was Florence?

Busacca explained to Walker how he had parked his car on the previous night and Walker re-enacted Tom's actions as he explained them. The car was parked slightly less than diagonally and nosed in toward the rail fence and curb. Mike and Walker got out of the car, Walker walking to the rear to assist Busacca from the back seat since he was still handcuffed. They walked over to the corner post of the fence and Walker and O'Connor made a close examination of the ground that was pointed out to them by Tom Busacca.

"There's nothing here. . . . and there hasn't been anything here for some time," said Walker, turning to O'Connor. "There's no trace of blood, no footprints or recent tire marks in the dirt."

"Tom, are you sure this is where you brought your wife, or are you guessing?" asked O'Connor, doubting in his own mind that this was the area to which he brought his wife. Mike held little or no hope that Florence would be found alive if she were to be found at all.

Tom just shook his head in the positive. He was a man of few words, but insisted that this was the place.

"Let's drive farther east," suggested Walker, "and see if he remembers anything else. Nobody has been here in quite some time."

They got back into the squad car. O'Connor took over the driving at this point. The long night was catching up to both of the detectives. Neither had even

stopped for coffee or a breather since Walker's arrival
at the squad room some four and a half hours ago.
Tom Busacca wasn't the most genial or cooperative
person to be with. Time seemed to be slipping away
from them and the hopes of finding Florence Busacca
alive were diminishing rapidly with every minute.

They continued driving east on Sunrise Highway to
where it intersects Hospital Road. Busacca kept insisting that he hadn't traveled that far. But there was
something strange about his demeanor. He seemed
upset over the fact that the police insisted it could
have been farther east. Did he travel farther out on
the Island? More confounding questions, and a reluctant, unwilling witness, or better—murder suspect.

The driving around was wasting valuable time. The
detectives ended up back at Jersey Avenue and the rail
fence. At that point O'Connor called for assistance
from the Suffolk County Police K-9 Corps and their
Air Bureau. They then took a much-needed break.
They had passed a diner about two miles east of them
so they decided to get some containers of coffee for
themselves and Tom and return to Jersey Avenue to
await the assistance from Suffolk.

It was about eleven o'clock when the first police car
arrived with a patrolman and a sergeant. O'Connor
introduced himself and explained the highlights of the
strange events that were unfolding before them. The
sergeant, a young polished officer, looked on intently.
He assured the detectives of all the help he could mus-
ter. At that point the two K-9's arrived with their
handlers and both trainers were briefed and asked to
check the wooded area to the north of their location

and around the two structures that were formerly model homes. Within minutes the distinctive sound of rotor blades penetrated the morning calm. The helicopter had arrived. It made an unusual sight for the motorists who slowed to a crawl, obviously trying to figure out what all the activity was about. The big iron bird made its landing on the short dead end street, its spinning blades touching off spirals of dust and debris, causing the officers to clutch their hats and turn their backs from the cyclones of wind that swirled around them.

It was decided that O'Connor would go with the chopper over areas along the route the men had taken from Nassau County and adjacent to Sunrise Highway. Walker would stay with Tom and the K-9 troop. Suffolk motor patrol personnel were instructed to check both sides of the highway along the shoulders of the road and report any unusual items found; more specifically, blood-stained items of clothing and rags.

O'Connor and the helicopter pilot returned to Jersey Avenue after about a half hour aerial search.

"See anything?" asked Walker, sensing the disappointment in Mike's face.

"Nah, the foliage is too heavy and the pilot's got to get back and refuel. He's been up all morning. Anything here?"

"No, not a damn thing. Not one trace of clothing, blood or anything. I think at this point he's putting us on. She's farther east."

"We've got to start somewhere," Mike cut in. "He's telling us only what he wants to; and that ain't much!"

An officer seated in one of the patrol cars called the

young sergeant over. There was a hint of urgency in his voice. O'Connor and Walker looked at one another. They watched as the officer explained something to the sergeant and gestured toward the west. Walker felt a moment of excitement. Maybe all was not lost; from what little information that had been given to them by Tom, perhaps they were now going to receive some valuable clue to the wife's disappearance.

The sergeant hurriedly walked back to the detectives. "We just got a call that Officer Loeffler found a shirt just off the shoulder of Sunrise, and it looks like it may have blood stains on it."

"What color is it?" inquired Walker, his excitement reflected in his voice.

"I think he said it was light blue. It's off the westbound lanes about two miles west of here."

"Mike, you stay here with Tom. I'll go take a look. I'll keep you posted. Let's go!" Walker said to the sergeant. He turned back to O'Connor. "Let's get some help out here, Mike! It's going to be a long day."

Walker and the young sergeant pulled up behind a Suffolk County patrol car, its red lights flashing. It was 12:20 P.M. It was important to record all time at this point. Questions will have to be answered and anything relative to the case would have to be documented as to time, place and persons involved. It would have to pass the scrutiny of a defense attorney, judge and jury, and satisfy the requirement of the district attorney's office.

Loeffler was out of his car as the two men approached. He motioned to an article of clothing in the grass off to the side of the road. Walker walked over and looked at it. His excitement turned to ecstasy. He turned to the officer. "How long ago'd you find this?"

"About ten minutes ago. Twelve-o-one, to be exact. I made note of it."

Walker examined the shirt. It was relatively new. It hadn't been thrown or dropped there too long ago. It was a blue oxford cloth, long-sleeved shirt with button-down collar. It was stained on the front button flap and sleeves with what appeared to be dried blood.

"I want you to mark the area where you found this and, asking the sergeant's permission, I would like you to stay here until our Crime Scene Unit arrives to take some photos. They're on their way now." Walker knew that the unit would be responding after Mike had contacted the Homicide office for assistance. He was counting on it.

He placed the shirt in a clear plastic bag that he had brought along; he and the sergeant then returned to Jersey Avenue. He was informed by O'Connor that Sergeant Bill Dempsey and Crime Scene were responding to Holbrook and would be arriving shortly. Walker showed the shirt to O'Connor. They were both all smiles, reassured. With all of Tom Busacca's reluctance and ambiguous statements, they were getting somewhere. Their tenacity was beginning to reap rewards.

"While you were gone, I asked Tom to tell me about anything he may have discarded along the road on his way back home," Mike said, as they walked toward the car where Tom had been seated during most of the search effort. "He said he threw out a shirt, some rags and some clothes in a plastic bag that he claims he threw under a parked car in Long Beach."

"Good," replied Walker. "Let's see if he can describe the shirt he was wearing. If it is his, then we're in the ball park."

Walker and O'Connor approached the car, followed by the sergeant. Tom was in the back seat, void of expression. O'Connor opened the front passenger door and got in. Walker sat in the back next to Busacca, keeping the bag containing the shirt out of Tom's view.

"Tom," O'Connor began, "you told me you threw a shirt out of the car somewhere along this road. Can you describe it to us?"

Tom looked first at O'Connor, then at Walker. That same vacuous expression continued to manifest itself and Walker grew increasingly annoyed at the perhaps cold, calculated, unfeeling arrogance of the man.

"It was a blue shirt . . ." Busacca fumbled for words, his voice faint and childlike.

"What shade of blue?" Walker quickly asked not wanting to give him time to think of anything but the correct answer.

"Light blue . . . like yours." Tom pointed at Walker's shirt. "It was just like yours. Buttons on the collar."

"Oxford cloth?" asked O'Connor.

"Yeah . . . just like his."

"Where'd you buy it?" asked O'Connor, keeping the pressure on Busacca, not affording him the opportunity to fabricate anything.

"Macy's department store," replied Tom without hesitation. "Yeah, I bought it at Macy's."

Walker had forgotten to look at the label in the shirt but everything else fit. He held his breath as he took the shirt from the plastic bag, making a silent, humble entreaty to God as he did so. He glanced at the label in the collar. "SUPRA MACY." He couldn't hold back the broad smile as he looked at Mike, then at Tom.

"Is this your shirt, Tom?"

"Yeah, that's mine." His eyes closed as he lowered his head in abjection, withdrawing once again.

Walker placed the shirt back in the bag, satisfied that it was indeed Tom's shirt. He reached across the seat and shook O'Connor's hand. He then got out of the car and told the sergeant the good news.

12:45 P.M. and a positive identification. A positive direction. It was time for a refueling of the body's energies. They would have to settle for a hot dog and soda from the Sabrett pushcart up the street. Lunch under the umbrella.

It was 2:15 P.M. when Detective Robert Horan and Police Officer Larry Gilbert arrived on the scene with the Nassau County Crime Scene van. On board they had all the equipment necessary to process any type of crime scene, but their only task at this point would be to photograph the shirt in place where it was found, and the area where Tom claimed he had left his wife the night before. They would then take custody of the shirt and turn it over to the Scientific Investigation Bureau where it would undergo a series of tests and examinations to determine if in fact there was blood on it and if so, the blood type broken down to its most intrinsic properties, if enough was found.

Walker gave Horan and Gilbert instructions as to what photographs he wanted. He accompanied them to the spot where the shirt had been found and where Officer Loeffler was waiting. Walker commended him for his patience and told him that Busacca had identified the shirt as being his. Walker wanted to express his appreciation for the officer's alertness and patience while waiting at the site for Nassau officers.

The shirt was photographed at the place where it had been found. Photographs were then taken of the surrounding area with emphasis on landmarks that could be later identified. All of this would be important in the eventual prosecution of the case. Walker was thinking optimistically. He had to. He dismissed the Suffolk officer, thanking him again for his alertness, and with Horan and Gilbert, returned to Jersey Avenue. Sergeant Dempsey had arrived while Walker was away, and he and O'Connor had left the area with Tom to look farther east for Florence Busacca. There would be no argument from anybody that at this point they were looking for a body and not a badly beaten woman. The thought disturbed Walker. Tom Busacca had been playing games with them. His procrastination and infantile attitude may have been a deliberate attempt on his part to hobble the investigation, to make certain that his wife was not found. If that was his intent, then he had probably won that round.

O'Connor and Dempsey drove up to the Crime

Scene van. Horan and Gilbert were finishing up their photos.

"Hi, Bill! Anything new?" Walker asked.

"Hello, Roger . . . This fuck'n guy's putting us on. He knows where the hell she is and he knows she's dead and buried somewhere."

"Mike told you about the shirt, right?"

"Yeah, and we've got to get a statement from that kid at the gas station when he gets to work. We're going to get some more men out here."

At that moment, Assistant District Attorneys Barry Grennan and Edward McCarty arrived at the scene. Dempsey was talking to the Crime Scene officers and O'Connor was with Thomas Busacca. Barry approached Walker but had not been seen by O'Connor or Dempsey as Mike got out of the car and yelled over to Bill.

"Hey, Bill, this guy says he wants to talk to a lawyer now!"

Dempsey spun around, resentment in his voice. "Fuck him! He can call a lawyer when he tells us where his wife is!" His eyes then met the District Attorney's.

"Hi, Bill!" Grennan smiled. "I'll talk to you in a minute." Barry turned to McCarty, "Let's get the hell out of here for a while." Grennan smiled again.

McCarty, following the cue from Barry Grennan, looked back and gestured toward Dempsey, then walked away from the van toward the fence where a marker was still in place, a reference point used by Crime Scene during their examination of the scene.

"Mike, we've got to get a statement from the kid at

the gas station, and also look for the original copy of the gas receipt from last night when this guy bought gas there," Walker suggested.

"Yeah, you guys take care of that and then take this fuck back to the office and process him," interjected Dempsey. "Dolan's sending out more guys to continue the search. There'll still be a few hours of daylight left after the four to twelve crew gets in."

O'Connor and Walker drove the short distance to the Sunoco station where Tom had purchased gas. They parked away from the building, avoiding any possibility of the young attendant observing Thomas Busacca before he could be shown either a photo lineup or a live lineup of the accused. It was important that they think ahead to the prosecution of the case as to the manner in which Thomas Busacca had been identified.

Walker's luck doubled up on him. Raymond Burkhart, the nineteen year old gas attendant, was working and was able to produce the original copy of the receipt from the credit card that Thomas Busacca used the night before. It was dated August 29, 1986, and showed the purchase of 10.3 gallons of gasoline for $7.00. A statement was taken from Burkhart and a receipt was given to cover the confiscated gas receipt. That had now become a part of the expanding Busacca file.

"We'll be in touch with you in the next few days," Walker explained as he was leaving. "We'll have you look at some mug shots and see if you can pick this guy out of a photo lineup."

The ride back to Nassau County was a quiet one.

The hectic pace, their fruitless search for Florence, and the insolence of Thomas Busacca, had drained their strength and resolve. They had not found Florence, but had found evidence that would support a case against her husband. But charged with what? There was the absence of a body to sustain a murder charge and only circumstantial evidence to support an assault, but no victim. A long, arduous investigation lay ahead for the investigators. The search for clues would continue in Suffolk County until all possibilities were exhausted. Motive would be drawn out through investigation. Cases of this nature almost always have their underlying causes, the answers to which would have to be extracted from family, friends and neighbors who knew the couple.

Mike pulled into the rear parking field at Police headquarters in Mineola. It was 5:19 P.M. It was a day that had begun some eighteen hours ago for O'Connor with no promise of ending soon. He had caught his second wind, and it was determination that was keeping him afloat now.

The detectives walked up the stairs to the Homicide office. For a change, the light green and off-white walls were a relief from the outdoor exposure to the dust and din of traffic that had enveloped them most of the day. It was a welcomed chance to sit down, if even for one undisturbed moment, to ponder the events and circumstances of the day.

Young Lawrence Busacca was brought to the Homicide office to see his father. He wanted some answers. A slender, dark haired youth of fifteen, Larry was uncommonly composed, in light of what he had discovered and what his mind must be going through.

The young man was taken into a small office where his father sat handcuffed to a desk. Larry glanced at this father and a very faint "Hi" was barely audible. He sat down quickly in a chair that had been placed at a distance from his father. The detectives left the room but the door was left ajar.

"Where's Mom?" young Larry asked.

After a moment of silence Tom responded, "I don't know."

"What happened?" Larry pressed.

"I don't know," came the response.

The young man asked several more questions calmly, clearly, but received no answers. Tom just sat and stared blankly. It was as though there was no one in the room. He had withdrawn into that shell. He was not willing to confide even in his son, not willing to disclose the deep, dark mystery that was locked perhaps forever in his own head. Larry was taken home. His desire to know the fate of his mother left wanting, unfulfilled, his face etched in despair.

Thomas Busacca was given the opportunity to call his attorney. It was 6:35 P.M. He would eventually reach the office of Jerry Halpern.

"Roger, while we're waiting for Halpern, we might just as well start the paper work on this guy," said Gene Dolan. "I've been in touch with Barry Grennan. He says the charge will be Second Degree Assault. If we develop anything further, he'll present it before the Grand Jury and try for a murder charge."

The ritual of processing began for Thomas Bus-

acca—a litany of questions that made up the pedigree
of the individual. He had no prior criminal record, no
outstanding warrants. It was unimaginable that this
ungainly maladroit would appear on anyone's Ten
Most Wanted list. But then again, Walker reasoned,
the man was obviously capable of beating his wife to
death. The thought prompted Walker to check the
secureness of the handcuffs that had Busacca re-
strained.

O'Connor walked over to the prisoner. "Come on,
Tom. Let's check your property." He unlocked the
cuffs and took Tom to an adjoining office. "Take everything out of your pockets. Put the stuff on the
desk."

Without a sound, Busacca complied. As he handed
O'Connor a handful of coins, Mike's expression suddenly changed.

"What's this, Tom?" Mike demanded, showing him
a gold plated earring. Without waiting for an answer,
O'Connor showed it to Walker and Dolan. There was
blood on it, and more questions were provoked by the
discovery. A bloody shirt, an earring with blood,
fleshy tissue and a blood splattered room—all indications of a dreadful beating.

Mike slipped the earring into a clear plastic evidence envelope and gave it to Walker. It would be
turned over to the lab people with the other evidence
thus far found. It was all adding up, bit by bit. A
bloody earring in his trouser pocket. Curious, thought
Walker, very curious.

The night went slowly now. The body's reflexes
were trying to close down, the mind screaming out

for relief, the muscles aching, coordination becoming
dulled. Tom's lawyer made his appearance, talked to
his client and left.

O'Connor directed Larry Gilbert to photograph the
scratches on Busacca's face and the blood on his legs,
to take specimens of the blood from Busacca's face
and fingernail scrapings from each finger to determine
if there were traces of flesh or blood beneath the nails.
He was then taken to the Nassau County Medical
Center by Walker and Detective Gary Abbondandello, who had relieved Mike O'Connor, whose
twenty-four hours plus of continuous work had begun
to take its toll on his sharpness and coordination. Fatigue had invaded his body and had closed down sys-
tems that were vital to his subjective and intellectual
functioning. In just a little more than seven hours he
would have to be back for Busacca's arraignment in
District Court in Mineola. He signed off duty and
went home to a much needed sleep. It had been an
exhausting day.

It was 2:25 A.M., August 31st, when Gary and
Roger returned to Headquarters with a sample of
Tom's blood sealed in an evidence, tamper-proof kit.
It was placed in a Scientific Investigation Bureau
locker in the Main Office of the Detective Division by
Walker and secured with a padlock. All proper nota-
tions had been made in the logs to insure continuity
of handling. The locker was accessible only to the per-
son who was to perform the test or the Commanding
Officer of the unit.

It was 2:50 A.M. before the defendant was finger-
printed and photographed by Police Officer Rosenber-

ger of the Identification Bureau, and at Walker's behest, a voice print was also made for the record. Thomas Busacca was then taken to a detention cell at 3:20 A.M., August 31, 1976. Some twenty-four hours after his arrest, he was behind bars.

It was almost 4:00 A.M. before Walker walked out of Headquarters to his car. The temperature was in the sixties and the early morning calm was a refreshing inducement to his fatigued and aching torso. It was, for an instant, an energizing of the will to last just one more hour, the time needed to travel the thirty-five miles to his apartment in Westchester. In just four hours he would be joining O'Connor at Busacca's arraignment. Three hours of sleep would go a long way with Walker. He was one of those persons whose body did not require a lot of sleep. Just a little catnap would do.

It was not until 12 o'clock noon on August 31st that Thomas Busacca, besieged by the media and photographers, was taken before the Honorable James P. Griffin, First District Court in Mineola, and arraigned. The District Attorney's Office had amended the charge from Second Degree Assault to Murder Second Degree. Thomas was held in lieu of $50,000 bail and transported to the Nassau County Correction Center in East Meadow, where he would remain until his trial.

The charge of Second Degree Murder came as a surprise to Walker and O'Connor. The body of Florence Busacca had not been found and Thomas Busacca had done all the talking he was going to do. He was now under the wing of his attorney.

"Barry, how the hell can we sustain a murder charge against him?" queried Walker.

"We'll find her," retorted Grennan. "I have confidence in you guys."

It was later pointed out to Barry Grennan that in New York State there had never been a murder conviction without the body, and only once in the entire United States.

Obviously a lot of work had to be done. The body of Florence Busacca could be anywhere from Sheepshead Bay, Brooklyn, to Montauk Point on Long Island.

Chapter Four

ON THE AFTERNOON of the 31st, the investigation was in full swing. Mike O'Connor joined Bill Dempsey in Suffolk County and Roger Walker joined Jack Marjoribanks in Baldwin to begin the process of obtaining dental and medical records of Florence Busacca. Physicians' and dentists' names had been obtained from the children, Lawrence and Gerri. It was now necessary for Walker to visit that scene that he had only been able to envision from the description given to him by O'Connor and Marjoribanks.

At 2:45 P.M., Walker and Marjoribanks arrived at 1442 Circle Drive West, a wood shingled, one and a half story unadorned house, situated on a small parcel of land that was bordered by hedges and shrubbery in a quiet neighborhood. The two detectives sat in the car for a moment, Marjoribanks pointing out details that had been described to him, and that he himself had observed. There were two police officers on duty inside the house, and they logged the detectives in as they entered the house through the front door. The house and its property were now considered a crime scene and could only be entered by authority of the police.

Jack Marjoribanks led Walker toward the kitchen and rear porch. They passed through a small dining room, a den, and then the kitchen.

"Wait'll you see this," Jack warned, as he reached out to open the door leading from the kitchen to the porch.

Walker approached slowly, contemplatively, his mental picture crowded with presumptions. As he stepped down and into the porch area, his furtive glances became fixed upon the door sill that led to the driveway, then to a larger sanguineous area under a window seat. He felt cold; pain came to his stomach. "Christ!" he uttered under his breath. What he had been told was an oversimplification of the fact. The room gave the appearance that someone had centered himself in the middle of the room and then from a brush made swiping motions at the walls and ceiling with red paint. If he had seen this earlier, he would have thought it was sheer lunacy to speculate that Florence Busacca was alive. They had been suckered by a scheming, cunning, pertinacious old man who had now enveloped himself in an impenetrable shell of muteness.

"Where're the kids staying?" Walker finally asked, collecting his thoughts.

"They're at a friend's house for the moment, not too far from here," Jack replied.

"It's unimaginable they came home to this," Walker continued. "Can you appreciate their horror, the ter-ror that must have gripped them?" he said rhetorically. "Christ!" He moved about the small porch, careful not to touch anything. Jack stood silent, waiting for the impact to clear from Walker's mind.

Jack described the items that had been removed by the Crime Scene Unit and taken to the lab in Mineola and turned over to Detective James Grannelle: Samples of dry blood, and strands of hair stained with blood that had been removed from the driveway, a fragment of bone found in the trunk of Thomas Busacca's car along with an iron pry bar smeared with blood, and a blood-splattered shopping bag containing Florence Busacca's pocketbook, which itself was saturated with blood. Every piece of tool, article of clothing, or equipment that was in the trunk gave evidence in its own mute way of the horror that Florence Busacca had suffered on the 29th of August. Detective Robert Horan had made a thorough and comprehensive examination of the scene. Photographs were taken in color to graphically depict the heinous nature of the crime and to leave an impact upon the minds of viewers that, indeed, Florence Busacca could not be, by the wildest imagination, considered alive.

Walker was shown the chair under which an upper partial denture had been found and next to that some keys belonging to Mrs. Busacca, and an area where a fleshy piece of material, possible evulsed fat, had been found and removed. Spatterings of blood were evident on the bamboo shades, the windows, the walls and storm door and measured more than six feet above the floor. A trail of blood went from the porch steps for a distance down the driveway, where its concentration was so great it seeped into the cracks of the concrete and slate slabs. This was no simple family spat. This was no simple family fight. This had been a confrontation that had led to a brutal death, and it would be from here that the pieces of the puzzle would begin to fall into place. It would take a concerted effort on the part of the Homicide Squad, Scientific Investigation Bureau, where blood typing would be done, the Crime Scene personnel and all the detectives that could be put on the case to follow up on leads which were certain to come in.

Walker and Jack Marjoribanks then walked back into the kitchen. Walker had been told about a small slate blackboard that had been hanging on the wall near the door to the den. It apparently had been used as a daily memo of activities or appointments.

"It was hanging right here," Jack said. "According to the daughter, he had written the note 'Mom's @ Marge's.' He apparently did it in an attempt to put the kids at ease and buy some time needed to get rid of the body. As far as I can tell, Margaret Newman screwed that up by coming over to the house looking for Florence and caught him in the middle of cleaning up."

"Where's the board now?"

"Crime Scene took it with the other evidence. There were other messages on the board but that one had apparently been put on that evening or day after the kids left and Gerri said it was her father's handwriting."

"Jack. . . . tomorrow I'd like to get together with the kids and go through the house as thoroughly as possible and see what we can come up with. Especially anything missing that may have been used as a weapon."

"Okay, Rog, I'll make arrangements to pick them up in the morning."

On August 31, 1976, Detective Sergeant William Dempsey, Deputy Commanding Officer of the Homicide Squad, organized a massive search effort for the body of Florence Busacca. The search began on the 31st and ended on October 8th, 1976, encompassing hundreds of square miles, five thousand manhours and the assistance of the Suffolk County Police, their Marine Bureau and K-9 Units; Long Island State Parkway Police; the Conservation Department, Long Beach Police Department and Nassau County's own Marine and Air Bureau. The areas searched along the roadways were done on foot and on certain days covered as many as ten miles.

On September 1st the search team's efforts in the area of Patchogue, along Sunrise Highway, would yield another piece of promising evidence. On the north side of Sunrise Highway, between the Patchogue-Yaphank Road and Bellport-Yaphank Road, just two feet off the traveled portion of the highway, Police Officer Michael Connaughton, found a one foot square piece of quilt that was saturated with blood and matted hair. The discovery extended the search area by several miles. The piece of evidence was turned over to Detective Robert Edwards and taken immediately to the police lab in Nassau County. To find that the blood on the piece of quilt was A-B negative would be an important element of the investigation. But eastern Suffolk County is replete with pine barrens, swamps and wooded areas not to mention the miles of beach front along the ocean to the south and Long Island Sound to the north, and perhaps Florence Busacca would never be found.

On August 31st, Walker and Marjoribanks had obtained Florence Busacca's dental chart from Doctor Melvin Fuerst in Baldwin. The Doctor had also been shown the partial dental plate that was found at the scene and he identified it through records as belonging to Mrs. Busacca. Doctor Fuerst had not seen her since October of 1975.

Back once again at 1442 Circle Drive West, Walker, along with Marjoribanks and the two Busacca children went through the house in search of anything that might assist them in the search for Florence Busacca. A hair brush belonging to the missing woman, hair curlers and a comb were taken for hair samples, to be compared or typed with the unknown samples found on the quilt, the piece of cartilage and in the trunk of the defendant's vehicle. That task would fall to S.I.B.'s Charles Frass, an expert in hair identification.

Every available Homicide detective, squad detective, uniformed officer and men on special detail were recruited into service as the search for Florence Busacca broadened. New leads and information telephoned in were checked each day. Two dogs, belonging to the New York State Police and specially trained in locating dead bodies, were brought to Nassau County from Oneida, New York. Nothing was being overlooked. Neighbors, close friends, fellow workers, teachers and instructors who had tutored the

missing woman were constantly visited to determine
if any of them had received any word from Florence
since her disappearance. Medical and dental records
were obtained by Detective Henry Andreoli also learned
that Thomas Busacca had told an acquaintance that he
was aware that a "divorce was in progress."

From information later gathered during the investigation, those who knew of the divorce plans did not
know that Tom also had his suspicions about what
was inevitably going to happen. A sixth sense told him
that the marriage was about to end.

On September 7, 1976, Detective O'Connor, accompanied by Detective Albert Martino and Alfred
Vincinere of the Nassau County Homicide Squad,
went to the Busacca home once again to continue their
search for evidence. This time they had something on
which to focus their attention, a blue floral print quilt
that would match the piece found on Sunrise Highway several days earlier. At 12:15 A.M., Al Vincinere
made the discovery that was usually reserved for television mysteries, and another piece of puzzle fell
neatly into place. While searching a linen closet in the
downstairs hallway, he found a piece of quilt that appeared similar to the one already in police custody.
Barely ten minutes later, the three detectives had even
more reason to be ecstatic, for in a basement laundry
room, Detective Martino found another piece of the
quilt. These were significant discoveries in a case that
had not yet produced a plethora of evidence. Police
Officer Lawrence Gilbert of the Crime Scene Unit was
called back to the house to photograph these newly
found pieces of evidence in the areas in which they

had been located. Martino and Vincinere then transported their precious cargo to the Scientific Investigation Bureau at Headquarters. Excitement began to generate in the Homicide office and a more positive posture of optimism was beginning to replace the uncertainty and bewilderment that had subdued the attitudes of the investigators. If the sections of quilt could be positively matched, it would represent a very vital piece of circumstantial evidence on which this case would be tried if the body of Florence Busacca were not found. The expert called upon to conduct the comparison was Detective Henry Galgan, S.I.B.'s specialist on physical comparisons.

The scope of the investigation was broadened to include timed drives from the Busacca home to the vicinity of the Sunoco Service station in Holbrook and to Jersey Avenue, in an attempt to ascertain the feasibility of Thomas Busacca's ability to perform all that he alleged he had done within the time span he in fact had. The most direct route of travel was timed and the most circuitous that the defendant claimed he took was timed at speeds between fifty-five and sixty miles per hour. On one occasion the defendant's car, driven by Detective Walker, was driven over the routes described by Thomas Busacca.

On September 27, 1976, the Homicide Squad received a telephone call from Lieutenant Drew, Suffolk County Police Department's Third Squad Commander. The information he supplied caused a stir of activity in Nassau County. A woman's skull had been found on the south side of Montauk Highway in the vicinity of Patchogue. The skull was delivered to the

Suffolk County Medical Examiner's office and a dental
record of Florence Busacca was rushed to the Suffolk
morgue for comparison. It was not to be. The dental
record proved that the skull did not belong to Mrs.
Busacca. It was later determined that it had been removed from a crypt near where it had been found.

News releases and appeals to hunters and fishermen
to report any suspect site that resembled a grave were
issued. Major newspapers in the area gave extensive
coverage with photographs of the missing woman.

Having exhausted all of his preliminary investiga-
tions and being aided by a number of other investigators, Walker decided to sit down with the Busacca
children and then with Margaret Newman and get a
first hand account of what had occurred on that fateful day. He had not as yet met the children except for
the brief moment when Larry was brought to police
headquarters to confront his father.

He met the children at the family home. It was the
first time he had met the defendant's daughter Geraldine, a petite young lady with large brown eyes that
peeked out from behind her waist length brown hair
that partially hid an attractive face. The older of the
two children, Geraldine exhibited an extraordinary
manner. She was intelligent, was well versed, with an
uncanny ability to recall the most trivial detail of an
incident or event. Geraldine was a professional singer
and song-writer. Her voice compared to that of Bar-
bra Streisand or Liza Minnelli.

The three sat in the living room and Walker listened intently as they recited their stories. First one
then the other would correct each one's account as

they told him with a calmness that was almost unnatural, one of the most unusual stories Walker had ever heard.

Larry had arrived home about 9:40 P.M. in the company of his girlfriend and her father. He heard the dog barking inside the house and went to the front door which was ajar although the screen door was locked. The living room light was on as was the hall light. He then went to the side door which led to the mud room and went into the house. The mud room light was out but he made his way in, the hall light giving sufficient light for him to make his way into the kitchen and then the den. The television was on in the den but the light was out. He walked through the house and found no one. He then walked back to the mud room where his friend was waiting outside with her father. As he stepped down into the mud room he froze. There on the floor he saw a partial upper denture. He picked it up and recognized it as his mother's denture plate. He wondered what was going on and became concerned. At this time Gerri rushed into the house past Larry and went into the bathroom. His friend and her father left. They were not aware of what he had found. When Gerri came out of the bathroom he showed her the denture and she screamed. She turned the porch light on and Larry heard her scream again. This time it was a long, blood-curdling scream. He ran to the porch and saw his sister on her knees. He looked down and saw blood on the folded-up carpet, on the walls and on the window bench. Gerri found her mother's car keys under a chair next to a clot of blood. Gerri went immedi-

ately into the kitchen and checked the knives because
she was afraid her father had done something to hurt
her mother. He had previously written notes threat-
ening her and her mother.

When they finished their story, Walker sat in
stunned silence. It was incredible. He spoke briefly
and then decided it was now time to see Margaret
Newman. What she would have to say to him could
only be anticlimactic. But he had also been warned
that Mrs. Newman was a very emotional woman;
highly charged and filled with an intense anger.
Walker decided that he would take a veteran detective with him on his assignment. Henry Andreoli, a
veteran of Homicide for some twenty-five years,
would be able to keep the interview under control.
Walker was counting on it.

They arrived at the Newman house, which was only
two blocks from the Busacca residence. Margaret was
one of Florence's closest friends. They had performed
on stage together in the opera. She was extremely agitated and looked haggard from the lack of sleep. Her
eyes were dark, her face drawn.

She invited the detectives in and offered them coffee. They declined. Mrs. Newman ushered them into
a posh, well-furnished living room complete with a
large, expensive-looking piano. The detectives introduced themselves and they sat down. Mrs. Newman
dabbed at her eyes with a piece of tissue that she clutched
nervously in her hands. She broke the silence.

"How could this have happened?" she said, addressing no one in particular.

"Mrs. Newman," Walker began, "I know this may

be difficult for you and I understand that you have given a statement already. . . . but I am the investigating detective and I would like you to tell me what happened on Sunday, as best you can remember. There may be areas that are more clear to you now than they were before. So if you would, in your own words, tell Mr. Andreoli and me what you remember." Walker sat back and waited for the woman to gain her composure and then she began her story.

Florence Busacca had made an appointment to see Mrs. Newman's husband, an attorney, for the purpose of preparing an affidavit that would begin divorce proceedings against Thomas Busacca. Florence was supposed to be at the house at seven-thirty that evening. At eight-thirty, when she hadn't arrived, Margaret drove to the Busacca home to determine why Florence was late. As she turned into the driveway, she saw Tom's car there. She also saw a figure in the mud room area turn off the room light. The figure then became outlined in the doorway that leads to the kitchen. She could only identify the figure as that of a male and assumed that it was Tom. She said the figure had risen from a stooped position when her headlights first flashed on the mud room. She got out of the car and walked to the front door and tapped on the screen door several times with her car keys but received no response. The main front door of the house was ajar, but she didn't see anyone in the house. She began yelling and banging louder on the door, "Floria . . . where the hell are you?" After a short time she heard Tom's voice coming from the bathroom area and in a calm voice asked, "Who's there?" She told him who she was and asked him where Floria was, to which he responded, "I'm not dressed! Florence is on her way over to you." Margaret drove the short distance back to her home, but Florence was not there. She began to telephone places where she thought Florence might be but was unable to locate her. She was now very concerned and nervous, and a telephone call from Larry, Florence's son, telling her that he was unable to get an answer at his house and thought perhaps his mother was with her reinforced her anxiety. It was Larry's second phone call that began the chain of bizarre events that followed.

The search and massive manhunt for the body of Florence Busacca ended on October 8th, forty days after it had been initiated. No other evidence was found. No other lead was fruitful. The police department and the district attorney's office was now confronted with a challenge unprecedented in the history of New York State jurisprudence. Many in both departments thought it unlikely that a guilty verdict could be sustained without the physical presence of the body of Florence Busacca. In only one precedent case in the United States, which took place in California, was a verdict of guilty rendered against a man charged with murder without the presentation of the bodies of two people he had allegedly murdered. Walker and Grennan were still confident, undaunted.

Chapter Five

THE INVESTIGATORS GATHERED for a critique of the investigation's progress. One compelling piece of information which had been provided by Margaret Newman was focused upon, and certainly needed amplification: Mrs. Newman had stated that when she turned into the driveway of the Busacca home, Thomas Busacca was on the back porch and "rising very rapidly," running into the kitchen and turning the porch light off after him. Investigators determined that an attempt had been made on someone's part to clean up the blood from the porch floor and walls.

The Scientific Investigation Bureau held the answer. Could it be determined that attempts had been made to wipe up blood and a means available to record it? "Yes" was the unequivocal answer from Detective James Granelle and Officer Jay Caputo.

The test, used since the early twentieth century and the oldest presumptive test for blood on record, was considered. The chemical used was called luminol, one of the oldest and best known chemiluminescent compounds which reacts with blood to emit a fairly intense, bluish light. It does not, however, make a distinction between human or non-human blood. The luminol test utilizes the peroxidases-like activity of hemoglobin heme to produce a visible change in the reagent, color production for benzedine and phenolphtalein and light production or luminol. Questions were raised as to the prolonged period of time since the crime had been committed and the present state of the scene some five weeks later. "The older the blood, the better the test," asserted Granelle, reassuring everyone that the test would work.

On October 6, 1976, at 8 o'clock in the evening, Detectives Walker and Granelle and Officer Jay Caputo went to 1442 Circle Drive West to conduct the test. The porch area in which they would be working was approximately 8' by 9'.

"One good thing about this test, Roger, is that it won't interfere with any subsequent test you may want to have performed," said Granelle.

The luminol test had to be performed in the dark for the luminescence to be visible, hence the reason for Jay Caputo and his photographic equipment being made ready to record the results.

Granelle started the test. He sprayed all the areas of the walls and floor with luminol reagent. The light on the porch was turned off, and, in the absence of light, the luminol, where it had come into contact with blood, glowed, and a positive reaction was recorded. It was an exciting moment for the investigators. The swirling, wiping motion was no less than brilliant. Tom Busacca apparently had made a desperate attempt to clean up the blood until he was interrupted by Margaret Newman.

Caputo, using thin strips of masking tape, outlined the areas that reacted to the luminol. Then he proceeded to photograph the areas with the porch light on, at which time the swirls could not be seen, and with the light off, clearly making visible the wiping and swirling motion.

The test was a total success. It enabled investigators to note blood patterns that had not previously been recorded because of their minute size.

The success and accomplishments of the luminol test, which had corroborated certain aspects of the investigation, and had delighted the District Attorney's office because of its graphic implications, was rendered useless as evidence in the case against Thomas Busacca. In a ruling made during a pre-trial hearing, Judge Lockman had set a limit on the time period the police could have considered 1442 Circle Drive West a *crime scene*, allowing them continuous access to the premises. Unfortunately, the date he set was prior to October 6, 1976, making the luminol test null and void. The successful test was, however, an interesting experiment with a little used weapon by the men of the Crime Scene Search Unit and the Scientific Investigation Bureau.

In another part of the lab, working methodically was Detective Henry Galgan, a criminalist in charge of physical evidence and assigned to the police lab; who had worked on the three pieces of quilt, the one found along Sunrise Highway and the two pieces found at the Busacca home. By performing a physical microscopic examination of the three pieces; observing their fiber and thread make, and by performing chemical tests on the threads and fibers and then making a physical jigsaw match of all three pieces of cloth, he found that weave of all three pieces was similar in that it consisted of forty-four threads per inch count in one direction and a sixty-thread count in the opposite direction. All three pieces of cloth were consistent in that they were composed of a woven cotton and cotton matting stitched into a center portion of two layers. He found it consistent in the floral design both in color and the design itself. He found that two of the pieces of cloth were similar, both having no binding on it whatsoever. He also found the threads to be of approximately the same diameter, within the area of one-thousandth and two-thousandths of an inch in diameter. He was able to assemble them into a configuration of matching edges. When the matching edges were in place, photographs were taken of the reassembled pieces for the purpose of preservation and trial.

Galgan's expert opinion concluded that the two pieces of cloth were originally one piece of fabric and were separated by cutting. The third piece of cloth was once one part of the other two pieces of cloth. All three pieces at one point in time formed one portion of a quilt.

Galgan's findings and conclusions lifted the hopes of Walker and Grennan. It was a mighty powerful piece of evidence. Perhaps New York State would have its first conviction without a body.

Walker and O'Connor spent the next several weeks reviewing and cataloging the reports that had come in from the field. They had their own reports to prepare as well. Both men spent long hours in the lab

where they expected most of their critical evidence
would be found. A trial date had been set for March,
1977, and enough evidence, as circumstantial as it was,
had to convince a jury of twelve men and women that
Florence Busacca was, in fact, dead, and that, beyond
a reasonable doubt, Thomas Busacca did kill her on the
night of August 29, 1976. Barry Grennan, the Assistant
District Attorney who would prosecute the case, suggested that they begin their trial preparation in January.

Since the official termination of the search effort in
October, several interesting developments occurred.
The first was word received from a maintenance mechanic at the Nassau Correctional Facility in East
Meadow where Mr. Busacca was incarcerated. The
man told the investigators that he had had occasion
to see Tom Busacca in the clinic of the facility. He
had known both Tom and his wife for several years.
He had read that Tom had been arrested and his wife
was missing so therefore was not too surprised to see
him. The man walked over to Tom and said hello to
him. He seemed surprised to see the mechanic.

"I didn't know you worked here!" he said, looking
up from his seat. He then said, "It's too bad I wasn't
with you. I wouldn't be in this trouble now."

The man asked Tom what had happened and Tom
only made a gesture. He asked Busacca, "How bad
did you hurt her?"

"Pretty bad," he answered. "It looked like she was
nailed to the cross."

Tom then turned away and the mechanic walked
away slowly, digesting what he had just heard.

The second development occurred on December 17,

1976, and confounded the investigators. A black inmate stated that Tom Busacca had told him that he had killed his wife and had mutilated the body, putting some parts in the Great South Bay and the remaining parts in Peconic Bay. He also indicated that Busacca had asked if he, the inmate, knew anyone who could handle a contract to take care of two witnesses in his case. The inmate told Busacca he would see what he could do and subsequently notified the District Attorney's office. Detective Tom Allen was assigned to handle the report and question the man further. It was too unbelievable to be taken seriously. But the investigators and the District Attorney would be remiss in their duties if they ignored it. On the contrary, the story was consistent with all else that had happened, and the third development was the kicker.

On January 21, 1977, Walker received a telephone call from a young female who stated that she was the hitchhiker that Tom Busacca had stopped for the night of August 29, 1976. After having read several newspaper articles of the incident and seeing Busacca's photograph in newspapers, she was convinced of it. Walker and O'Connor went to the girl's house and took her back to the homicide office where she was interviewed and a written statement taken from her.

She said the man had picked her up as she was hitchhiking on Sunrise Highway in the vicinity of Babylon, and told her he was going all the way "east." She was surprised when Busacca suddenly stopped the car after only a few miles and ordered her out of the car. "This is as far as I'm going," he told her. She recalled how the man appeared very nervous and disheveled and constantly stared at the floor at her feet; glared at her with piercing eyes. She became a little anxious and was relieved when asked to get out of the car.

Detectives Walker and O'Connor worked long hours, and their share of sleepless nights wove into place a profile of Thomas Busacca and his wife. Subpoenas had to be obtained to seize some hospital records, dental records and the bank accounts of both Florence and Tom Busacca. The investigation went smoothly, and people went out of their way to extend a helping hand to the investigators.

Some of the facts brought out during the investigation concluded that Florence Busacca had a rare AB negative blood type which contrasted with her husband's type O positive. This distinctive difference would greatly enhance the Scientific Investigation Bureau's efforts to classify, identify and separate the blood splatters found in Thomas Busacca's car and home. The rarity of the wife's blood type was an added bonus. It was also learned that a savings account belonging to Florence Busacca had a small balance of $464.92 remaining in it and had not been drawn on after August 29, 1976. Her passport was still in the safe deposit box at the bank.

Florence had been married to Tom for twenty-five years, and of those years, her husband had only held employment for about five years, total. Support had either been generated from his parents or her own aggressive attitudes toward work. The family relationship was strained, the social atmosphere electrified. Florence resented the fact that while she labored to make ends meet and saw to it that the children were not deprived of the very essential commodities of life, her husband amused himself about the home, seduced by the television, much in the manner of a child, and growing lean on the subsistence that was acquired by others.

Because she had to secure a job to ward off the complete destruction of the family, it meant that the thirteen-year-old son in the family of two children would be left practically unsupervised at a time when he needed parental guidance and attention. She soon began teaching voice at her home in Baldwin, and this put her in a more comfortable position to see to the needs of the family. Her good fortune was short-lived however. Her health began to deteriorate, as her mental anguish was compounded by the continued contemptible demeanor of Tom. He never seemed embarrassed to turn to her for a handout. Utility bills were being neglected and his only response would be a note to the company explaining his family's crises:

> Our family is in the last throes of a combined personal disaster and related short money income source. I am forced to change my full-time job due to my employer's business failures. I am now left with my part-time job which I've done for the last six years as a teacher. I received part of my salary and am submitting my own check as part of what I owe Lilco—partially at least. As things break, I'll be catching up with my bills.

But such conjured-up ideas were a figment of the man's surrealistic imaginings. There were no prospects for employment; there were no part-time jobs of any significance. It was the determined volition,

the love for her family, that kept Florence Busacca
from a complete breakdown. She had to be strong to
save the sensitivities of a young man who needed her
in order to communicate within the family circle that
was now being threatened. The continual arguing that
he had to constantly bear witness to had, in her judgment, begun to affect his scholastic standings. He came
to her one day and confided that he had become quite
disturbed over the turmoil that had suddenly settled
over the family like an ominous dark cloud, penetrating every room and making rational conversation impossible.

On one occasion, Florence found a note left for her
on a counter in the kitchen, which frightened her:

Florence!

. . . . As your Gerri came into this house today . . . I
suffered the pangs of a killer. Don't leave her alone
for me to get at her. Her arrogance, activities concerning you and I, or our friends have become part
of you.

TALK LATER

Florence Busacca was always finding notes that typ-
ified her husband's absolute loathing for his daughter
and she herself was the victim of maliciously written
notes:

Dear Wife,

You came pushing in to get the phone and there was
a student at the piano waiting for you, and Larry was

preparing to go out with friends, and *there I was having a steaming fit that started this morning in bed. You've been running and I suddenly feel the complete foolishness of pursuing you intellectually or sexually since you don't care to concentrate on either.* You acted on your realizations in the times you left our home life in the past. *The pain of living with that bank of memories is something I can no longer carry.* We've talked about all this, usually you've scoffed at me over moral questions and then money takes over the situation and as you have stated, *money is the crux of it all and we should never have been married. Now I believe you're right. You know I'm a jealous husband, then and now.* Your being out of my life at those times hurt drastically. And you've said that when Larry is fourteen you'll be leaving me was no help to our home life. This can be seen in the ugly mouthing of Gerri and her fleeing attitude. Even when she was beating you with her hands or trying to disembowel me that day (We both can't forget and I can't forgive) so our values were smashed.

. . . . I have felt that I could not stop you from doing some of the things I don't appreciate from you as an artist, insofar as having no money to back you up. To the unfairness of my administration backed layoffs and company closings is a thorn in my side that pains the most when we try to resolve our petty and deeper differences.

The investigators were now certain, without a doubt, that they were dealing with a disturbed mind, a man who had, for the most part, fantasized for a lifetime and was cruelly sheltered from the realities of responsibility and a productive mind by an overly protective father who stymied his son's personal ambitions with money and provisions whenever the basic necessities at home were imperiled. Tom was an only child and had never been weaned from his parents' unceasing attention. Their overindulgence had left their son an irresponsible, lethargic and slothful fifty-one year old child. By their own innocent actions, they had created an individual who could no longer function in the average social circumstances. He had become subdued and recluse; unable to engage in normal conversation; speaking in fragmented sentences that had little or no meaning and were not always understood by others.

On June 4, 1976, Tom Busacca met an acquaintance of the family on the boardwalk in Long Beach. He had his camera and some equipment and he smiled when he saw someone he knew. He engaged his friend in a conversation which delved into the area of family problems. He was painfully aware that his wife was seeking some kind of separation and bemoaned his lack of employment over the years. In a telephone conversation on August 9, 1976, he confided in another acquaintance that there were "family problems" and that there was a "divorce" in progress.

Depression began to swallow Thomas Busacca alive. He became a self-imprisoned man in his own home and Florence Busacca became increasingly nervous. She feared for her safety and the safety of her children, Larry and Gerri. Thomas rejected any plan for family counseling that had been encouraged by Florence. He said emphatically that there was nothing wrong with him. Besides, he didn't have time. Tom Busacca had nothing but time.

When Florence suggested to her husband that she

had thought of going to Paris with her sister, his only comment was, "Over my dead body will I allow you to go away. You think I'll let you run around having affairs?" He then called his sister-in-law and chastised her attempting to break up his marriage and coaxing his wife to have extramarital affairs. After the call, Tom was in a frenzy, to the point where young Larry suggested that his mother lock herself in her bedroom for the night. Larry did the same. It wasn't the first time that this young man had feared the ire of his father. He and his sister had on occasion placed thread at the top of the stairway, stretching it across the hall from room to room. When the thread had been broken or moved in the morning, they knew that their father had been prowling outside their bedroom doors. It frightened and sickened them.

Florence Busacca, once a performer who began her career at Carnegie Hall and gave concerts at Carl Fisher Hall and Judson Hall and was a member of the Opera Orchestra on radio on a number of occasions, was now struggling to preserve her dignity and defend the welfare of her children against a man who had gone mad.

On one occasion, his wife found a brief rambling note on a piece of paper left on the table for her to see!

Haven't asked for welfare or food stamps and how do I compose a letter to hold off creditors!!!

On another piece of paper she found printed in bold upper case print:

"DECIMATED: DIVORCE, SEPARATION OR DEATH"

Florence Busacca's fears turned to panic. She would now seek a separation and confide once again in her dearest, most trusted friend, Margaret Newman. Her husband was an attorney and agreed to draw up the papers for her.

On August 29, 1976, at 7:30 P.M., Florence Busacca was to sign the first draft of those papers to be served on her husband the following day. But she failed to return to the home of Margaret Newman at the given hour, and was never heard from again. Not a telephone call, letter, telegram, not a word.

Perhaps one of the most interesting observations written by Thomas Busacca and one which probably told a lot more about the man and his dilemma is the following:

> Compassion is a trait that money can disintegrate when in the eyes of our wives the money was the glue of comrades.
> If the money is by circumstances curtailed, see then how the gentle palms that counted your silver hair and your silver coin is now become a hammer of vengeance. Her scope and sexuality are remolded to the forms of the hammer's swing so beware its weight. She thrusts and smashes out irrevocable dismissals of friendship by impact.

Chapter Six

TRIAL PREPARATION BEGAN in mid-January, 1977, after the holiday mood had dissipated and a return to some semblance of normalcy prevailed on the Island.

Assistant District Attorney Barry Grennan would be prosecuting the case. A member of the District Attorney's staff for eight years, he had attended Boston College and graduated from Brooklyn Law School. He had been in private practice for nine years. A very serious but easy-going man, he had a love for sailing and entered his sloop 'Serenity' in many of the Island's yachting races.

Assisting him would be ADA Abby Boklan who would handle research of case law and maintain an orderly presentation of evidence and witnesses.

It was learned that Attorney Marvin Zevin would be defending Thomas Busacca. Zevin attended the Solomon P. Chase Law School in Cincinnati, Ohio; the Seton Hall College in Newark, New Jersey, and obtained an engineering degree from Cornell University. He had been practicing law since 1966.

The trial began on March 2, 1977, before County Court Judge John S. Lockman, in Mineola, New York.

Judge Lockman had been a judge since 1964, presiding over both civil and criminal matters. He had also served the other two branches of government: Executive, as Assistant District Attorney and the Legislative as Hempstead Town Councilman. Married and the father of five children, he is a member of the American Bar Association, the New York State Association of Trial Lawyers, and the Nassau County Bar Association for whom he has lectured and written articles. He attended Hofstra University and is a graduate of the United States Merchant Marine Academy and the New York University Law School.

Both attorneys made rather lengthy opening statements, each magnifying his personal aims and conclusions. Grennan painted a picture of a brutal, sadistic beating and murder. Marvin Zevin countered with his steadfast argument that Florence was alive and well and living in California or Milan.

The case would be determined by a panel of eleven men and one woman from varying walks of life, a cross-section of Busacca's peers.

Early on, Grennan presented the police witnesses who initially responded to 1442 Circle Drive West. Their testimonies went smoothly with the anticipated objections, upon occasion, from Marvin Zevin, notably the use of the word "blood" as what the men claimed they saw.

The going was not so effortless as the testimonies focused upon the neighbor Margaret Newman, the forensic scientists, the children, and the police laboratory technicians. Marvin Zevin was confident that this case could be won and he applied himself to that task with the tenacity of a bull dog.

Grennan decided that Margaret Newman would be his first civilian witness. She was, after all, the one person who saw Tom Busacca and spoke to him at his home, probably at the time he was attempting to clean up the blood. But Grennan was concerned about Newman's emotional state of mind. Here was a woman who was the closest personal friend of the victim and Grennan was concerned about extemporaneous remarks that could easily prompt a motion for mistrial. Grennan and Walker spoke to the woman and instructed her only to answer the questions asked and not to volunteer information.

They then entered the courtroom and the court officer called the next witness: "THE PEOPLE CALL MARGARET NEWMAN."

Margaret Newman took the witness stand and Grennan rose slowly from his chair. Please Margaret, he said to himself, no spontaneous and unsolicited comments. Hang in there.

The witness was sworn and Grennan began his examination, carefully wording each question so that it would be understood by the witness.

"Mrs. Newman, directing your attention to the twenty-ninth day of August, nineteen seventy-six, you were acquainted, were you not, with Florence Busacca?"

"I was."

"How long had you known her prior to that day?"

"Six and a half years."

"Did you know the other members of the family as well?"

"Yes, I certainly did."

"Who were the other members of the family?"

"Well, there was Geraldine, who I also taught, I am a concert pianist. And I also taught her. . . ."

It wasn't unexpected, Marvin Zevin was on his feet. "Your Honor, I object as nonresponsive and I would ask that you instruct the witness to answer only the questions asked."

"Sustained," agreed Judge Lockman. "Mrs. Newman, would you direct yourself just to answering the questions?"

"Yes, all right."

"My question is," continued Grennan, "who are the other members of the family?"

"Geraldine and Larry."

"And was there a husband?"

"Thomas Busacca!" replied Margaret Newman with contempt in her voice.

"Is that gentleman seated here in the courtroom?"

"Yes, sir."

"Did you know him in August, nineteen seventy-six?"

"Yes, I did."

"Now, Mrs. Newman, directing your attention to the twenty-ninth day of August, did you have occasion to meet with and be with Florence Busacca that day?"

"Yes," she said weakly.

"About what time?"

"Twelve o'clock noon."

"For how long were you with her at that time?"

"From twelve o'clock until about five o'clock when she left."

"And did you have an appointment to meet her again?"

"Yes."

"What time?"

"Seven-thirty that same evening."

"And where?"

"At my home."

"With whom were you to meet her?"

"Floria that's her real name . . . I call her Floria. . . . She was to be at my home at seven-thirty that evening in relation to a matrimonial problem."

"What is your husband's occupation?"

"My husband is an attorney and he was representing her in a divorce action."

"Your Honor, I'm going to move to strike the answer," complained Zevin. "It certainly goes beyond the simple question asked by the District Attorney."

"Yes," declared Judge Lockman, turning to the witness. "Mrs. Newman, would you please listen carefully to the question and answer only the question? Otherwise we may get into some difficulty. So listen carefully to the question and only the question; and only answer the question, don't volunteer anything."

"I will try, sir," responded the witness, tears beginning to well in her eyes.

"Is that why the appointment was for seven-thirty . . . to meet your husband in connection with this matter?" continued Grennan.

"Yes."

The question and the response was objected to by the defense counselor and the judge sustained the objection and had the answer stricken from the record.

"Did you have a conversation with Mrs. Busacca as to why she was returning at seven-thirty?" queried Grennan.

"Yes, I did have a conversation with her."

"Did she tell you why she was returning?"

"Yes."

"What did she tell you?"

An objection was again raised by Zevin and sustained by the court.

"I may answer?" inquired Mrs. Newman.

"You may not!" admonished the judge.

"Did she come to your house at seven-thirty?" urged Grennan.

"No, sir."

"What did you do when she didn't arrive at seven-thirty?"

"Just waited. I waited until eight o'clock."

"What did you do at eight o'clock?"

"I started calling her home."

"Did anyone answer?"

"No."

"What did you do then?"

"I waited another few minutes and called again."

"Did anyone answer this time?"

"No."

"Then what did you do?"

"I decided to go to her home and bring her back with me. We were only three blocks away from each other."

"Did you go there?"

"Yes, I did."

"About what time?"

"Twenty-five after eight, eight-thirty."

"What happened when you got there?"

"I pulled into the driveway. There was another car there, and at first I saw nothing except the porch light that was on. The porch leads into the kitchen. And I turned my motor off, and turned my bright lights on."

"What did you see?"

"Well, I saw Thomas rising. . . ."

"Where?"

"From the porch. On the porch. I saw him rising very rapidly. Obviously he was. . . ."

"Objection?" shouted Marvin Zevin.

"Sustained."

"You saw him rising very rapidly. What did you see next?"

"I saw him running into the kitchen quickly and turning off the porch light and standing in the kitchen door."

"And then what did you do?"

"I then got out of my car and walked around to the front of the house, the door was ajar so I could see to the right of the living room but I couldn't see to the left."

"Did you attempt to enter?"

"Yes, but the screen door was locked."

"The inner door was ajar?"

"Yes, the inner door was ajar."

"What did you do then?"

"So I had my car keys, I started to rap on the door and I called 'Floria?' and no one answered. And I rapped again on the door and called again, a little bit louder this time, but no one answered. And I banged on the door again. This time the dog came barking and I told him to shut up. Finally, I banged on the screen door with all my might, because I must say I was very angry. I screamed very loud and then Tom said, 'Who is it?' and I said, 'It's Margaret, Tom!' and Tom said, 'I'm not dressed. Florence is on her way over to your house.' My reply was, 'That's good, because the coffee is getting cold.' I ran, jumped into my car and went speeding home, pulled into the driveway, and rushed into the house. I have a nurse that's employed by me and I said to her, 'Betty, where's Florence?' and she said, 'She's not here.' I said, 'Impossible. Tom said she was on her way over here.' She says, 'Well, she's not here.' and that was that."

"What did you do then?" asked Grennan.

"Well, then I sat down and the next thing I remember distinctly, I couldn't see the clock very clearly and I said, 'Betty, what time is it?' and she said, 'Nine o'clock.' "

Zevin's objection was sustained and the jury was instructed to disregard it.

Lockman turned to Mrs. Newman once more. "Mrs. Newman, you know you're not a lawyer and you don't understand these things. You cannot tell us that conversation. Whatever anybody said to you, you can't tell us unless there are certain exceptions that apply. So, whenever you get to a part where somebody said something, just say that you had a conversation. You can tell us what you said, but not what somebody else said."

"I see," acknowledged the witness.

Grennan continued his direct examination. "How long did you wait?"

"About twenty minutes."

"Then what happened?"

"Then I got a phone call from Larry and he said. . . ."

"Objection!" said Zevin, forcefully.

"Sustained."

"After the phone call from Larry, what did you do?"

"I tried to locate Floria. I thought perhaps she was. . . ."

An objection was made by Zevin and sustained by Judge Lockman. He once again instructed the witness that she could only testify to what she did.

"What efforts did you take to locate Florence?" inquired Grennan.

"I called a neighbor. I thought she was at this particular house with her daughter."

"Did you have any success?"

"No, sir."

"What did you do next?"

"Then I started to really worry, because I didn't know where she was."

"Your Honor," interrupted Zevin. "I don't know what to do. I am continually objecting. The questions are proper but the answers are not responsive. I don't want to continue to object. I am at a loss as to what to do."

"Mr. Zevin. . . ." interjected Margaret Newman.

"Please, Mrs. Newman," chided the judge, "I have cautioned you about this. I want you to just restrict yourself to the answer. You can't tell us what somebody said, and you can't tell us what you thought. You can't tell us anything of what we call the operation of your mind. That is not permitted. You can tell us, however, if the question is 'What did you do?' or 'What happened next?' You can tell us what you did."

Margaret Newman was doing everything that Grennan feared she would. The fact that any one of her extemporaneous remarks could be grounds for a mistrial or a reversal upon a later appeal was a very real and ever-present concern. It bothered him as he continued his direct examination.

"A period of time then went by. What happened next?"

"I received another phone call."

"From whom?"

"From Larry."

"Did you have a conversation with him?"

"Yes."

"What happened after the conversation?"

"I couldn't understand him, he was screaming so loud and. . . ."

"What did you do?" Grennan insisted, trying to contain her answer. Mrs. Newman then indicated that after speaking to Geraldine for a brief moment she went back to the Busacca home.

"What did you see upon your arrival at the Busacca home?" inquired Grennan.

"I saw two hysterical children screaming and crying and I couldn't. . . ."

Judge Lockman looked sternly at the witness. "Excuse me. The jury will disregard that. I thought you wanted her to tell you what she saw in relation to the facility and not the children screaming and crying. This is prejudicial. The jury is to disregard it. It has nothing to do with your responsibility. Strike it from your minds."

It was definitely not the answer that Barry was seeking. But the scene of two hysterical children would leave an indelible impression upon the minds of the jury. But how many more of these outbursts would Judge Lockman tolerate from the witness?

"Mrs. Newman," Grennan continued, "What were these children doing when you met them?"

"They were pacing back and forth. They were very frightened."

"Were they screaming and crying?"

"Yes."

"Objection!" bellowed Zevin.

"Sustained," scolded the judge. "The jury will disregard it. We can't possibly have a fair trial here, member of the jury, if we put this kind of information before you. You are supposed to get facts that relate to the trial, not the reactions of various people. And I ask that you desist from that, Mr. Grennan. I thought I made it clear that I didn't want that before this jury."

"May I approach the bench, Your Honor?" asked the District Attorney.

Marvin Zevin and Grennan approached the bench so that their conversations would not be heard by the jury.

"Judge, these people are going to be witnesses as to the state of mind they were in at the time and that is part of this case," implored Grennan.

"State of mind is only to serve one purpose," admonished Lockman, "and that is to prejudice this jury."

"No, sir," insisted Grennan.

"It has nothing to do with this case!" said Lockman sternly.

"Their observations are going to be put in here and what the condition was at the time that they arrived home."

"No way," countered the judge. "Its prejudice outweighs any probative value at this stage."

"I can only put the witness on once."

"On no! If it comes out later that they failed to make observations because of a state of mind, at that stage you will be able to do it. But at this stage, it serves one purpose, and that one purpose is to inflame the jury. It is the only possible point."

"Then I ask the right to recall the witness."

"That, you have a right," conceded Lockman. "No question about it. The case is inflammatory enough without additional fuel to the fire."

The questioning of Margaret Newman proceeded. Whether by desire or by design, the impact of the witness' unsolicited remarks to his questions could not be purged from the minds of the jurors, though instructed by the judge to disregard and 'strike it from your minds.' Such an instruction tended more to focus attention to the very matter the Court sought to expunge.

"Mrs. Newman, upon entering the Busacca house," Grennan pressed, "what else did you see?"

"I saw a lot of blood all over the porch, blood in the bathroom, blood all over a piece of carpeting that was pushed under a bench, blood in the driveway. There was a lot of blood."

Grennan proceeded to lead Mrs. Newman through

a myriad of questions, bringing out that she was a concert pianist and also an accompanist to Florence Busacca. They were both business and social acquaintances and saw one another almost daily.

"Mrs. Newman, did there come a time in nineteen seventy-six when Florence Busacca took a trip?"

"Yes."

"And when did that trip take place?"

"In June, I believe."

"And did you do anything in connection with that trip with regard to her family?"

"Yes."

"What did you do?"

"I told Floria that I would take care of the children. That I would call daily and check on them. That she should not have any fears, because she really didn't want to leave the children. That I would feed them and take care of them. That she wasn't to worry."

"Excuse me, Mrs. Newman," interrupted the judge. "I can understand. You know, I went through law school and spent a whole lifetime, and I have trouble with these rules so I can see that you would. But you can't tell us things like 'she was concerned' or things that she may have said. What you can tell us is that you took care of the children, that sort of thing. Mr. Grennan is trying to show the relationship and it is very difficult. But Mr. Zevin has a very serious responsibility here. He has a very important function and he has to protect his client from any evidence that is improper. And when you say that 'she' said something, that's improper. When you say what you thought, that's improper. It is my job to see that this is a fair trial and we can't have a fair trial if that continues."

"I'll try, sir," said a tearful witness. "Except that the only thing is that what I am expressing is the truth. So that's. . . ."

"See!" cautioned Lockman. "That is the sort of thing that is going to prevent us from having a fair trial."

"Well, I took care. . . ."

"Please, don't say another thing," snapped the judge, his patience wearing thin. "All right. Members of the jury, we are going to have a short recess. Don't discuss the case, please."

The jury was ushered out of the courtroom by the court officer. Lockman turned to Grennan as they left.

"Mr. Grennan," pleaded Judge Lockman, "can you talk to the witness within the framework of what I told her?"

"I certainly can, Your Honor," replied Barry Grennan. "But I want to be heard in this area. In view of the opening with Mr. Zevin, I believe now it is an issue or what properly is in issue, particularly where he indicated in his opening that Florence Busacca would be a singer in La Scala, perhaps, or California, and would abandon her children. I think now what is proper before this jury is, would this woman in the past, when she did disappear, in the sense that she took a vacation, what arrangements have been made for them now that we don't know where she is."

"Mr. Grennan, you know very well what I am talking about. I'm not talking about what you are attempting to do. I am talking about the manner in which you are doing it. There are rules of evidence which have been developed over the centuries to protect all of us. These rules are being trampled on in this courtroom and I am *not* going to permit it. Now, you tell the witness what she can say and what she can't say in a courtroom. That's what I'm directing you to do and this is your last chance to do it."

"I agree with that," declared the prosecutor, "but in this area, Mrs. Busacca's area of concern for her children, I believe, because of the opening, I can obtain proof of it. I can see that the witness is way beyond the rules of evidence and I'll make every effort to have her stay within the bounds of those rules."

"I missed your point," said the judge. "Your point is that you should be permitted to establish a conversation with the missing Mrs. Busacca concerning her attitude toward her children?"

"That's correct," answered Grennan. "Her conclusion that she is concerned is one thing, but what arrangements Mrs. Busacca made for her children when she went to Paris on a prior occasion and what arrangements were made on this occasion of the 29th to, as Mr. Zevin indicated, take a trip to La Scala or California, are now relevant and come within the exceptions."

"It's relevant? It runs smack into the hearsay rule," cautioned Lockman.

"There are exceptions to the hearsay rule."

"Which exception do you apply?"

"The state of mind of Mrs. Busacca should be admissible. Mr. Zevin is contending that she voluntarily absented herself without taking any precaution for her children and what her relationship with her children was. The only way to prove that is what relations, expressions of concern she made, which otherwise is hearsay. I'll concede."

"I thought the state of mind exception only dealt with the state of mind of the witness, not with the state of mind of the missing person," pondered Lockman.

"I think, Judge, that 'Richardson' would indicate that it's of the declarant."

"I see now what you are driving at, Mr. Grennan, but it was the manner in which she was stating these things. I can appreciate that she is very upset. This has been a terrible experience for her. But we have to do something to preserve the semblance of a fair trial.

"Gentlemen. Section two-o-five of the Tenth Edition of Richardson states that you can show by a statement of the missing declarant something that the declarant said to show the state of mind. That is, the state of mind of the declarant. So, on that basis, this is what will be permitted under the citations of Loetsch v. New York City."

"Now, Judge, the same argument which I didn't pursue at the time prevailed with regard to what her intentions were on the twenty-ninth when she was to sign divorce papers. That was her announced intentions."

"How does that show a state of mind?" questioned Lockman.

"To obtain a divorce."

"In other words, you want to introduce a statement that she made?"

"I am going to do it another way," decided Grennan.

"Mr. Grennan, I am telling you that if you raise

hearsay, you have a problem before me. I am a very strict adherent to the rules of evidence."

"I know you know them well. That's why I was taken a little aback by this."

"Flattery will get you nowhere, Mr. Grennan. In this case the law is in your favor and I will permit you to ask the witness questions with regard to what Mrs. Busacca told her to do for the Busacca children. That does not include what she said to Mrs. Busacca. That's admitted under a different theory, because that is what *she* said.

"Now, under the circumstances, will you give me an offer of proof of what she is going to say?"

"She's going to say it was an arrangement to take care of the children in the sense of calling every day, seeing that they were fed and so forth."

"She has testified to that already," charged Zevin.

"But much of that was stricken, wasn't it?" suggested Lockman, looking at the District Attorney. "I will permit testimony regarding the arrangements that were made for the children, but I don't want to get involved with the situation that Mr. Zevin is complaining about very rightfully, where she gives statements like 'I'm here to tell the truth!' That I can live without and this record can live without it."

"I agree, Your Honor. I'm doing the best I can."

"I know that."

"Incidentally, that answer was not responsive to my question; it was to yours."

"Right. . . . you really know how to hurt a guy," Lockman smiled. Tranquility had momentarily returned to the courtroom. It was a moment to regain one's composure and assuage frayed nerves.

The task of restraining Margaret Newman was more taxing than Grennan had imagined. He glanced at the clock at the rear of the courtroom. For a moment the turmoil of the day left his mind, giving way to an expanse of blue skies and billowing sails, the rush of ocean waves rising and falling majestically, nurtured along by an untiring wind and gentle spray forced over the bow by the biting, spear-like nose of the sleek racing boat. His reverie was suddenly shattered by the judge. The jury had been returned to the courtroom.

"Mr. Grennan? . . . You may proceed, Mr. Grennan," prodded Lockman.

Grennan moved toward the witness and then turned to Judge Lockman. "Judge, I would like to make an offer before the Court at the bench, if I may, with regard to the conversation Mrs. Newman had with Mr. Busacca while his wife was in Paris. I want to eliminate any possible conflict.

"I am not suggesting that there is anything wrong. It is the telephone conversation only that I am offering. Mr. Zevin has a copy of it."

Judge Lockman studied the document which contained the conversation that Grennan was uneasy about. He then turned to Marvin Zevin. "I'll permit it," he said. "Mr. Zevin, you have an exception."

"And you'll deny my motion for a mistrial after it goes in?" inquired Zevin.

Lockman studied the document again, wanting to be sure before he committed himself and to be certain that allowing it would not result in reversible error.

"I assume you're offering it on the issue of intent, Mr. Grennan," clarified the judge.

"On the issue of intent, motive, insanity, and state of mind of the defendant," replied Grennan.

"All right. I'll deny your motion for a mistrial and if you don't want to make it in front of the jury, you have it now if you want to," advised Lockman.

"Consider it deemed now," responded Zevin.

"The motion for a mistrial is deemed now and denied, based on Mrs. Newman's testimony relating to a conversation she allegedly had with the defendant. The motion for mistrial is deemed made at this time; it is denied, and Mr. Zevin has an exception."

Grennan once again approached the witness. "Mrs. Newman, will you please relate to the Court that conversation that you had with Mr. Busacca while Mrs. Busacca was in Paris?"

"I called the house and Thomas answered the phone. I asked him how everything was and how the children were. He said that they were okay, and then we were talking about some trivialities. He said something to the effect that he didn't know why she had to go to Paris because he was going to rent a trailer during the month of August and take the family away and considering that, I owed. . . ."

"No!" cautioned Grennan, "Just what you said and what he said."

"So I said, 'That's not a vacation, trailering. It's hard work. Floria would have to cook and keep the trailer clean. That's no vacation.' I told him that where she is is the best place. She's being served, doesn't have to worry about cooking and cleaning. He told me. . . . excuse me, but it is embarrassing," said the witness.

"Mrs. Newman, we understand that it may be embarrassing, but it has to be said in the words that were used," encouraged Lockman.

"He said . . . 'All she's doing in Paris is screwing around.' I said to him, 'I'm going to forget you even said that because we know what a wonderful wife you have; we know what a wonderful person she is and she has never in her entire life ever had a lover, even looked at another man.' He laughed and said, 'I guess you're right, but I have a very big penis and I'm sick and tired of being castrated by my family.' I told him that nobody was castrating him. The only thing that Floria wants out of life is for you to get a job and bring home some food and take care of the family. That's all she wanted."

"I didn't see that in the minutes, Mr. Grennan," declared Lockman. "That is stricken."

"Your Honor, it is not in this statement, but I ask that it stay as an issue of recent fabrication," retorted Zevin, who would use it to impeach the witness' credibility and the veracity of her entire testimony. "Her own collective thoughts have permeated her mind to the extent that she now finds it difficult to extract the spoken words from her own reflective thoughts."

Mr. Zevin's request that it remain on the record was granted. He then asked that in light of the remarks unsolicited from Mrs. Newman, that his application for a mistrial be reconsidered. The jury was sent out.

"Mr. Zevin, since your earlier motion for a mistrial was denied, a completely new set of facts have emerged from her answer which was completely different from what had been presented at the offer of proof. In other words, I said, given the facts that were presented to me, that Mrs. Newman could testify to the conversation with the defendant. I did not know that she was going to say that she told him 'you ought to get a job,' and make those other statements that I consider prejudicial. That I didn't expect and it wasn't presented to me. If it had been presented to me, I would have excised that conversation. The jury shouldn't be hearing her opinion that he ought to have a job. He's on trial for murder, not for being unemployed."

"This is a conversation with him," argued Grennan. "What she said to him and what he said to her."

"But when she says something that is prejudicial, it is excised. Why should the jury be inflamed by his wife being upset, that he has been unemployed for four years? Why do we have to inflame them with that? There is enough inflammatory material in this case which is not the people's fault, just the facts of the case. It is an inflammatory case in its very nature," exhorted the judge.

"Judge, just by way of explanation to the Court on the question of murder, when Gerri and Larry Busacca testify, they're going to tell you about an argument in the house in the early morning of the 29th, the day of the murder, between Mr. and Mrs. Busacca, relative to him not supplying money for the family and so forth. I intend to offer that on the issue of motive," suggested Mr. Grennan.

"That's a different situation than a gratuitous remark from a nonmember of the family that he 'ought to get a job' in the context of a man that had been unemployed for four years," replied Lockman.

"But this is what she said: 'that the only thing Florence wants is for you to get a job.' He said to her, 'I'm tired of being castrated.'" She is responding to that, Judge. Quite frankly, I thought she would terminate the conversation at that point. However, it is still admissible, but not in this area," said Grennan apologetically.

"I disagree," countered Lockman. "I think the prejudice outweighs the admissibility, so I'm going to rule. . . . First of all, Mr. Zevin wants it stricken. Her statement to him that he's to get a job and all his wife wants is for him to get a job."

"Your Honor," argued Zevin, "I don't believe that simply telling the jury to strike it and forget it at this stage is going to have any effect at all upon the jury. I renew my motion for a mistrial."

"I'm going to question the jury before I decide your motion. I'm going to ask them that if it is stricken, can they can strike it from their minds," maintained Lockman. "You have an exception, of course, but if I'm satisfied, in other words, if the jury says that they can strike it from their minds, I will deny your motion for a mistrial and you will have an exception."

"I have in mind the entire voir dire and Mr. Zevin's remarks in the course of the voir dire as to the unemployment of Mr. Busacca. This is no surprise and great prejudice all of a sudden coming out," disagreed Grennan. "As a matter of fact, he went into it in the voir dire."

"What he does, Mr. Grennan, is one thing, but to

have a woman who is very emotional and emotionally involved in the case, and this is not meant to be criticism of Mrs. Newman, because my heart goes out to the lady . . . She has gone through a tremendous experience but we have to have a fair trial and we can't have a fair trial if the emotional aspects of the defendant's being unemployed are inflamed unnecessarily by a witness. It could be that later on you could well be right, that later you are going to be able to bring it out on a different issue. But at this stage, it is completely unnecessary and I'm going to find out from the jury if they can put it out of their minds, and if they can't, I will reevaluate the motion for a mistrial."

"You see, Judge," insisted the District Attorney, "I am aware of the defense. I know things that the Court cannot know. I have seen a transcript for instance. I have read a psychiatric interview of the defendant that goes into some depth on the question of unemployment. I know what the children are going to say on the question of unemployment. I know the defendant's own psychiatrist has reflected, at least in his formal report pertaining to the unemployment. For those reasons I would suggest to the court that it is not as prejudicial as it would appear. I would say that I did not anticipate that answer in the detail that it went. So I consent that it be stricken, but in weighing and considering this application and what we are about to do with the jury, knowing what is to come in the future, I would ask that you reserve on it or consider reserving decision."

"I cannot reserve on a motion for a mistrial, Mr. Grennan. It must be decided immediately. There is no provision for that in the Criminal Procedure Law.

"Your point is extremely well taken, Mr. Grennan, but I have no alternative but to work with the record that is before me at this point in time, and on the record before me at this point and time, I must satisfy myself that the jury will put that out of their minds.

"Later on, as you say, it may become an issue. But at this stage, before I rule on the motion for a mistrial, I will question them regarding their ability to put it out of their minds. Now, Mr. Zevin, you won't have to make the motion again in front of the jury if you would not care to. The motion has been made. If I continue the trial, you'll know automatically that I have denied your motion and you will have an automatic exception to that denial.

"Now, before the jury is brought in, do you want it stricken? In other words, let us assume that I deny your motion for a mistrial. Do you want it stricken then, or do you want it to stay in, which incidentally, I'm wondering, if it is not stricken, where is your motion for a mistrial? It is somewhat inconsistent, but it could be that that is your position."

"It is going to be my position," said Zevin adamantly. "It is my position that an instruction to the jury is inadequate."

"Is your position, should I deny your motion, that you want it stricken or not?" asked Judge Lockman.

"I request that it be stricken," replied Zevin.

The District Attorney was not satisfied with the solution given by the judge. "Your Honor, you don't understand my position. The first motion should be for a mistrial or not. Failing that, if that were not granted, if he wanted to strike it, I consent. But you can't strike it and have a mistrial on something that has been struck."

"No, Mr. Grennan, rather than bringing the jury in, for example, if I am going to deny his motion for a mistrial, and then send them out again so he can then move to strike it, I'm deeming it stricken now. If I deny the motion for a mistrial, I'm deeming it stricken on his motion."

"That is precisely why I brought to the Court's attention what I believe the trial to hold in the future. That bears on whether this reference to unemployment is so prejudicial to declare a mistrial. Particularly in view of Mr. Zevin's own opening where he made reference to the defendant's unemployment," continued Grennan, not seeing the judge's reasoning.

"But you characterize it as flaming and with that, judge, most respectfully, I cannot agree. I would argue that it is not inflammatory in that sense."

"Well, in context of this very good friend of the missing Mrs. Busacca, I consider it inflammatory when she makes these statements. That is my interpretation of it. I have observed the witness and I have observed the jury and in observing the witness, that is my interpretation of the effect of what this witness is saying to that jury," said Judge Lockman uncompromisingly. "Now bring the jury in, please." Lockman turned away from Grennan, not caring to engage any further in conversation on the issue. He had taken his position and he would not be swayed.

Mr. Zevin's motion for a mistrial was denied and Mr. Grennan ended his direct examination of Mrs. Newman. As she waited to be cross-examined by Mr.

Zevin, the witness lowered her head and dabbed her eyes. It had been a long day, and reliving the horror of that fateful August 29th conjured up the tragedy that she had wanted to forget, but knew in her heart she would relive, over and over, for a long time to come.

Marvin Zevin would not be considerate of the witness, not gentle, nor tolerant. It was his client who was on trial for murder and his personal passions and sensibilities could occupy no part of his given task. Many things are unpleasant during a trial, any trial, however complex or elementary. Innocent people who lived quiet, uneventful lives sheltered from the violence, the intensity, of an ungentle world, are suddenly thrust into its maelstrom and find it an unpalatable intrusion into their social standards of living.

No, he would not be tolerant, he would not be yielding, but he would be sympathetic.

"Mrs. Newman," he began, "it's a fact, is it not, that you didn't like Tom Busacca?"

"That is not so, sir."

"But isn't it a fact that before the Grand Jury you testified that you did not like him?"

"Yes, Mr. Zevin, but let me explain something. . . ."

"No, Mrs. Newman, just answer the question yes or no!"

"Yes, sir, that's what I said, I guess, but I must explain. . . ."

"Mrs. Newman, on August 29th, what time did you arrive at the Busacca home?" asked Zevin, not permitting her to explain her reasons.

"Between eight twenty-five and eight thirty."

"But in your handwritten statement, didn't you say you arrived at the Busacca home between nine and nine fifteen P.M.?"

"Yes, but I was wrong at that time. . . ."

"Please, Mrs. Newman, don't do this. Just answer the question," scolded Lockman. "I tried to explain to you that everybody in the country has the right to have a lawyer to conduct his examination the way he wants to do it, not the way the witness wants it. Now, this is his right under our system to ask his questions his way. Many of his questions just call for a yes or no answer. Just answer his questions; don't add anything and don't volunteer."

"I was wrong, sir," replied a very distressed witness.

"Mrs. Newman, you were anxious for Mrs. Busacca to sign the divorce papers, were you not?"

"I wasn't anxious for anything, Mr. Zevin. This was Mrs. Busacca's idea, not mine."

"Did you not testify before a Grand Jury that when you went to her house you would rush her back to sign the papers?" pressed Zevin.

"No, I was going to rush her because my husband was very annoyed and he said that she's not here and that he was going to bed. So, I rushed over to get her to bring her back. But not for any personal reasons but because of my husband's already being very angry with me."

"Was he anxious that she get a divorce?"

"He was anxious to go to bed, Mr. Zevin," snapped the witness, becoming a bit piqued.

"It was not essential that the papers be signed that night, was it?"

"No, but it was Floria's wish."

"Was it your wish?"

"I was not married to Tom!" the witness retorted, becoming obviously irritated at the questioning.

She reiterated her testimony, outlining the events as they had occurred on August 29th, and as she was reminded of the ugly details of that evening, her composure began to crumble and a feeling of hysteria began penetrating the façade she so carefully tried to maintain. She looked drawn and uncomfortable, an appearance that did not go unnoticed by Judge Lockman.

"Mrs. Newman," asked the judge softly, "would you like me to have a recess?"

"No, it's all right," she replied. "Anxiety pangs."

Zevin's cross-examination continued, taking the witness step by step through the nightmare, the hell-on-earth that she had experienced. There was so much more she wanted to say but was stopped repeatedly by the judge. Zevin attacked the inconsistencies in her statement made to the police, her Grand Jury testimony and the answers she was now giving.

"Mrs. Newman, while Mrs. Busacca was in Paris, did you have a telephone conversation with Mr. Busacca?"

"Yes."

"And during that conversation, about screwing around in Paris, you advised him that if Floria wanted to have an affair, she didn't have to go to Paris, that she could have it right there in Baldwin?"

"Yes . . . and I was laughing, you see, when I said that to him because I thought it was rather funny, and I said exactly that, Mr. Zevin. 'Gee, why would she travel three thousand miles to have an affair. She could have one right here in Baldwin if that's what she really wanted to do.' I asked him how he could say such a thing about his wife."

"She wasn't sleeping with him, was she?" asked Zevin.

"No."

"Whose choice?"

"Her choice."

"What was your relationship with Mr. Busacca?"

"Always a very neutral one. I would go over to the home and I would say "Hello" to him and have coffee together. I had no close relationship with Tom. He and I had nothing in common with one another, so really great discussions we never had. My relationship was with Floria. I can say. . . ."

"Did you find Mr. Busacca to be a basically non-aggressive, non-violent, non-ambitious vegetable?" interrupted Zevin.

"Yes, sir."

"You never saw any aggressive tendencies on his part?"

"None at all."

"You never saw him in any violent act?"

"No, sir."

"You never found that he had any ambitions?

"No ambition."

"And he acted like a vegetable?"

"Yes, he sure did."

Margaret Newman described Tom Busacca's photography work as the only ambition he had and he was good at it. But he did not prosper from it, the only thing he did well. He simply could not live on film.

"Mrs. Newman, did you find Tom coherent?"

"Well, my conversations with him were never very long. At times I found him difficult to understand. There was a problem verbalizing with Tom."

"During social occasions Tom would bury himself in the basement, would he not?"

"Yes. . . . he is an introverted kind of personality and did not socialize very much. Wasn't interested in it; and either he'd be sitting watching television or he would be down in the basement. No one ever knew what he was doing. I often asked Floria what he was doing and she never knew."

"Did Mr. Busacca drink very much?"

"No, he wasn't a drinker."

"Did you participate in a seance in regards to Mrs. Busacca?"

For the first time during the line of questioning, Grennan was on his feet. This was an area that had been considered off-limits during the preliminary hearings and he was objecting to its introduction.

Both Zevin and the District Attorney approached the bench.

"I don't understand why the question is not permissible," pressed Zevin.

"It's completely irrelevant to the proceedings. Let me put it another way. I don't understand the basis for the question," advised Lockman.

"Well, I understand that she did participate. If she believes in seances and she believes in communications from the dead, if you like, it may, number one, go to her competency, her sanity, her ability to testify; and number two, if she did not communicate with Mrs. Busacca and she does believe that, obviously, Mrs.

Busacca must be alive because Mrs. Newman would be able to communicate with the dead."

"Well, you're saying that people that believe in seances are incompetent to testify?" asked Lockman.

"She may well be," said Zevin contemptuously.

"On neither ground will I permit you to question her."

"Your Honor," interjected the District Attorney, "the question was asked at the hearing and it is now not being asked in good faith. She was asked if she contacted Mrs. Busacca and she said no. And she was even asked 'spiritually,' I might add, and she said no. So I don't think there is any good faith to that question."

"That would prove that Mrs. Busacca was still alive if she believed in seances," retorted Zevin.

"Well, we all laughed about it at the time we raised it," replied Lockman.

"I'm not sure it's a joke," a serious faced Zevin replied. "I'm not even sure if you can communicate with dead people, Your Honor. I remember the one thing they say about scientists: 'Scientists are the people who have no imagination to believe that things can be done and they're done by idiots and not by scientists.' There may be another world up there."

With that the testimony of Margaret Newman ended.

Chapter Seven

IF MARGARET NEWMAN had been a difficult witness, Grennan was taken aback at the commotion created by a seemingly harmless photograph of the victim that he attempted to introduce into evidence through his next witness, Dr. Melvin Fuerst. Doctor Fuerst had repaired the upper denture that he had earlier identified. Zevin's motion to deny the photograph into evidence was sustained by Lockman.

"Without foundation alone, Your Honor, I would object to its introduction. We don't know when. . . ."

He was interrupted by Lockman. "All right, I sustained the objection."

"Your Honor, it is not being offered as to when, only as to who the individual was and who he treated in the period of time that he treated her," argued Grennan.

"We haven't established that period either," replied Zevin.

"I will," retorted Grennan, annoyed at the objection over such a picayune item. But little did he realize, nor could he have foreseen, the near disastrous complications and discussions that this photograph of Florence Busacca would unleash.

"Dr. Fuerst, do you recognize the individual in the picture as being the individual that you treated in the period of time, dentally speaking, Florence Busacca?"

"Yes."

"I renew my offer to have the photograph marked into evidence."

"Same ruling," insisted the judge. "You don't know when the picture was taken or we don't know when it shows how she looked. It may have been the way she looked twenty years ago. I don't know how she looked twenty years ago and I don't know how it is relevant to this case. Maybe it would be."

"I have to be heard in that area," Grennan persisted. "Judge, my position on this picture is that it matters not when it was taken. What matters is this doctor recognizing the individual in this picture as being the person he treated. That is why it is being offered."

"But right now, I don't know what it is being offered for," queried Lockman. "If there was no objection, there would be no problem. Right now I don't know what you're offering a picture of Mrs. Busacca for."

"As being the person the doctor treated. We have a missing person."

"And the picture may have been taken twenty-five years ago and it may not be the way she looks today," maintained the judge.

"And it doesn't matter, Judge, if the doctor says he recognizes this individual as being the person he treated. As a matter of an aside and as a matter of further offer, I am informed by Lawrence Busacca that this picture was taken approximately one year ago by Mr. Busacca. However, it is my position that if the doctor says the individual in this picture he recognizes is the person he treated, it matters not when the picture was taken."

"He treated her when?" asked Lockman. "You mean you could bring in a picture . . ."

"In the period of time that he treated Florence Busacca."

". . . . You could bring in a picture of someone the way they looked forty years ago and have somebody say this is Florence Busacca?"

"If he recognizes the individual, yes," replied Grennan confidently. "But that is not when the picture was taken."

"You have my ruling. You have an exception," advised Lockman. "You can establish from the last time he saw her if this is a fair representation of how she looked a year ago or two years ago, and you may be able to get it in. I don't know if there will be an objection or not. I can't conceive of any, but if this picture shows the way she was within the last year, maybe while the jury is out we could cross this bridge."

"My next objection," Zevin interposed, "would be the seizure of the item, the illegal seizure of the item without a search warrant."

"What'd ya have to say about that?" asked Lockman turning toward the District Attorney who was taken by surprise by Zevin's remark, knowing that this would ignite the issue of search and seizure.

"I say to you. . . . I don't know who the item belongs to. It was delivered to the police department in my presence by Lawrence Busacca," explained an uncertain Grennan.

"At whose request?" questioned Zevin.

"Not only that, but we must have something on record on that. I don't know where Lawrence Busacca got it from," interrupted Judge Lockman.

"It was not seized from the defendant," disputed Grennan.

"And we had a proceeding to resolve all of these problems and I told you at the time I wanted all the problems resolved and no loose ends."

"At that time I didn't have the picture. I received this photo, I might point out, Wednesday night of this week. Upon my request, Lawrence Busacca brought a picture of his mother."

"Well, on the ground that Mr. Zevin has raised, I would also sustain the objection. There is no foundation that this was not seized illegally, on this record."

"Judge, it wasn't seized at all," protested Grennan.

"You say that Lawrence Busacca, the son of the defendant, produced this picture?"

"At my request."

"Where did he get the picture from?" asked Lockman.

"The police did not seize this item. They requested it of an individual. It was delivered to them. I can't hold a suppression hearing on things we didn't seize."

"But you knew you had it!" scolded Lockman.

"I didn't have it until Wednesday night, Judge, on my request."

"You have my ruling, Mr. Grennan."

"I respectfully except, and I ask a further opportunity to argue on this point. It happens to be a photograph of the person who is missing, about whom this very case exists."

"But there is an objection now that the police obtained the photograph illegally and it is all hearsay because it is not based on any sworn testimony before me. But you may say you have obtained it legally and I say you have to lay a foundation by showing how you obtained it."

"And you will not take it subject to the connection through Lawrence Busacca, and I represent what I have to the court in good faith, I might add."

"Make an offer of proof as to what Lawrence Busacca will testify to."

"Very simply that I requested a photograph from him of his mother three nights ago; and pursuant to my request he delivered to Detective Walker, in my presence, and this photo was developed from the negative."

"Do you know where he got the negative from?" asked Lockman.

"No, sir, somewhere in the house I would assume."

"It might have been someplace he had no right to go. He doesn't have a right to go into his father's bureau drawers or rifle through his father's things. I don't know where he got it from," maintained the judge.

"I don't know either, Judge, but we have to ask him, of course."

"You have my ruling. On the present state of the record it is inadmissible," concluded Lockman.

"I must except most strenuously and most respectfully. However, in the area, I would ask, in view of the argument that we have, to continue to lay a foundation at least with Dr. Fuerst with regard to the photo," petitioned Grennan.

"Well, would you explain to me how you're going to do that so I can make a ruling?"

"I am going to ask if the photo resembles the person in the period of time that he treated her?"

Judge Lockman looked puzzled. "You're going to ask him if he recognizes the person in the photo, giving a time limit, in other words of five, ten, fifteen years or when?"

"In the period of time he treated her."

"We don't know that," added the judge.

"We will establish that."

"Suppose you establish when he treated her first," proposed Judge Lockman, "and whether this picture represents how she looked during that period. I will permit that subject to connection. However, you can offer it in evidence but I will not permit it to go into evidence if there is an objection."

"Your Honor, I would ask that the picture be turned over prior to the jury's coming in here," advised Zevin.

The jury and the witness returned to the courtroom. They had been subjected to a great deal of colloquy between attorneys but would soon come to realize that this was the internal workings of a trial that is rarely scrutinized by the general public.

Dr. Fuerst explained that he first treated Florence Busacca in October, 1974, and again in October, 1975. Grennan showed the photograph of Mrs Busacca to the doctor and solicited from him that it resembled the woman whom he had treated. He had not seen or treated her since August 29th, 1976. Fuerst was shown X-rays of Florence Busacca's mouth taken by him on one of her visits, and he was able to identify them. Mr. Zevin objected to the introduction of the dental records but was overruled.

"May I be heard, Your Honor?" asked Zevin.

"You may."

"Since there exists both a civil presumption of life for five or seven years in the State of New York, and these are the items of Mrs. Busacca. . . ."

Grennan exploded to his feet, his face flushed, thrusting his arm forward and pointing a finger at Marvin Zevin. "Judge, I object to this instruction and request now . . . !"

"In the presence of the jury?" cautioned Lockman.

". . . and I ask for an instruction to the jury. I think that remark should have properly been made at the bench and I think Mr. Zevin knows that. And I ask specifically for an instruction to be given the jury to disregard Mr. Zevin's remark and for an instruction with regard to the content and the substance of what he said."

"All right, the jury will disregard Mr. Zevin's remarks."

"May I make my position clear at the bench, Your Honor?" requested Grennan.

"You certainly may."

"In his remark a moment ago, Judge, he made reference to a civil presumption of life for a period of seven years. I believe that the court should now give an instruction to the jury with regard to this so-called civil presumption."

"Frankly, I'm not familiar with it," admitted Judge Lockman.

"Neither am I," conceded Grennan.

"You are not familiar with the fact . . ." stated Zevin.

"I know about 'Enoch Arden'* but . . ." interrupted Grennan.

"Well, I know about 'Enoch Arden,' but there is a presumption that they're alive," interjected Lockman. "I always think of the negative aspect of the presumption. You're saying that since the presumption is that for seven years, they're alive. All right. I see your point. That's interesting."

"And therefore, I go to the next step and I say that there is a confidential relationship which can't be waived with regard to these dental records," insisted Marvin Zevin.

"You know, Judge," pleaded Grennan, "if you had turned the comment around and had the D.A. say it, we would have had a mistrial motion within instants. I believe an instruction is called for."

---

*'Enoch Arden' was a Florida Case which established the time period after which a person could be declared legally dead.

Judge Lockman shifted in his chair. His fingers pushed aimlessly through his mane of white hair. He looked directly at the District Attorney. "I keep saying this to you. With all due respect, it's not an equal battle. The defendant has more rights than the People."

"I know, but we try to make it as fair as we can, and I think that in fairness, an instruction from the Court is called for."

"I agree with you. I am going to instruct them on something I don't know though. I don't know frankly whether that rule applies to this case. I don't know. I hadn't thought of it before. Are you going to request such an instruction?"

"No," answered Zevin. "I'm referring specifically only to the items that the District Attorney now requests to be admitted."

"I understand your position, Mr. Zevin, but Mr. Grennan is concerned about the remarks that you made. Now I told the jury to disregard it. If you feel that I need to tell them what the law is at this stage— I don't now whether that presumption applies in this case or not."

"You can tell them as far as they're concerned at this time there is no such law," suggested Grennan.

"I will tell them that they are to disregard everything Mr. Zevin said and I'll ask their assurance that they will put it out of their mind. Will that satisfy you?"

"Yes, if that's all we can do at this time, I have to be satisfied."

"No, it's not all you can do. You say what you feel

and you tell me what you want and why," responded Lockman.

"I'd have to be satisfied with such an instruction. I'm still upset that Marvin said it, quite frankly, Your Honor."

"I was careful to note the word CIVIL," Zevin said, with a sheepish, timorous expression that attempted to hide a smile. At least for the moment, he had implanted in the minds of the jury the presumption of life for seven years when a person was declared missing. Whether its application was germane to this case or not was the Court's obligation to resolve.

"But I don't see how it applies in any way to the subject matter under discussion at the moment, having to do with the admission of X-rays, photographs. . . ."

"No," interrupted Lockman, "his point is. It's unfortunate he said it in front of the jury; his point, I think, is a valid point. He is saying that since there is a presumption that she is alive, being alive, the only one that can waive the physician-patient privilege is Mrs. Busacca. How else is he going to preserve the record on that point except to make it? I created the situation by denying his motion and he had to speak up or the witness would have started to testify. Let's do one thing at a time."

Judge Lockman directed that the jurors be brought back into the courtroom. He asked that they strike the comments made by Mr. Zevin from their minds. The only law that would apply in the court and that they would have to contend with was the law that came from him, not from the attorneys. He then called the two attorneys up to the bench. There was another matter to be settled, the matter of physician-patient privilege.

Mr. Grennan made his position clear. "It's being offered in this criminal case; we are offering it on our theory that she is dead, in the same way for any dead person's identification purposes. Their dental records are made available to the police and others, and I don't believe Mr. Zevin has standing to take such an objection.

"I am looking at the Section 427, tenth edition of Richardson on evidence which states, last paragraph: 'b. a dentist shall be required to disclose information necessary for identification of a patient.' "

"Mr. Grennan, what is the purpose of your offering this testimony?"

"We have what will be identified as Mrs. Busacca's upper plate, which is coming next, referring to his X-ray charts and to the plate he is able to identify as the plate belong to Mrs. Busacca. In addition to which, Judge, one of the X-rays, although I could never tell you which one depicts a portion of the body which will be subsequently offered into evidence."

"He can identify it?" asked Lockman, interestedly.

"He will establish, to my belief, he will establish that the piece of the body that we have, in fact came from Mrs. Busacca's body."

"He can identify a piece of the body?" asked Lockman, his curiosity heightened by the remark.

"He will not be concerned with identification of the piece of the body except for the fact that the X-rays he has portray a portion of the body of Mrs. Busacca," explained Grennan.

"Mr. Zevin, do you understand that?"

"No, Your Honor."

"I don't either, Mr. Grennan."

"Another individual will refer to the same X-rays and referring to the exhibit will be able to tell us that it came from that body," Grennan tried to clarify.

"In other words, he's going to identify those X-rays as being Mrs. Busacca's?" queried the judge.

"As the X-rays he took of Mrs. Busacca," corrected the D.A.

"And you are eventually doing this on the identification of a certain tissue or bone or whatever? You need this as a link?"

"That's correct, Your Honor."

"Do you want to be heard, Mr. Zevin?"

"Yes. I believe that the sentence means or stands for the proposition that if you had a skull that was unidentifiable, then the dentist's X-rays would be admissible as a comparison to the X-rays of the skull in mind to show that this skull and this skeleton represents that individual. The X-rays here are not going to be used to identify a person. They are going to be used to establish the person's denture plate or perhaps a piece of bone from a person. But they're not going to be used to identify that person and that's, I think, a clear distinction."

"Your objection is overruled, Mr. Zevin."

Doctor Fuerst continued his testimony, identifying dental X-rays as those he had taken of Florence Busacca.

Marvin Zevin then requested and was granted a voir dire. "Doctor, in your dental office, do you have a dental technician who works for you?"

"Yes."

"What did you do after that with relationship to the film?"

"Well. . . . I take a set of X-rays like you see, however many there are, put them in a bag like that, mark the bag with the patient's name and date and then put them into a box until we develop them."

"You do the developing personally?"

"Yes."

"How many sets do you develop at a time; as many as you take that day?"

"Usually, yes."

"Have you ever put the wrong negatives in the wrong envelope after they've been developed?"

"It happens sometimes, yes."

"Where do you store them?"

"In a box with others that are kept in the darkroom."

Fuerst went on to say that after a patient comes to the office, the X-rays are then put into the individual's folder. His wife was the only other person with access to the X-rays. The doctor then turned the X-rays over to the detectives. Doctor Fuerst then went on to identify Mrs. Busacca's upper partial denture that had been found at the scene. It had been matched against the X-rays and against a chart from Florence's folder. In 1974 the doctor had added a tooth to the plate. He described it as a "peculiarly individualistic plate, not hard to recognize."

"Dr. Fuerst," continued Grennan, "did Mrs. Busacca have a second plate?"

"I don't think so. She wanted this plate back right away."

"Judge, may I approach the bench with an offer of proof?"

"You certainly may."

Grennan and Zevin approached the bench.

"In this case, Judge, the defendant's opening, he went into great detail about the woman voluntarily absenting herself; about her going to La Scala; going to California. I believe now the conversation or her reaction to the plate being removed from her mouth, as to having it back in a period time, that she wanted it back in, and whether she had another plate indicates her state of mind in going off to California and so forth, without an upper plate. It is in that area I intend to go with this doctor. I believe it is absolutely required that we establish whether she had an upper plate or not."

"There is no question that if you could overcome certain problems to do with the hearsay rule, whether she had another plate or not is relevant to this lawsuit. But how are you going to get around the hearsay rule in this conversation? I mean, you can't keep saying 'state of mind' and ride roughshod over these rules."

"I'm advised that she did have another plate," submitted Zevin. "Now I may be incorrect, but that's what I'm advised."

"Then I'll tell you quite frankly the doctor tells me that number one, she wanted it back the same day and she told him she hid in the period of time that it was out of her mouth one day," countered Grennan.

"How does he know that? She told him this?" asked Lockman.

"Yes."

"That's my point. That's hearsay."

"I'm not finished. Your Honor. He wanted to make her another plate. She couldn't have it done although she wanted it. He said she said she couldn't have it done because she couldn't afford it. And in that area, the witness yesterday, I instructed her not to testify in view of what occurred yesterday. But the balance of his conversation as to whether she had another plate or not, I think that is relevant."

"As I said, I agree with you, Mr. Grennan. But I don't know how you're going to overcome the hearsay rule."

"We are concerned, Judge, about the defendant's position that she ran off starting life as an operatic singer somewhere. Would she do this without her teeth?" argued Grennan.

"Another thing I'm concerned about. Mr. Zevin says, and obviously in good faith, that he thinks she did have another plate. It would be terrible to have some conversation that is not accurate," pondered Judge Lockman.

"He thinks she's alive, too. But the family doctor would also have knowledge as to whether she had an upper plate or not."

"Let me ask you this, Mr. Zevin. Can you give me any basis for the belief she has another plate. What your client told you probably?"

"I was going to ask for a ten or fifteen minute recess so I can inquire of my client to see whether or not there is a basis for that statement."

"The two kids tell me she only had one plate," said Grennan. "And they will apparently testify to that as well, and I believe his testimony with regards to the intention of making another plate should be testified to. But she only had the one, which is relevant and material."

"I assume they went through the house with a fine toothed comb and didn't find another plate," suggested the judge.

"We can't say what we didn't find negatively," pointed out Grennan.

"I understand, but I want to know for my own edification. I assume you went through her belongings and her toiletware and so forth. The problem that we have remaining is the hearsay rule. How does this become her state of mind?"

"Her state of mind he put in issue. He is saying that she voluntarily took off," Grennan declared.

"On the state of mind? I'm having a little trouble with the concept. You mean the state of mind that she hasn't run away?" pressed the judge.

"No, her state of mind at the time she ran off, and I'm saying I have to go into that area and prove to a moral certainty that she didn't voluntarily depart. I believe that some circumstantial evidence in that area is the fact that she didn't have another plate. This has to do with her mental attitude.

"He says she voluntarily disappeared. I say the proof that she didn't voluntarily disappear is the fact that

she didn't have another set of teeth in her head. It
negates the intent," expounded Grennan. No witnesses are going to be easy with Marvin, he thought.
Because there is no body, everything will become an
issue. Zevin would keep the woman alive for as long
as possible. Tom Busacca had not told him anything
to the contrary.

Judge Lockman turned once again to Barry Grennan, his stern face beginning to display signs of wear-
iness. First there was the very difficult testimony of
Margaret Newman whose spontaneous remarks irritated and frustrated him. Now, an issue has been
raised that he feels should have been resolved during
the suppression hearing. This was not the time to air
matters that could possibly influence the jury and has
in fact kept them out of the courtroom more than in
the courtroom where they should be listening to testimony from witnesses.

"Now, Mr. Grennan, I have repeatedly asked you,
and it seems to me that this is a problem in a case that
is going to involve a lot of problems with rules of evidence. And I asked you to analyze your case and present these problems to me. Here we are with a jury
sitting here and you come up with this most profound
question and I warned you. . . ."

"Judge," interrupted Grennan, annoyed at being
singled out as the bad guy, "that may be, and if there
are some areas I overlooked, I apologize to the court.
However, we are faced with the problem and I believe it is admissible."

Judge Lockman decided that there was no better
time than now for a recess, an opportunity for all con-

cerned to divest themselves of mounting strain, a tenseness that was beginning to manifest itself in the exchanges between counsels. Judge Lockman would have been the first to admit that he certainly needed the respite. The jury was led from the courtroom after an admonition.

Marvin Zevin took the time to confer with his client who had sat impassively through most of the proceedings. His only reactions had been made evident during the viewing of the color photos of his automobile trunk and Margaret Newman's remarks relating to what he considered very personal matters.

The court was reconvened after a forty-five minute recess and the jury was seated. Barry Grennan continued his direct examination of Doctor Fuerst, an examination that seemed hours old and one that the District Attorney thought would be a matter of procedure. Marvin Zevin was not going to succumb to a matter of routine. He was going to attack every misguided word or expression and direct inconsistent testimony in an effort to impeach the witness' credibility and leave a reasonable doubt in the minds of the jury. That's all he wanted: a reasonable doubt. Therefore, it was incumbent upon him to leave his client in the most favorable light that this case could possibly engender.

Doctor Fuerst went on to testify that to his knowledge, Florence Busacca had no other set of dentures, only the plate that he had prepared for her. Florence's dental records, with certain modifications because of legal technicalities, were then entered into evidence.

Upon cross examination of the witness by Marvin

Zevin, it was brought out that there was a possibility that another dentist had made an upper plate for Mrs. Busacca and that Fuerst was only one of several dentists that she may have seen in her lifetime.

The witness was excused and trial was adjourned until Monday, March 7th, 1977.

Walker met Grennan as he emerged from the courtroom. "Come on, Barry, Mike and I'll buy you a drink after you deposit that stuff upstairs."

"I need one," exclaimed Grennan. "Christ! What a fuck'in day. We've got work to do tonight, Roger. Zevin isn't letting much get by and I'm not going to be suckered into anything by him. He's nit-picking and he's got a judge that he'll score with at times."

Chapter Eight

GRENNAN WANTED TO bring on the black inmate who allegedly had conversations with Busacca and to whom Tom had made certain admissions of guilt. Detective Allen had been working with the inmate but couldn't glean much more information from him. He wanted to tell his story on the stand, wanted immunity from prosecution and release from prison. It was a tall order, but worth the gamble if it was true. The inmate was a two-bit nickle and dime thief whose release to society would be short lived at the very least. Let the jury decide if what he has to say has any credence or substance.

The twenty-eight year old inmate from the County jail was Grennan's first witness for the day. Walter Smith, Jr. had been on the same tier as Tom Busacca and they occupied adjoining cells. He was to testify that he heard Thomas Busacca call out in his sleep one night that "I did it! I did it!" and when questioned with regard to it the next day, he told Smith that he had killed his wife.

"Mr. Smith, why were you in jail?" asked Grennan.

"I had signed someone else's name on a car rental agreement."

"You forged a name?"

"Yes, sir."

"And you received a car in connection with that?"

"Yes, sir."

"And prior to that occasion, had you been convicted of any crimes?"

"Yes, I was—attempted criminal possession of a forged instrument, and I served three years for it."

"And in connection with the crime for which you were in jail, have you received immunity, sir?"

"On January twenty-fifth, nineteen seventy-seven, I did. Prior to November sixteenth, no."

"And was that from me?"

"Yes, sir."

"Tell us, what were some of the other conversations you had with Thomas Busacca?"

"Well, we were discussing different cases and, you know. . . . I was explaining at the time, about in Nassau County, in his case, that, you know, without a body and everything, and with circumstantial evidence, that can't convict a man. We discussed that."

"He discussed that with you?" urged Grennan.

"Yes, sir."

"Well, Your Honor, I don't think he said a discussion," corrected Grennan. "I think the statement was that Mr. Smith made that statement."

"Well, could we have that clarified?" asked the judge. "Is that the thrust of it?" Lockman turned to the witness. "You're the one that said it?"

"Yes, sir," replied Smith. "You know, like he

brought out, you know, his case, different cases, and in general."

"It is very important, though, that it was you that said it," cautioned Judge Lockman. "It wasn't Mr. Busacca?"

"No, it was I that said 'under circumstantial evidence.' "

"Mr. Smith, would you continue with your conversation?"

"We talked about other areas. Not primarily as to his case but different areas, you know and about newspaper articles, television, et cetera, and things like that; and we became very close friends to a degree, as friendly as two people could become in jail."

"There came a time when you discussed with him his wife?" asked Grennan.

"That happened about two o'clock one morning, when we were locked in."

"Objection," cried Zevin.

"I don't follow," said the Judge.

"Your Honor, I believe we all know what is going to be said next. I'm objecting to the two o'clock statement, Your Honor."

"Do you want to be heard on this, Mr. Grennan?" asked Lockman.

"Maybe I can clear it up if I ask one question," answered Grennan, turning to the witness. "Did you then have a discussion with Mr. Busacca in the morning?"

"Yeah! The following morning, yeah."

"Tell us that discussion."

"I had brought out a statement that he made during the night and I brought it to his attention."

"And what did he say?" asked Grennan.

Zevin was on his feet once again in protest. "Your Honor, now I continue my objection. It doesn't cure the issue."

"Overruled," replied Lockman.

"Tell, us, Mr. Smith, what you said to him and what he said to you in the morning."

"Well, he had cried out during the night about 'I did it, I did it,' and I brought that to his attention."

"What did he say?"

"He said. . . ."

"Objection!" Zevin interrupted. "Now, Your Honor, I would make an application for a mistrial."

"All right, members of the jury, there will be a short adjournment. Don't discuss the case," admonished Judge Lockman.

Lockman also directed that the witness leave the courtroom and the two attorneys approached the bench.

"Mr. Zevin, I thought we had discussed this in chambers," questioned the Judge. "That's why I. . . ."

Zevin interrupted. "Your Honor, we have, and I maintained then, I believe, that the statement 'I did it, I did it,' and while Mr. Busacca was asleep, is highly prejudicial and not probative of anything. He could have caught a fish."

"And Mr. Grennan then said that he wanted this to show the basis for the conversation and he acknowledged that 'I did it, I did it' in no way was an admission of this crime and that I was to admonish the jury at that time. That's my recollection of the conversation. You didn't have to agree with it, incidentally. That goes without saying," advised Lockman, "but this is the way it comes back to me that we had discussed dealing with this particular problem. Not that you were a party to it; you were there when we had the discussion but you didn't agree to it. Needless to say, you have a right to take your exception to move for a mistrial and take whatever steps you feel are necessary. But my recollection of the way I said I would handle this particular problem. . . ."

Barry Grennan interrupted. "Mine goes further, Judge."

"Go ahead," conceded Lockman.

"You had asked me about it and I said, 'As far as I'm concerned, it is not offered for the truth of it but only for a prelude to the conversation I'm about to go into,' and you said you would then so instruct the jury that those statements at two o'clock were not admissible and the question. . . ."

"They had nothing to do . . . 'I did it, I did it', could be talking about anything in the world. Anyway, someone who says something in his sleep, it wouldn't be admissible. But you're offering it only on the issue of whether the conversation took place. It couldn't have taken place in a vacuum and therefore, of course, I would deny the mistrial motion. However, I did want to excuse the jury while we had this discussion. So the motion for a mistrial is denied and at this time I would admonish the jury as to the 'I did it, I did it.' I'm not going to repeat it. I'm going to explain to them that in no way can anything said by a person in his sleep be used against him."

"Such an admonition was made to the jury by Judge Lockman. The purpose in admitting the conversation into evidence was to show that as the District Attorney contended, a conversation did take place between Thomas Busacca and the witness, and the remarks made by Busacca when asleep were the basis for the conversation that took place in the morning.

Barry Grennan then continued his direct examination. "Tell us, if you will, Mr. Smith, that conversation you had with the defendant that morning."

"I had mentioned to him what he had said the night before, that night prior to that morning, and he turned around and told me he had killed his wife and had mutilated the body and severed the head and deposited it in two bodies of water in Nassau County, Great South Bay and Peconic Bay."

"Did he say what he had used?"

"Yes. He used a knife and possibly a meat cleaver."

"Do you know when this conversation took place?"

"I would say roughly about December fifth or December sixth."

"Mr. Smith, did there come a time that you thereafter met with myself?"

"Yes, sir, I believe either December eighth or December ninth."

"Prior to that date, had you met with any district attorney or police official in connection with this matter, or had any conversation with law enforcement people prior to that conversation?"

"No, sir."

"Was there any further conversation with Mr. Busacca?"

"No, sir."

"You may examine, Mr. Zevin."

Marvin remained seated for a long moment staring at the witness, perhaps in an effort to intimidate him. Then he rose slowly from his chair. He had just heard an incredible story, he thought to himself. A story that was given by a convicted felon to gain immunity and was now walking the streets.

"Mr. Smith, what is a hamster?"

"A small rodent."

"At the jail what is a hamster?"

"I can't answer that; I wouldn't know."

"What is a 'honky'?"

"It's a term they use for white people."

"What is the term they use for black people?"

"Blacks, different names, I guess."

"Never heard the term 'hamster' used for black people?" pressed Zevin.

"No, sir."

"How long have you been at the jail?"

"From November 16th to January 20th."

"During that entire period you never heard the term 'hamster' used to refer to black prisoners in the jail?"

"No, sir."

"But you have heard the term 'honky' used referring to white prisoners in the jail?"

"From time to time it was used."

"By whom?"

"Objection," shouted Grennan.

"Sustained."

Zevin moved closer to the witness box. "Did you have lunch and dinner with Mr. Busacca in the jail?"

"Yes, we ate from time to time."

"How often?"

"During that period I cannot answer that question. I can't enumerate how many numbers of times."

"Every day?" persisted Zevin.

"I can't answer that," replied Smith, obviously becoming a bit annoyed. "I can't give a pinpoint number of how many times."

"Isn't it a fact that down in the jail, whites and blacks do not mix?"

"No, sir."

"They have lunch together? Integrated?"

"There are five tables to a floor and you sit where you want to sit. I sat where there was a table to sit at," argued Smith, piqued at the line of questioning.

"Mr. Smith, you are indicating to me that at lunch time, white and black prisoners mix indiscriminately?"

"I can only speak for myself. I ate with who I felt like eating with."

"Isn't it a fact that you never heard the term 'hamster' used because you never spoke to white prisoners?"

"That's not true, sir."

"You had a lot in common with Mr. Busacca?"

"We got along in jail together. We both had a lot in common. Didn't make any noise and. . . ."

"How old are you?" interrupted Zevin.

"I don't think he has finished the answer to the question, Your Honor," implored Grennan.

Smith finished his answer. He and Tom Busacca

were not on drugs. Their conversations were not "street talk."

"How old are you?" asked Zevin.

"Twenty-eight."

"How old would you guess Mr. Busacca is?"

"About fifty-four or fifty-five."

"What color are you?"

"I am an American black," Smith answered indignantly.

"What color is Mr. Busacca?"

"He is an American Caucasian."

"Not an Italian Caucasian," mocked Zevin, suppressing the desire to smile.

"Sir, I cannot answer where he is from because I do not know where he is from or anything else."

"Do you have any children?"

"I wish not to answer that question," snarled the witness.

"You will have to answer the question, Mr. Smith," said Lockman dryly.

"Yes, sir."

"You have one child, is that correct?" Zevin continued. He compared the ages of Busacca's children and his own five year old. He brought out Smith's criminal record and time spent incarcerated in upstate prisons.

"Didn't you know that being charged with a felony and being a prior felony offender, you had to serve the mandatory jail sentence if convicted?" asked Zevin, working his witness into the ropes.

"Yes, sir."

"Are you serving a mandatory jail sentence?"

"No, sir."

"Did the District Attorney dismiss the charges against you?"

"I was offered immunity. The charges were taken care of. . . . dismissed. Yes, sir."

"You also had a parole warrant against you, right?" hammered Zevin.

"Yes, sir."

"The parole warrant was lifted?"

"Yes, sir."

"So," smiled Zevin, turning to face the jury, his hands outstretched and clasped in front of him, "for your cooperation the charges against you were dismissed; the parole warrant was lifted and you were permitted to walk out of jail! Is that correct?"

"No, sir." Smith hesitated and looked in the direction of the District Attorney and then at Marvin Zevin. "No promises or anything were made to me. My parole warrant was lifted through the efforts of my family, not through the efforts of the District Attorney's office."

"Your lawyer had no effect in getting that parole warrant lifted?"

"My lawyer worked on it."

"But your father was the one who accomplished it; is that correct?"

"My family accomplished me being . . . getting reinstated back on parole," answered a perturbed witness.

"When was the parole warrant lifted?"

"The 18th of January."

"When did you first speak with the District Attorney?"

"December ninth, nineteen seventy-six."

"When were the charges against you dismissed in Nassau County?"

"January. . . . I guess it was about January twenty-seventh."

"Now, do you remember testifying with regard to this matter on January twenty-fourth, nineteen seventy-seven?"

"Yes, sir."

"Had you discussed your testimony with the District Attorney prior to that date?"

"Yes, about January twentieth."

"And prior to January twentieth, the District Attorney of the County of Nassau did not know what you were going to testify to; is that correct?"

"Yes, sir. He didn't know. He asked me if I were brought to testify would I and I said I would."

"And that was all of your testimony in the presence of the District Attorney, Mr. Grennan, prior to January twenty-seventh, nineteen seventy-seven?"

"Yes, sir."

"Isn't it a fact, Mr. Smith, that Mr. Grennan was down at the jail approximately December 9th and you told him the story at that time?"

"I told him what was told to me. Yes, sir."

"On December ninth?" pressed Zevin raising his voice questioningly.

"But I didn't talk to Mr. Grennan again," responded the witness, looking confused and seemingly looking for some direction from the District Attorney.

"Was Mr. Grennan present when you made that statement on December ninth?"

"Yes, sir."

"So, Mr. Smith, it wasn't January twenty-eighth when Mr. Grennan first found out what you were going to testify to, was it?"

"On December ninth I had no knowledge I was going to testify at all."

"Did you meet Mr. Grennan on December ninth?"

"Yes, sir."

"Did you make statements on December ninth?"

"Yes, sir."

"The same statements you made in court today, right?"

"Yes, sir."

"And you had discussed the testimony, hadn't you?" asked Zevin, not letting up.

"I discussed the case. Yes, sir."

"Do you remember testifying here January twenty-fourth and these questions and answers: 'Have you spoken to anyone about your testimony?' Answer, 'No, sir!' Question, 'No one at all?' Answer, 'No one at all, sir.' Question, 'So when you took the stand today, the District Attorney didn't know what you were going to say?' Answer, 'No sir.' Now, that wasn't true, was it, Mr. Smith?"

"At that time," answered a beleaguered Walter Smith.

"Was it true that the District Attorney didn't know what you were going to say when you testified here on January twenty-fourth?"

"No, sir, it wasn't, because I had spoken to him on January twentieth."

"Mr. Smith, in that whole series of questions the answers were not true, were they?"

"I am not able to answer the question in that form."

"What cell were you in at the jail?" asked Zevin, not insisting on an answer to the previous question. He hoped he had made his point for the benefit of the jury.

"Two nineteen."

"Would you describe it?"

Walter Smith described the small cubicle that he had occupied at the jail: not untypical of all jail cells—bunk, commode and wash basin, a recessed ceiling light which was turned off at ten o'clock at night.

"After ten o'clock, is there any lighting?"

"From the hallway there're fluorescent night lights."

"About how far away from the cell?" asked Zevin.

"About twelve or fifteen feet."

"Would you say the lighting at night is rather dim?"

"It is adequate enough to read by at night."

"Mr. Smith, you're very bright because you anticipated my question, because I knew what your answer was going to be," countered Zevin arrogantly.

"I object, Your Honor!" roared Grennan.

"Sustained," replied Judge Lockman. "The jury will disregard that."

"I ask that the answer be struck from the record," enlisted Zevin.

"I ask that the comment be stricken," suggested Grennan.

"The comment will be struck and the answer will stand," said Lockman sternly, his eyes showing his displeasure of Zevin's remarks.

"Now, as you lie in your bunk, which way is your head?" continued Zevin.

"Facing the hallway."

"Facing the light?"

"Correct."

"So as you were reading that night, you were lying in your bunk, your head facing the gallery, and with the book in your hand you were reading that night, right?"

"Yes, sir."

"You were reading a book while you were facing the light, a fluorescent fixture about twelve or fifteen feet away?"

"Approximately."

"Was it pretty dim?"

"It was adequate enough to read by."

"What were those two bays you mentioned?"

"Great South Bay and Peconic Bay."

"Do you know where they are?"

"Suffolk County. I don't know exactly where."

"As far as you're concerned, they may be right next to one another or far apart, you just don't know where they're at?"

Zevin continued to interrogate the witness, trying to exact minute details of areas in Suffolk County, the names of other inmates on the tier, their interests, families, and the number of whites as opposed to blacks that he had been exposed to. All of this is an attempt to make Smith's testimony controvertible.

"You've been upstate in jail, Mr. Smith?"

"Yes, sir."

"Is it your position that you never heard of people

cooperating with the District Attorney's office and deriving a benefit?"

"Yes, sir, I've heard of it."

"Didn't you expect that to happen in this case?"

"Yes, sir."

"That you wanted to get out, right?"

"Every man who is in jail would like to get out, sir," volunteered Smith.

Marvin Zevin's deft cross-examination of the witness played upon Smith's egotistical demeanor. Zevin was baiting the witness and was getting the nibbles he wanted. He had to show that this witness had come forward as an opportunist, using Thomas Busacca as his vehicle out of jail. This admitted felon who reads the Wall Street Journal, the New York Times, various law journals and talked about astronomy, space exploration, origins of space, man's evolution on earth and a host of other things with his client, this felon who talked of astrology and organic chemistry was, in Zevin's mind, trying to perpetrate a fraud upon the People to gain his freedom. Smith had testified that he had been in and out of Busacca's cell many times during the period of time that they were on the tier together, but Zevin challenged him to describe the interior of Tom's cell that he had visited so often. He was unable to do so. Marvin Zevin was confident he had scored well with this witness. He ended his cross-examination. Mr. Grennan was reluctant to examine the witness further. He did not want to create a chasm into which he could fall.

There was a long way to go, many more witnesses to follow and an abundance of controversial evidence to be guided through Zevin's multitudinous questions and objections. And, indeed, there were numerous pieces of evidence that were ruled by the court to be too inflammatory in nature to assure a fair and just trial.

Judge Lockman called a lunch recess and Barry Grennan used the occasion to brief his next witness, Detective Michael O'Connor, and caution him on the use and characterization of the word "blood."

"But everybody knows blood when they see it," Mike was to say.

"But the judge says you're not an expert and it can only appear to you to be blood," Grennan responded jokingly. "Don't forget that. The judge is already on my ass about remarks that he considered, especially in this case, inflammatory."

O'Connor's testimony was completed in a surprisingly short time. Zevin's cross examination was minimal and likewise low key.

Perhaps Zevin was anticipating the appearance of the missing woman's sister, Aida Raucci. She would be the first family member to testify at this trial.

All heads turned toward the courtroom doors as her name was called. A small delicate woman, impeccably mannered and stylishly dressed, entered the witness box. Her oversized glasses exaggerated her dark eyes; her voice was hoarse but soft, just above a whisper. She was sworn in by the clerk.

"State your name to the Court, please, and spell your last name," he directed.

"Aida Raucci, R-A-U-C-C-I."

"Mrs. Raucci, you are the sister of Florence Busacca, are you not?" asked Grennan.

"Yes."

"And her maiden name was what?"

"Florence Raucci."

"Miss Raucci, directing your attention to July, nineteen seventy-six did there come a time when you took a vacation with Florence Busacca?"

"Yes."

"Who paid for it?"

"I did."

"When did you first have a discussion with her, relative to going to Paris?"

"Sometime in April. I had seen an ad in the paper for a charter flight and I knew I could go cheaply and I did not want to go alone."

"What did she say when you asked her to go?"

"She. . . ."

"Objection," protested Zevin.

"Sustained."

"Your Honor, may we approach the bench?"

"You may," consented Lockman.

"Her initial answer, from what the lady tells me, is that 'I don't see how I could leave my family,' and then there's a considerable discussion to persuade her to go. I believe it is relevant on the question of voluntary, the alleged voluntary disappearance of Florence Busacca," asserted Grennan.

"I agree with you," replied the judge, "but how do you overcome the hearsay?"

"As an exception, as her state of mind."

"To show the state of mind of the client?"

"As not voluntarily absenting herself from her family."

"In April of nineteen seventy-six?" argued Zevin.

"Your objection is overruled," submitted Judge Lockman.

"I want to raise one other issue while we're here," advised Zevin. "When the District Attorney asked his first question of Miss Raucci, he first asked it in the present tense and then changed it to the past tense. I did not object but I think it would be highly prejudicial if he kept up that line."

"I agree," cautioned Lockman.

"I didn't understand," questioned the District Attorney.

"In other words, you can't ask a question as though she is dead; that is for the jury to determine."

"I have to ask it as though she's alive when I don't believe that and the witness doesn't believe that?" asked Grennan, perplexed at the thought.

"That's right, you have to do it or phrase it in such a way that you're not planting in the jury's mind that she is dead. You can afford it," quipped Lockman.

"Exception," replied Grennan.

"Your exception is noted."

"Miss Raucci," continued the D.A., "what did Florence Busacca say to you when you asked her if she would accompany you on a trip to Paris?"

"She said it would be very nice. It would be very difficult for her to leave her family. What would she do about her family."

"I can't hear the witness, Judge," advised the D.A.

"I can't either, Your Honor," agreed Zevin.

"You'll have to keep your voice up, Miss Raucci," said Lockman sympathetically.

"What did she say?" pressed Grennan.

"She said, 'Who would take care of Larry and Gerri and Tom?' "

"Did she discuss with you arrangements for taking care of the children?"

"Yes, she told me that she would probably leave Mrs. Newman in charge to call every day and check on the children."

"When did you return from Paris?"

"July seventh or eighth. It was a six day trip."

"Since August twenty-ninth, nineteen seventy-six, have you heard from, or had any conversation with Florence Busacca?"

"No, sir."

Mr. Grennan's direct examination was intentionally brief, sparing this woman the pain and emotional stress of recounting her missing sister's last days as she remembered them and the horror of arriving at 1442 Circle Drive West in Baldwin and not being permitted inside her sister's home which had now become a crime scene. Grennan had made his point with this witness, the fact that she has not heard from nor seen her sister, who used to call five times a week, since August 29, 1976.

Mr. Zevin's cross-examination related to Aida Raucci's relationship with the defendant, his artistic talent and his employment opportunities. Florence Busacca had been a working woman, a voice teacher and a housewife. Zevin also got the witness to acknowledge that the trip to Paris by Florence had been kept secret from Mr. Busacca for as long as possible.

Barry Grennan made an attempt to extract the rea-

son for the secrecy from the witness but Marvin
Zevin's objection was sustained. Both men were
summoned up to the bench.

"Do you know what that answer is going to be?"
asked Judge Lockman.

"I have just an idea. I believe it is admissible," responded Grennan.

"I want to be sure though. That's why I called you
up," cautioned Lockman.

"Now I don't honestly know the answer, but if the
witness indicates a fear, I believe it's admissible."

"Why?" asked Lockman.

"Because if the victim indicates a fear of harm to
herself by the defendant prior to the crime, I believe
it is admissible."

"Are you pressing this?" asked the judge. "Because if
you are pressing it, I'll ask you to find out what she
is going to say and then I'll analyze it. Its prejudice
may be so enormous. I just don't know, Mr. Grennan,
but I'll certainly analyze it. Go over and ask her what
the answer would be."

"Judge, continually I am back and forth to my witnesses in front of the jury. I don't like the impression
that that has created," argued Grennan.

"I don't blame you," conceded Lockman. "I'm not
trying to cut you off on this . . . ah. . . . I just think
that the prejudice of it . . . ah . . . there are a lot of
problems involved in this particular point."

"Well, . . . I can get to it through Gerri and Larry
anyway," yielded Grennan.

"Well, we'll let it go."

"That makes it easy for me and I appreciate it," confessed Lockman.

Mr. Zevin and the District Attorney returned to their respective places and Barry continued his redirect of the witness.

"Miss Raucci, did Florence Busacca in the year seventh-five or seventy-six say to you that she aspired to the 'Big Time'?"

"No, sir, impossible at that age. Her voice was shot," replied the witness, matter-of-factly.

"Did she know that?"

"Yes, of course!" she said tersely.

"One other question, Mrs. Raucci. Do you need a passport to get to La Scala in Italy?"

"Objection!"

"Withdrawn," replied Grennan sheepishly.

"However," interjected Zevin, "we can take judicial notice of the proceedings if you like because I have gone to Italy and I will be glad to put on the record that. . . ."

"That you needed a passport?" queried Lockman.

"I left the United States without showing my passport and I entered Rome airport without showing my passport."

"You left the United States without showing your passport; that doesn't mean you don't need one. I object, Your Honor," snapped Grennan.

"Yes, the jury will disregard that. Strike it from your minds. First of all it wasn't under oath," chided Lockman.

With that, the testimony of Miss Raucci ended.

Police Officer Larry Gilbert was the District Attorney's next witness. Gilbert had photographed the defendant at the Homicide Squad office, and also had taken blood samples from Busacca's shins and left cheek. He enumerated the procedure that followed and explained that taking of fingernail scrapings from each of the defendant's fingers and thumbs, securing them for the S.I.B. personnel for analysis. His direct testimony was brief, but a necessary link in the long chain of circumstantial evidence that had to be fastidiously woven into an incontrovertible, credible fact. A fact that the twelve members of the jury could not find wanting.

Marvin Zevin then began his cross-examination.

"Where did you take the photos of Mr. Busacca's legs, Officer?" he began.

"In the Homicide office in Headquarters," responded Gilbert.

"Is it also used as a source of coffee . . ."

"There is a coffee machine in there," the witness quickly volunteered.

"And did someone come to get coffee while you were taking photos?"

"Not that I recall."

"Perhaps I can refresh your recollection," Zevin submitted. "Didn't someone come down there to get a cup of coffee and there was some question as to . . . you know . . . don't come in here, we're taking color photographs, or something like that. . . . Does that refresh your recollection?"

"No, it doesn't."

"While you were taking photographs, did Mr. Busacca attempt to turn around so he couldn't have his photo taken?"

"No, he didn't. He was very cooperative."

"What was he wearing?"

"He was wearing a shirt and pants."

"While you were taking photographs of his legs?"

"That's correct."

"Did he roll up his pants' legs so that you could take photographs?"

"He lowered his pants."

"And did he have on any underwear?"

"No, he didn't."

"Did he hold his shirt in his hand?"

"I don't recall . . . I think he had the shirt on."

"Your testimony is that his shirttail then hung to below his knee, to midway to the floor?" pressed Zevin.

"Actually not," objected Grennan. "I object to the question. He says he doesn't recall."

"No, no," disagreed the defense counsel. "He has testified. . . ."

"The objection is overruled," said Lockman. "You may answer the question."

"Yes, he had his shirt on and it hung fairly low. In the photograph you can see that he had his shirt on," yielded Gilbert.

"Are you saying that between the time you took these photos, nothing happened to his shirt . . . he kept it on?" impelled Zevin.

"I don't recall. He may have taken his shirt off," said Gilbert, not having the slightest notion what the line of questions was leading to.

"Why would he take his shirt off?"

"He was told or he was asked to remove his pants. I don't know the reason why he took his shirt off, but evidently he took it off," answered an annoyed witness.

"At whose directions?" asked Zevin emphatically. "You were there!"

"Well, he took his pants off so I could photograph his legs," countered Gilbert. "I didn't tell him to take his shirt off. I guess he just took his shirt off."

"He just wanted to stand around nude. That's what you're telling us?" demanded Zevin.

The question was objected to by Grennan and sustained by the court.

"Was he standing around nude?"

"He was standing around partially nude."

"When you say 'partially nude' you mean he had his socks on?" asked Zevin contemptuously.

"His socks on and his shoes on."

"What else?"

"That's about what he had on."

"Did you take any photos of his torso?"

"Just what's in the photographs. His legs, his neck and cheek area," insisted the witness.

"So you have no explanation why he was standing around nude during the period that you took this photo?"

"Well. . . . he had to take his pants off so that I could photograph his legs."

"Now, we will go back to the coffee machine. Is there a policewoman named Mary on this squad the night you took these photos?"

"Not that I recall."

"What was her name?"

"I have no idea," replied Gilbert, not understanding the line of questioning at all. What the hell do I know about the coffee machine, he thought to himself.

"Are there policewomen down at Headquarters?" pursued Zevin.

"Yes, there are."

"Were they working that night?"

"I can't recall."

"Did they come into the room to get a cup of coffee?"

"I can't recall; I don't think so; not while he had his pants down."

"Did they come to the door to come into the room?"

"That I can't recall."

"Which detective was there?"

"Detective Walker."

"Which other detective?" barked Zevin, unrelentingly.

"I can't recall any other detective there," maintained Gilbert.

"And didn't you hear the detective specifically invite the young lady in to get a cup of coffee?" snarled the defense counselor.

"No, I didn't."

"You specifically remember that you didn't?"

"There were only three of us in the room."

"Who was at the door outside?"

"I wasn't outside the door looking out."

"Now, have you refreshed your recollection as to why he had to take his shirt off?"

"No, I haven't."

"Do you usually take nude photos of prisoners?" mocked Zevin.

"No. . . . but usually they wear underwear," retorted Gilbert with an air of disgust.

"When you ask a man to drop his pants, do you normally ask him to take his shirt off?"

"No."

"But in this case his shirt somehow got off," insisted Zevin.

"Somehow it did."

"Did he do it without anyone asking?"

"Evidently he did."

"Now, in your experience, taking photos of legs when people drop their pants, do they normally take all their clothes off?"

Again an objection by Grennan, which was sustained by Lockman. Walker and Grennan were puzzled. If only they knew what Zevin was leading up to or what particular incident, real or imagined, he was alluding to.

Officer Gilbert testified that he had taken many photographs of the legs of prisoners both in jail and in hospitals but he had never had the experience that the persons stripped down completely in front of him. It was not considered abnormal by Gilbert for Thomas Busacca to have stripped down in the manner that he did.

"You considered his stripping to be normal?" asked Zevin.

"For the purpose of the photograph, yes."

"The proper word, Mr. Zevin, is rational," suggested Judge Lockman.

Mr. Grennan had a question for the court. "Judge,

may I ask any person to make a conclusion as if he is rational for what they did?"

"Certainly, the layman's opinion as to the rationality of the performance of the individual is at issue in this case," explained Lockman.

"Is that a question of this officer?" sought Grennan.

"That is what he's asking. Am I correct?" said Lockman turning to Zevin.

"Yes, sir," replied Zevin.

"Then I don't object to it," agreed Grennan. The ruling allowed him maneuvering room for his future edification.

"Was there a detective there that night whose first name was 'Gary'?" asked Zevin.

"I don't think he was in the same room. There was somebody there in the earlier part of the evening, but I was mainly concerned about the photographs and the samples I had taken."

"At the time you took the photos, Gary Abbondandello was not there? Is that the detective's last name?"

"Yes."

"Was he there?"

"I don't recall."

Marvin Zevin terminated his cross-examination. However, the District Attorney was determined to clarify the issue that Zevin had attempted to raise with respect to Tom Busacca's nudity in the presence of a female officer whom he intimated was "invited" into the room while the photographs were being taken.

Grennan recalled Detective Walker, who had sat bewildered through Gilbert's testimony.

"I don't know the purpose; I'm sure there is good

reason, but Detective Walker has been here since he testified," advised Zevin.

"The jury has observed and you will be allowed to comment on it in your summation," Judge Lockman suggested.

"He is also going to be allowed to remain afterward?" argued Zevin.

"After Detective Walker has completed his testimony, he can remain unless you, at anytime, feel that something is being testified to that he may be called to rebut, in which event either of you can call it to my attention and I will make the ruling."

"I'm in no position to know that," continued Zevin.

"Well, in the future, Mr. Grennan, whenever you feel that Detective Walker may be recalled, I'm going to ask you to excuse him. You have a right to have him after he has completed his testimony, as long as you are not going to recall him. Certainly, we all understand that things happen in a trial, but you don't expect and can't possibly anticipate all these things. On the other hand, it is important, as you have indicated, that you have him to help with the voluminous files that you have. That is why he is permitted to stay here. In the future, as soon as you anticipate that you are going to recall Detective Walker, I want you either to ask him to leave or call my attention so I can make a ruling," instructed Lockman calmly.

"Yes, sir. With regard to the matter he is being called on, I wasn't aware of it until thirty seconds before I called his name," exclaimed the District Attorney.

Walker took the stand once again and was again questioned by Grennan.

"Detective Walker, were you with Thomas Busacca at all times on the thirty-first when Officer Gilbert was taking photographs involving the defendant's legs?"

"Yes, sir."

"At any time, officer, did a woman come into that homicide while he was naked?"

"No, sir."

"No further questions," said Grennan, bouncing the ball to Zevin's court.

"Where were you standing, Officer?" prodded Zevin.

"I was in the room with him."

"That room has a sliding glass window, doesn't it?"

"No, sir."

"There's no sliding glass window?" asked Zevin, seemingly surprised. "Is there a window?"

"In what office are you talking about?" asked Walker.

"Between the office where the photo was taken and any other office or hallway," pressed Marvin Zevin, his knowledge of the Homicide office floor plan obviously lacking in detail.

"There are no windows and no glass at all in that office where the photos were taken," explained Walker.

"Is there one in the homicide squad?" asked Zevin.

"Yes."

"Where were you standing?"

"In the coffee room where the photographs were taken."

"Did any female officer approach the outside of that room?" demanded Zevin.

"I didn't see any female officer in that area at all," responded Walker.

"Were there any female officers on duty that night?"

"I don't know," snapped the witness.

"No further questions, your honor," mumbled Zevin, returning to his seat next to the defendant, Thomas Busacca, who had remained stoic throughout the processing of witnesses, offering an occasional timid glance at the jury and the courtroom spectators.

The prosecution's next witness from the Scientific Investigation Bureau was Detective James D. Granelle, the unit's forensic serologist which he defined as being a scientist who deals with the identification of blood and biological fluids, usually in a crusted or stained form. Granelle held an Associate's Degree in Biological Technology and a Bachelor's Degree in Biology.

Granelle explained the methods of his testing and the associated photographs taken during the examination.

There were labelings on the photos that Zevin objected to, but the matter was resolved to the satisfaction of both sides.

Photographs of the car, taken at Granelle's direction, were introduced for identification. They were large blow-ups in color that delineated the expanse of blood in the trunk and on the rear bumper of the car. Photographed also was an area of fabric impressions in some blood that had dried on the rear bumper.

Detective Marjoribanks saw a sight that made his heart pound and his flesh crawl. Blood was dripping from the trunk lip and onto the bumper of the Busacca car.
(Nassau County Police Department)

The blood-soaked trunk of Tom Busacca's car.
(Nassau County Police Department)

The blood-spattered mudroom of the Busacca home. *(Nassau County Police Department)*

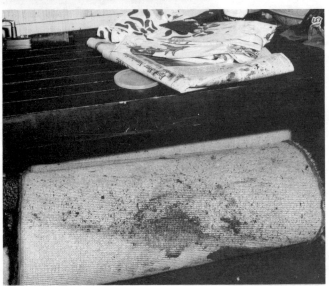

A newspaper stained with blood, and a blood-soaked carpet rolled up under the window bench in the mudroom, as photographed by Detective Robert Horan. *(Nassau County Police Department)*

The trail of blood in the driveway extended from the porch to the approximate position of Busacca's car parked in the driveway.
(Nassau County Police Department)

Several strands of hair, matted together by blood, were found in the middle of the mudroom floor.
(Nassau County Police Department)

Jersey Avenue and Sunrise Highway in Holbrook, Long Island, where Busacca alleged he left his wife propped up against the rail fence. *(Nassau County Police Department)*

The Busacca home on Circle Drive West. *(Nassau County Police Department)*

The mudroom, after the luminol was applied: *above,* as seen by the naked eye, and *below,* with the light off– the luminol is reacting to the iron in the blood and making it glow with a bluish light.

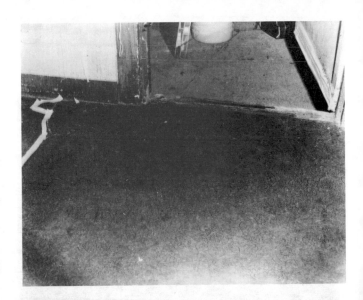

The mudroom after the luminol application. *Above,* in normal light, and *below,* the bluish glow visible in the dark.

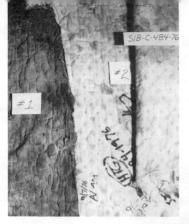

An examination of three different pieces of quilt (#1 was found on Sunrise Highway, #2 in the Busacca home), performed by Detective Henry Galgan, resulted in a jigsaw match. *(Nassau County Police Department)*

On November 21, 1980, an off-duty Long Island Railroad police officer, while walking along a lonely stretch of beach in Hampton Bays, N.Y., came upon a white sandal protruding from the sand.

The police officer casually kicked at the sandal and discovered the skeletal remains of a human foot inside it.

Two rings were found in place on the skeletal finger and matched those belonging to Florence Busacca.

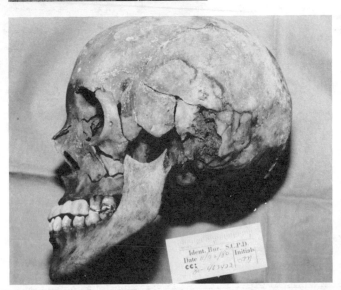

The skull of Florence Busacca was recovered from the dunes.

Granelle continued his direct testimony, describing his procedure for obtaining the blood samples and testing them in the laboratory, tests that he himself performed. His examination of the trunk, as well as the car itself, was painstaking and lengthy. The interior of the trunk, as well as the car itself, was ladened with objects, camping equipment, fishing rods, fishing tackle, maps and automobile tools, and obviously thrown in with no regard to organization. All of these items had to be invoiced and examined.

Marvin Zevin asked to approach the bench with the District Attorney. "I believe, Your Honor, that all of these will be introduced to show the presence of A-B type on the particular items found in the trunk. I think the testimony is that Mrs. Busacca was in the trunk of the car. There is no surprise that there is A-B type of blood. I believe we continually introduce items which have A-B staining on them, and there probably is not going to be any proof that these items were used as weapons or in any other way; and it is going to be totally prejudiced."

"You don't concede that she was in the trunk of the car, do you?" asked Lockman, surprised at the remark from Zevin.

"The testimony was that she was in the trunk of the car," qualified Zevin.

"By your plea of not guilty, Mr. Zevin, you are putting into the issue every one of these things. If you said to me that you concede she was in the trunk of the car, I think you have a legitimate point. But, without conceding that point, Mr. Grennan has a right to prove until the cows come home."

"I will concede that she was in the trunk," replied Zevin, a dejected look frozen on his already weary face.

"No. . . . every bit of circumstantial evidence, I believe, is relevant to the case," objected Grennan. Now that the tide was flowing in his favor, he was not going to be denied the march to a conviction. A conviction that many thought he would not get, and some continued to doubt. But, now, Barry Grennan's voracious appetite to win and win big, gave him renewed resolution and stamina. The defensive facade of Marvin Zevin was showing signs of debilitation. Just a matter of patience, thought Grennan. Patience and tenacity.

"I have to agree with you," said Lockman, "and, therefore, Mr. Zevin, I don't want you to make a concession only to accomplish nothing by it. In other words, if you concede and I change the ruling in your favor, then it makes sense. But it makes no sense to make a concession when I'm going to rule against you."

"If you are going to rule against me, I'll withdraw it."

"Based on what he said, I'll have to," explained Lockman. "I completely overlooked that point. Since the issue is whether she is dead or not, and there is no body, he has a right to rely on every piece of circumstantial evidence that he can bring in," instructed the judge.

"But, where it is clear, Your Honor, that I am willing to make that concession, that these items. . . ."

"That she is dead!" voiced Grennan.

"No, that she is alive and well. That concession that I'm referring to is that she was in the trunk of the car and to go through each item being offered with that concession, I deem it prejudicial. If Your Honor is going to permit him to do that, I withdraw the concession."

"For the reason that I have stated, that he has the burden of proving beyond a reasonable doubt that she is dead; he has no body; he is attempting to do it through circumstantial evidence; and he has to be permitted to use every piece of circumstantial evidence available to him; and, therefore, your objection is overruled."

"Exception, Your Honor."

"Noted," replied Lockman.

The District Attorney's next tactic was to have the witness bring out and identify items from the defendant's car that were stained and saturated with what had been tested and proved to be A-B blood. The items were bolstered by oversized and, imposing color photographs, the clarity of which made them even more repulsive than the items they represented. The photographs had not lost their original color as had the physical evidence which, with time, had darkened and gave more evidence of the quantity than the quality of hue.

At this point, the day had taken its toll on Barry Grennan. He requested that the trial be adjourned until the following day. A sympathetic Judge Lockman was in full agreement.

Chapter Nine

ON WEDNESDAY MORNING, March 16, 1977, Detective Granelle resumed his testimony on direct examination by the District Attorney.

Granelle went on to describe the chemical test made on the fingernail scrapings of Thomas Busacca and on two cloth swatches, which contained fresh blood samples taken from Busacca's cheek and legs by Police Officer Gilbert the night the defendant was booked. Hair samples were also taken from the defendant.

"With respect to those items, Officer, would you relate to us the tests you performed and the results of those tests?" inquired Grennan.

"I performed tests on the two cloth swatches on number one, the reddish-brown stained cloth swatch, and the test revealed the presence of human blood group A-B. On number two, my test failed to reveal the presence of any group or specific substance," replied Granelle.

"All right, now. . . ." started Grennan, but was interrupted by Mr. Zevin.

"Well, Your Honor, he hasn't completed it. He

hasn't told us about three and four," complained Zevin.

"I'm sorry," acknowledged Grennan. "I thought you had finished."

"The fingernail scrapings I tested. It revealed the presence of human blood on the left thumb and left ring finger. I had negative results or failed to reveal the presence of blood on the left index, left middle and left pinky. On the right thumb and right pinky, the test revealed the presence of human blood. The right index, right middle and right ring finger failed to reveal the presence of blood and it failed to reveal any specific species."

"Were you able to determine blood type from the scrapings?"

"No, sir."

"What happened to the items after testing?"

"All the items, with exception of the hair samples, which were submitted to Detective Frass, were destroyed during testing."

The witness went on to enumerate the various tests he performed and the results of those tests. One of the most significant tests performed was the ring-precipitant test which confirmed the presence of human blood, and the grouping examination which revealed the blood to be group AB.

Grennan concluded his direct examination and requested that the jury be given the opportunity to view the evidence that had been submitted through Granelle's testimony. But not before Marvin Zevin objected to the words CRIME SCENE that had not been expunged from some of the photographs, which he maintained were inflammatory. They approached the bench.

Judge Lockman agreed. "I had said that I did not want the words CRIME SCENE put in front of this juror," he chided. "It is a very inflammatory-type case and there's no reason to fan those flames."

"If we remove those tags, is he conceding continuity?" asked Grennan.

"You mean CRIME RESEARCH REPORT?" asked Lockman, seeking clarification of the D.A.'s question.

"That's inflammatory," protested Grennan, his voice suddenly pitching upward two octaves and reverberating in the quiet courtroom, before he realized the magnification of his disbelieving response.

"I feel it is," responded Lockman. "That's what I thought his objection was."

"Also, there is the charge," added Zevin.

"Yes, the charge. That shouldn't be on there. Of course if he didn't have it on there, you would be complaining that you would have a right to ask that the jury not see it," said Judge Lockman.

"I don't mind their being taken out of the bags as long as the identification numbers are there. I would rather take them out of the bags and do it that way," submitted Grennan.

"That's what we'll have to do," agreed the judge.

The necessary changes were made and the exhibits were displayed to the jury.

Marvin Zevin then began his cross-examination of the witness. "Now, how many people in the world would you say have AB negative blood?"

"AB negative blood? . . . I know of the percentage

in the United States, but not the exact percentage in the world," said Granelle.

"How many people in the United States have AB negative blood?"

"Approximately one half of one percent."

"What does that work out to, approximately? One and a half million people?"

"I haven't had the time to figure it out. I would say approximately one million if there are two hundred million in the United States," deduced the detective.

"If there are two hundred fifty million people in the United States, using your usual point seven percent figure, what does that work out to be?" pressed Zevin.

"Roughly it would be about one million seven hundred fifty thousand."

"One million seven hundred fifty thousand people in the United States have AB negative blood, approximately?" asked Zevin, emphasizing the witness' answer.

"Approximately, yes."

"How many or what percentage of the people in the United States have type AB blood?"

"Approximately five percent, figure."

"And that would be approximately eleven million people?" continued Zevin.

"Yes, sir."

"Isn't it a fact, Officer, that in no case have you identified any of these blood samples as being the blood of Mrs. Busacca?" challenged Zevin.

"That's correct. Yes, sir," agreed Granelle.

"You also testified that only one sample of blood were you able to establish as RH negative?"

"Yes, sir."

"All the other samples were either RH positive or unhuman blood or inconclusive?"

"They were either inconclusive or I received no grouping on them," responded Granelle. "I established no other RH's."

"Now, with regard to those samples which were established to be human blood, they could be Mr. Busacca's blood, is that correct?"

"It's possible. I received no grouping on them."

The monotony of the interrogation and the infinite detail of the witness' lab tests sought by Zevin were becoming insufferable. Questions had been asked and answered over and over. Walker had heard them before during the suppression hearings, the felony hearing and the trial prep that had lasted for several weeks. It was a dialogue that was now firmly entrenched in his mind and he could anticipate the questions and echo the responses with adroitness. It finally ended, but the District Attorney was now afforded the opportunity to reexamine the witness.

"Detective Granelle, you tested a series of swabs, did you not, from Officer Gilbert, from the defendant's legs?"

"Yes, sir."

"Could that have been Mr. Busacca's blood?"

"No, sir."

"You tested a shirt, did you not?"

"Yes, sir."

"Could that have been Mr. Busacca's blood?"

"No, sir."

Zevin objected, contending that no evidence had

been offered from which he could answer the question. Grennan reminded the judge that a stipulation had been entered into, for the record, that Mr. Busacca's blood type was O positive and Mrs. Busacca's blood type was AB negative. Grennan was then permitted to tell the witness of the stipulation and proceeded to establish from him that tests were conducted to determine whether the blood types were either AB or O.

"In any of your other tests, Officer, in any of the blood samples that you examined, did you find any O positive blood?" asked Grennan.

"No sir. . . . one exception, sir," Granelle corrected, "on report number six. A wet blood sample that I received I had O positive blood on."

"The wet blood sample. Who did you receive that from?" queried Grennan.

"That was received from a blood kit for the Main Office refrigerator on August thirty-first at nine fifty P.M."

Granelle then once again detailed the procedure used to identify blood types. "God! This could go on forever," thought Walker. He sat back and studied the jurors. They had also heard enough. Once more around and they could conduct their own absorption elution tests or lattes crust tests and hemochromagen examinations. . . . not to forget the ortho-toloidine test.

As expected, Marvin Zevin followed with his recross examination. "Officer, in all of the items that you tested in which you found blood or human blood but were unable to give a type or RH factor, could that have been Mr. Busacca's blood?"

"That is a possibility, sir," replied a beleaguered Granelle.

"Thank you," said Zevin softly, nodding politely at the witness, then the jury.

"Could it have been Mrs. Busacca's blood?" asked Grennan, determined to have the last word but knowing it wouldn't end there.

"That is also a possibility, sir."

"No other questions."

"Who else's blood could it have been?" pressed Zevin.

"That could have been anybody's blood," replied Granelle, now becoming amused at the exchange.

"About four billion people on the face of the earth," said the defense counselor contemptuously.

"If that's the count, yes, sir."

"Thank you." Marvin Zevin sat down. There had to be an end to this. The jury was losing patience.

"Could four billion people have fit into fourteen forty-two Circle Drive?" solicited the District Attorney, his lips tense, hands on his hip and facing the jury.

"I doubt that, sir," responded Jim Granelle, suppressing a smile and ending the exchange.

Walker looked at Grennan and winked. Even Marvin found levity in the question.

Barry Grennan would now call Joseph Scalise, Forensic Medical Investigator and Criminologist for the Medical Examiner's Office of Nassau County for twenty-two years, forensic serologist with a baccalaureate degree in biology and a Fellow in the American Academy of Forensic Scientists and a lecturer. His background qualified him as an expert witness in his field.

Mr. Grennan handed the witness a glass vial containing a bone fragment that had been found in the trunk of the defendant's vehicle. Scalise had been able to identify it morphologically as bone, under a microscope, by examining the spicules and then blood typing it. Another glass vial containing a fleshy material and preserved in formaldehyde was shown to the witness. This he identified as skin, subcutaneous tissue and cartilage with a blood type of AB. It had been found in the driveway of the defendant's home. It was a piece of human ear.

An unsettling calm descended upon the courtroom as the District Attorney offered the two items into evidence. Eyes strained to focus more clearly on the glass vial that contained what the prosecution contended to be a bone chip and a piece of flesh from the body of Florence Busacca.

Grennan then went to the table and was handed a third glass vial by Detective Walker. The witness identified it as scalp tissue and hair, with a blood typing of AB. Three dramatic and compelling pieces of evidence were now put into evidence. It was a very disturbing moment for Marvin Zevin. The impact of this evidence could not be mitigated. Its presence before the court and jury rendered all other testimony impotent by comparison.

Marvin Zevin began a cross-examination of the witness, one in which he was uncertain as to what direction it would take him. He asked the witness to point out for the court the area of the ear from which the tissue had supposedly been torn and Mr. Scalise accommodated by pointing to his own ear and describing it as the meatus, or area from the external opening of the ear down and commonly referred to as the ear lobe. Scalise was asked if there was a difference between the male and female ear lobe.

"Yes, there is," he responded. "The nuclei of the squamous cells have bar bodies and can be detected in fairly fresh tissue."

Scalise conceded, however, that of his own knowledge, he did not know if the distinction had been made. Zevin was able to point out through the witness that a person could survive without an ear lobe, that it was not an essential part of the living cell. Marvin Zevin took each item that had been introduced into evidence and one by one drew concessions from the witness that he did not, in fact, know from whom the material came and if, in fact, the piece of fatty tissue was indeed human.

Upon redirect examination, the District Attorney elicited from Mr. Scalise that it was not within the scope of his profession to make a determination of whether a person could live or die as a result of such injuries.

Scalise's testimony was completed and the District Attorney would now call Mr. Lowell Levine, employed by the Nassau County Medical Examiner's Office as Chief Forensic Odontologist. After the perfunctory questions, Barry Grennan went right after the heart of Dr. Levine's testimony. Showing him a series of exhibits, he asked the doctor if he had, after consultation with Mr. Joseph Scalise, formed an opinion as to the portion of the body that one of the exhibits had come from.

"It is an area of the body anatomically which we refer to as the canine eminence and this is probably the upper canine eminence," responded Levine. "The outer portion of bone fragment, first of all it is a bone shaped like a wedge or root, is of the contact bone variety. It is rather dense. The inside, with some bloody elements to it, is a little more spongy. The outside is concave; the inside somewhat convex. . . . The canine eminence is the most prominent ridge left by the root. It is left by the root of the canine tooth and if you put your finger up by it, you can feel the bump left by it, which all of us have."

Lowell Levine took the upper partial plate that was in evidence and pointed out the canine eminence to the jury and the court. He further determined that judging from the dental charts in evidence, they reflect the upper right canine eminence in place, consequently making the bone over that also in place. In his opinion, the bone that was in evidence came from the same person of whom the X-rays had been taken. Levine elaborated in depth the reasons for his determination and subsequent findings.

"Dr. Levine," asked Barry Grennan, "do you have an opinion with a reasonable degree of medical certainty as to how such a bone could be detached from a jawbone?"

"Yes, I do."

"Tell us your opinion and the basis therefore."

"There are only two ways that I know of that this bone would become detached. One is when we extract upper right canines, which occasionally come loose. This area will fracture and we break it actually in extracting the tooth and break out a fragment like that. The only other way would be a blow or blows of considerable force in that area to a standing tooth like that."

"All right, now, Doctor, do you have an opinion with a reasonable degree of medical certainty as to what effect the second manner of ejection of the bone would have on the person's ability to carry on a conversation?"

"Yes, I do."

"Would you state your opinion and the basis therefore?"

"Well, a blow of great force to that area would cause hemorrhage. You would have gum tissue which would be torn with this tooth fragment possibly adhering to it. You would have considerable swelling in that area and, of course, all the front teeth which are represented by the partial denture are gone. And if you stop to think about it, our upper front teeth play a considerable part in our ability to speak clearly and pronounce words clearly. For example, to say the letter 'F' or the 'F' sound, we are putting our lower lips against our upper teeth, and if our upper teeth aren't there . . . I'm sure you may have had the experience of trying to talk to someone in a hospital, for example, who had their false teeth out, and it is very difficult to understand them standing close by. Even so, with swelling, a blow such as that, or blows, would cause great pain. With the teeth missing, I can't see how you can carry on an intelligible conversation with the person."

After what had now become predictably a tedious cross-examination by Marvin Zevin that did little more than prolong the day and kindle everyone's desire to be elsewhere, Judge Lockman adjourned the trial, much to the satisfaction and delight of a weary panel of jurors. The trial was three weeks old and the chorus of witnesses, the long colloquies at the bench, and the technical testimonies that although necessary in nature, were confusing in fact to most lay persons and some of the members of the jury. What was apparently so elementary, so very simple, was left confusing and muddled and what was confusing and muddled was complicated more by a legalistic dependence on the scientific apparatus. Expert witnesses can be intriguing in the delivery of their testimony. But more too often, they become thrasonical in their responses and fail to appreciate the recipient's nescience of the terminologies associated with their fields of endeavor.

But, in the end it would all be ironed out, molded into persuasive, palatable arguments and presented to the twelve members of the panel by both the defense and the prosecutor, the most rational and sound abridgment being accepted.

Thursday
March 17th

The trial was now into its fourth week of testimony and on this particular day the courtroom was filled to capacity in anticipation of testimony from the defen-

dant's two children, Lawrence and Geraldine Busacca. Marvin Zevin had a more present concern,
however, and that was the testimony of the prosecutor's next witness, Dr. Leslie Lukash, Chief Medical
Examiner of Nassau County. Having acquainted himself with the scope of the doctor's Grand Jury testimony, Zevin was able to anticipate its potential
impact on the jury. It was replete with mention of
"fatty tissue" which gave credence to a presumption
of a savagely beaten woman. He, therefore, decided
upon a motion that he would put before the court, for
the judge's consideration, before the jury was present
in the courtroom.

"Your Honor," he began, "so that I don't interrupt
Mr. Grennan's examination later, I would like to make
an application at the bench."

The request was granted and both men approached
the bench and Zevin made his motion, a motion for a
mistrial on the basis of the Medical Examiner's expected testimony. His contention was that since the
"fatty tissue" could not positively be identified as that
of Florence Busacca's or even human in origin, it
should not be allowed before the court. Judge Lockman pointed out that it was for the jury to evaluate.
But Mr. Zevin pressed his objection and asked that his
motion for a mistrial be deemed made at the present
time and at each time the mention of "fatty tissue"
was made during the course of the testimony.

"Just to understand your position," allowed Lockman, "rather than interrupt Mr. Grennan's examination and rather than have the jury hear you make a
motion for a mistrial, which serves no purpose, cer-

tainly as far as the defendant is concerned, you are requesting that you have deemed made at this time, as of the time I permit the doctor to testify relating to hypothetical questions including fatty tissue. . . ."

"It is not going to be a hypothetical," argued Zevin. "I think he viewed the substance."

"In other words, if he bases an opinion on fatty tissue, as of that moment you want a motion for a mistrial?" asked Lockman.

"Yes, sir. Not only when he is going to testify, but I believe he was shown samples of fatty tissue and based on that as was everything else that he saw, he came to a conclusion. Now, I would move for a mistrial based upon any testimony involving the fatty tissue."

Zevin maintained that there had been nothing shown to prove that the fatty tissue belonged to Mrs. Busacca; that wasn't prejudicial and probative of anything.

His motion was denied and the testimony of Dr. Lukash would be allowed with respect to the fatty tissue, with the understanding that they could reconsider the application at any time during the testimony, if it was determined to be too inflammable in nature.

"On fatty tissue, you would have been deemed to have objected to any testimony relating to it, and, of course, any opinions based on it. And you also have been deemed to have made a motion for a mistrial with regard to any testimony relating to fatty tissue. If I don't sustain the objection, or I don't interrupt the proceedings, that means I have overruled your ob-

jection, and I have denied your motion for a mistrial,"
concluded Judge Lockman, leaning back in his chair
and securing the understanding but not necessarily the
acceptance of Marvin Zevin to his adjudication.

Dr. Lukash was called to the stand. A diminutive
man whose bull-dog looks was representative of his
professional conduct, he described his observations of
the defendant's automobile and home, and his own
consultations with Joseph Scalise and Dr. Levine. His
conclusion, based on what he saw, was that Florence
Busacca "had received multiple blows to the head,
causing deep lacerations to the skin and evulsions of
tissue with subsequent hemorrhaging. She lost a portion of her ear and fatty tissue from her skin. She lost
a portion of bone that originated in the facial area.
The blows that she sustained were of such severity as
to have ripped from the body the tissues mentioned."
It was his opinion that death was inevitable if she did
not receive immediate medical treatment at a hospital. If she were not already dead in the house, she
most certainly would have died in the car. He further
testified that his opinion with respect to the fatty tissue was based on three conclusions: the anatomical
similarity to a portion of the human ear; histological
similarity to human skin; and the fact that significantly it was typed AB, the same rare blood type of
Florence Busacca.

It was at this time that Barry Grennan chose to have
the jury view the glass bottle that contained the ear
lobe that had been so frequently referred to. The bottle was passed from one juror to the next, each responding with a degree of hesitancy accepting or just

simply touching the bottle. The only woman on the panel looked away repulsively after a fleeting glance, declining to handle the macabre object bottled in the formaldehyde solution. It was the most solemn moment of the trial that occasioned a heretofore stoic defendant to lower his head in consternation. Marvin Zevin sat back, his chin resting on hand and his forefinger massaging the upper lip. He studied each and every juror as the exhibit was passed and their forbidding expressions were clearly communicated.

The District Attorney then showed the witness the remaining two exhibits that were in evidence, and they were identified as being a piece of hemorrhagic fat and a piece of bone from the facial area. With that, Barry Grennan concluded his direct examination of the witness and Marvin Zevin began his cross-examination.

"Doctor, you were asked if the loss of part of the ear would be visible. Do you remember?"

"Yes."

"And you said, quote 'of course.' "

"Yes."

"I assume that you are referring to balding men like you and I and not a people like Miss Boklan who is sitting at the District Attorney's desk, unless she brushes her hair back as she is doing now, is that correct, sir?"

"Well, yes, to an extent, if the ear is covered up or if I wore a long hat it would be covered up, too. A big size hat."

"And, in our society, isn't it normal for women to wear their hair longer than men?" challenged Zevin.

"Although you may not be an expert in that area," he added contrarily.

"Yes. . . . right," submitted Lukash. "Ah. . . . but you see, Mr. Zevin. . . ."

"I think the question was really answered," interrupted Zevin.

But the witness continued. "Well, I just want to elaborate on this anatomical defect. . . ."

"I think that Mr. Grennan will permit you to do that later," responded the defense counselor wryly.

"Okay."

Barry Grennan rose slowly from his chair. "If the doctor feels, Judge, that his answer is not complete, I would ask that he be allowed to answer it," he proposed.

"It is a very simple question," suggested Lockman, "when you wear long hats or long hair over an ear, can you see the ear? It's a very simple question, isn't it, Doctor?"

"Yes."

"Just answer the question," continued the judge.

"Judge, I believe an expert witness is entitled to give more than a 'yes' or 'no' answer where he feels it is required," protested Grennan.

"Where the court feels it is required," corrected Lockman. "I don't feel it is required in a simple question like that."

Zevin continued. "Doctor, did you ever hear of a Dutch painter whose name was Van Gogh?"

"Yes," answered Lukash dryly.

"And isn't it a fact that Van Gogh, while in a schizophrenic fit, cut off his own ear?"

"So the story goes," replied Lukash, unimpressed.

"Did he survive?"

"So the story goes."

"Well, have you any reason to doubt the historic fact?" queried Zevin.

"Well, I don't think Van Gogh has anything to do with Mrs. Busacca, because if I were to cut off my ear and get immediate medical attention, that's one thing," replied the doctor. "But if Mrs. Busacca didn't have an anatomical removal of her ear; she had a defect that came from the swiping and from the blow that went right. . . ."

Zevin tried to interrupt, "Doctor. . . ."

But the witness as before, went on with his answer. ". . . across the side of her head."

"Your answer now goes far beyond my question and I ask that it be struck," appealed Zevin, gesturing toward the bench, searching for an receiving an admonition from Lockman.

"Yes," agreed the judge, turning to Dr. Lukash. "Doctor, you will confine your answers to the questions. It was a very simple question."

"Doctor, do you have any facts to indicate that Van Gogh ever received medical attention?" pressed Zevin.

"No," replied Lukash, his disdain for the line of questioning and the association between Van Gogh and Florence Busacca beginning to annoy him.

"Judge, I object," complained Grennan. "If we are going to discuss Van Gogh, I believe he is entitled to give his entire answer. We're not talking in this case on relevance, at least. . . ."

"Overruled," exhorted Lockman, again turning to

the witness, his voice composed but stern. "Again, Doctor, I'm going to ask you, Doctor, to restrict your answers to the questions. Many of these questions call for a 'yes' or 'no' answer."

Dr. Lukash's responses became less receptive as Zevin noted the more recent case of the kidnapped Getty heir, whose ear was cut off and sent to his parents, a question that prompted the witness to declare that he didn't know anything about Van Gogh or Getty losing their ears.

Zevin attacked inconsistencies in the doctor's Grand Jury testimony and his present testimony to which he now added to remarks made before the Grand Jury. He had stated at that time that, "failing medical attention, based upon the fact that she lost all this blood as evidenced by the distribution on the different items and also the evulsion of the skin, it is my opinion that she could not have survived this beating without medical attention." It was noted that the doctor never mentioned "emergency" at that time, nor the words "in a hospital," which he now used in his testimony.

Marvin Zevin then turned to the issue of blood splatterings. The court record was replete with testimony by witnesses with regard to the enormous amount of blood found at the scene and in the trunk of the Defendant's vehicle. Lukash acknowledged that the scientific reports examined by him and the pieces of evidence gathered by the police department confirmed that only some of the blood was found to be AB. Many of the samples could not be typed at all. Only one of the pieces of fatty tissue tested by Mr. Scalise was typed as AB.

Zevin called the doctor's attention to police reports that identified just one sample as AB negative, many as AB, more as human, and many that were identified as just blood.

"When you examined the scene, were you under the impression that all of that blood had been typed AB?" asked Zevin.

"I was under the impression that there was a sampling of it, of the blood at the scene and in the car that matched up to AB blood," responded Lukash.

"Thank you, Doctor. As an expert, after your examination, you found no evidence whatsoever of any injury to the skull. Is that correct?"

"No, there was. . . ."

"You weren't able to determine if there was any injury?" interrupted the counselor.

"No, there was no evidence to indicate that there was a fracture of the skull or a deeper injury."

"And, indeed, part of the blood that may be there may be from a bloody nose, correct?"

"Yes, part of it could have come from a bloody nose," conceded Lukash.

"Doctor, from your observations of the scene, as an expert, could Mrs. Busacca have been alive when she was placed in the trunk of the car?"

"Yes."

"And, did you find smearing in the trunk of the car?"

"Yes, there was smearing and pooling of blood."

"And the smearing could have occurred because someone was rubbing it?" said Zevin.

"Well. . . . it's very hard to speculate on that."

"You don't know whether it was smeared because someone was rubbing it or not?"

"Yes, how it got there or what the condition of the body was, whether she smeared it or it was on the clothes that were smeared, is hard to say."

The question of the fatty tissue was once again addressed by Mr. Zevin. ". . . Now, with regard to the fatty tissue, which was not blood typed, could you identify that tissue as being human or animal?"

"Well, the fatty tissue looked human to me," answered the witness.

"Can you establish scientifically whether this tissue was animal or human? Have you tested it?" persisted Marvin Zevin, making every effort to diffuse the brunt of the prosecution's assertion that most of the blood spilled belonged to Florence Busacca, and believing such testimony from an expert witness would foster the theory that she could not have survived the beating she received.

"Well . . . , we tested one piece scientifically and it was AB," said the witness.

"Aside from that one piece with the blood," continued Zevin.

"That one piece was not dissimilar to the other pieces. All pieces looked alike, and if you're talking about an animal, we have to talk about what animal," cautioned Lukash.

"Are there animals that have similar fat tissues?" asked Zevin.

"Well, fatty tissue. . . . there was a hair attached to the fat," qualified Lukash. "I know of no animal that would have that. Morphologically, tissue structure and adherent fat that would come from an animal. . . . no. It is my opinion that it is human fat tissue."

"Doctor, with regard to the fat tissue that had no hair attached to it, according to Mr. Scalise's report, can you identify that fat tissue as human?"

"Well, I identified it from my experience that it is human fat," replied Lukash stoically.

"By looking at it?" asked Zevin skeptically.

"By looking at it histologically and by microscope," explained the witness.

"But you didn't do any scientific testing on the fat tissue?"

"As scientific as I can be with my own mind and my own eyes. . . . He only tested one piece and it showed AB with blood adherent."

"But the other pieces which consisted of amorphous, tannish-yellow, greasy substance, was it identified as fat tissue?" Zevin went on.

"Well, one specimen, number four, was a small piece of skin adherent with fat. Specimen number five is a piece of fat, hemorrhagic fat that was blood type AB. Now, specimen number six, that had a small piece of skin substance adherent to the fatty tissue and likewise specimen number seven also had a small piece of skin substance adherent to it," expounded Lukash.

"Specimen number six is the specimen that consisted of amorphous, brownish-yellow, greasy material and histologically identified as fat tissue?" asked Zevin, referring to Mr. Scalise's notes from which Dr. Lukash was reading.

"That was with his eye," explained the doctor, "but I looked at it through a microscope."

"Do you have notes on this?" questioned Zevin.

"No, but I can bring slides and we can look at them."

"Have you made notes that have not been made available to me?" asked Zevin, glancing in the direction of the District Attorney.

"No, I made a few items which I have my little way of identifying things through my own recollection," responded Lukash.

Marvin Zevin faced the judge and then hesitantly turned to Grennan. "I don't know whether I should ask or suggest that the District Attorney acted in bad faith or what. I have asked for the notes."

The remark, made before the jury and the court, annoyed Grennan. He was on his feet in protest. "I object to his suggestion that I acted in bad faith," he declared, "because I wasn't aware of it. I produced every piece of everything in my possession."

"It is his obligation to produce that which he has and that which he ought to have," said Zevin scornfully.

"I wish you had not made that remark in front of the jury," chastised Judge Lockman, himself vexed by the comment. "The jury is instructed to disregard the remark," he continued. Lockman then turned to the witness. "Doctor, do you have those notes available?"

"Yes, these are just scribbling notes," answered Lukash.

The notes were marked for identification at the direction of the court, and turned over to Marvin Zevin.

Through the notes it was established that only one of the five specimens examined by Lukash was ever determined to have an RH factor of AB; the four others proved negative.

Marvin Zevin concluded his cross examination and returned to his seat, anticipating the redirect of Barry Grennan.

"Doctor," began Grennan, moving toward the witness stand, his fist buried habitually in his jacket at his waist, "The answers that you gave were in response to certain questions; is that correct?"

"Yes."

"The question that you were asked was, quote, 'Doctor, failing that medical attention' closed quote, but, did the question ask you specifically, in any case, further than quote 'Doctor, failing that medical attention'. . . . what your conclusion would be in each instance?"

"That she would not survive."

"Now, Doctor, referring again to the various exhibits that Mr. Zevin made reference to with regard to specimen number seven, which apparently was identified histologically as fat and cartilage, would you draw a conclusion from your microscopic examination of that tissue as to whether it was human or animal with a reasonable degree of medical certainty?"

"Yes."

"And what was your conclusion?"

"My conclusion is that all of the tissue including the fatty tissue was of human origin."

"And specimen number seven, Doctor, was ob-

tained from the area of the pocketbook, was it not?"
asked Grennan.

"Yes."

"Specimen number six, Doctor, came from the area
of the door saddle of the Busacca home?" pressed
Grennan.

"Yes."

"And were you aware that they did blood typing
that indicated the presence of AB negative blood right
in that area?"

"Yes."

"Specimen number five, Doctor, contained fat tissue and hair, did it not?"

"Yes."

"Was it identified, Doctor, as being animal hair or
what?"

"It was identified as human AB," responded Lukash
once again.

Grennan's redirect concluded with one final question. "Doctor," he began, "you were asked several
questions with regard to Van Gogh and Getty and so
forth. You didn't investigate that case, did you?"
Grennan could hardly contain a straight face as he
asked the question and drew a smattering of chuckles
from the capacity crowd in the courtroom.

"Not only did I not investigate the case, but it has
no bearing whatsoever," replied the witness moda-
ciously.

On the recross, Zevin did little to impeach the testimony of the Medical Examiner, whose stubborn
attitude and numerous appearances as a witness in such
trials cloaked him in an argumentative posture, will-

ing to debate any issue pertaining to his conclusions if the courts would so allow. Lukash may not have been correct in all instances of his medical profession, but his ability to cellar-door dance and the positive impression he was able to impart to the listener were his assets. His antagonists would consider him pompous, opinionated and vain, with an overly inflated ego.

Grennan and Zevin continued redirect and recross examinations, each expounding upon the crucial aspects of the doctor's testimony, reiterating the essentials and obfuscating that which one or the other considered damaging.

Judge Lockman recessed the trial for lunch. Upstairs in the office of the Assistant District Attorney was fifteen-year-old Lawrence Busacca, the defendant's son, waiting nervously for the moment when he would begin testimony against his father.

Before the jury was brought into the courtroom, Marvin Zevin made two applications. The first was to have the entire testimony of Dr. Lukash stricken from the record, but the application was denied. His second application was a motion for mistrial on the grounds that Dr. Lukash had characterized Mrs. Busacca as 'deceased,' which was a substitution of the use of his judgment, in front of the jury which was, according to Zevin, improper.

"It was just the one time?" asked Lockman.

"That is the only time I recall," responded Zevin.

"Do you want to be heard, Mr. Grennan?"

"I heard it, Judge," said Grennan. "Apparently the Doctor made a slip of the tongue. I don't believe it is sufficient to create a mistrial. We *are* trying a murder case," he argued.

"But you have a professional witness, a medical examiner with over twenty years experience."

"I understand that. He made a slip of the tongue. I don't believe it is sufficient ground for a mistrial. He instantly corrected himself, I believe. I think too, Judge, in view of his entire context of testimony, leading to this conclusion would really, certainly lessen the impact of what he had to say. Ultimately his conclusion is that she is deceased," maintained Grennan.

Zevin pressed his argument for a mistrial. However, the district attorney pointed out that during his testimony the doctor had concluded that Florence Busacca would have died had she not received immediate medical attention at a hospital, if in fact she was not already dead before being put in the defendant's automobile. He contended that that conclusion far outweighed his referral to the missing woman as being "deceased." Judge Lockman agreed and denied the motion for a mistrial.

The jury was brought into the courtroom. As Barry Grennan called his next witness, all eyes turned to get a glimpse of the defendant's fifteen-year-old son as he made his way into the courtroom escorted by Detective Walker. The slender brown-eyed youth with dark curly hair, olive complexion and handsome face, gave a fleeting glance towards the defense counselor's table, at which his father sat. Tom Busacca fidgeted nervously as he directed a timorous gaze straight ahead. It was the first time that the defendant had reacted with any degree of emotion, and as young

Lawrence took the witness stand, he stared directly into the eyes of his father, who appeared visually disturbed at his son's presence on the witness stand.

Lawrence had been the elder Busacca's only supporter in the small family. But this support was largely due in part to Tom's unceasing efforts to satisfy his son for fear of losing the young man's affection. Larry, as he was known by family and friends, took the middle ground as the marriage of his mother and father began to deteriorate and the discord mounted from day to day.

It was not long before there was an erosion of loyalty, a loss of respect and an atmosphere of suspicion that disheartened Larry, and the realization that his father's benevolence was simply a means to poison his mind against his mother and sister.

Chapter Ten

TOM SENSED THE change in his son's attitude and the tension that had gripped the household for months was now becoming unbearable for him. As young Larry and Tom were returning from a camping trip on the east end of the island, the elder Busacca broached the subject of the family's immediate plight and startled the youth by asking him, "If your mother or I were to separate, who would you want to live with?" Panic filled the hollows and recesses of the young man's mind. He had witnessed his father's irrational behavior of late and his growing contempt for his sister. He did not answer, but realized his father was staring at him, waiting for a response. "I don't know . . . really," he said, delaying a reply in hopes that the issue would not be pressed further; hoping that his father would say simply to "think about it." But Tom wanted an answer and wanted it now. Larry looked straight ahead and then blurted out softly, "Mom, I guess . . ."

Tom was visibly upset by the answer and the tenuous relationship that had been so fragile, so delicate had suddenly thrown his world into turmoil. The son to whom he had looked for love, understanding and moral support had turned away from him. The character of the man changed drastically and he backed deeper into his pagurian life style; the basement and darkroom in his home becoming his only world.

He left a note for his son in an attempt to reestablish a rapport:

Larry!

I am really sorry you parroted the words without knowing all the facts of why I react to such ugliness in our house. I may be under the roof, Larry, but that's all that your sister and mother allowed for many years now.

We need to talk at length, so may I suggest the movies and dinner out or let's go fishing for fluke.

If you don't care to talk to me again, I'll understand but your echo of ghosts of arrogance and insolence has now made me hurt and silent as I will ever be.

So long/tell you what, your mother knows I give her some pittance on thurs or fri for food. I'll go now to gather that money and you tell me when we can go out.

Dad.

The meeting never was to be, and now the young man sat face to face with his father in the charged atmosphere of a court of law. He had not seen his father since a visit to the county jail in early October of 1976. He had gone there with his sister to beseech his father to tell them what had happened to their mother. However, Thomas Busacca steadfastly maintained his innocence, and had so audaciously greeted them with the question, "Any word from Mom yet?"

Young Larry was afraid. He tried to look away from his father's stare. He did not want to look at the man who was accused of murdering his mother. He did not want to be associated with the man who had betrayed him, a man who had left him without a mother, and for all intent and purpose, without a father.

Barry Grennan began his direct examination of the young witness. Ears strained to hear the soft, nervous voice as Lawrence Busacca responded to the elementary questions. He then began his testimony.

He had last seen his mother at about 11:30 on August 29, 1976. Earlier on that morning, his mother and father had engaged in an argument concerning debts that had to be paid. Tom Busacca had suggested that he was going to permit the health insurance coverage to lapse, which angered his mother. However, his father had already allowed the policy to lapse. Larry left the house later that morning, leaving both parents at home.

Lawrence was then asked about the question his father had asked him in the car a week before.

"Larry," asked the District Attorny, "What was that conversation about?"

"My father had asked me, 'would you be willing to go into a marriage counseling place?' I don't know where and I said I would only go if my mother and sister would go also. I wasn't going to go in alone. He then said, 'If your mother and I separated, who would you go with?' I didn't say anything for a while . . . then I said, 'I'd probably go with Mom.' And before that he had said something about how strong my mother and sister were over him, and how they were pushing him to get a job and that's when he brought up, 'If we separate, who are you going to go with?' and I said, 'My Mom.' "

Lawrence left home at about 11:30 that fateful Sunday morning and after spending a day with his girlfriend, he made a telephone call to his home to advise his mother that he had decided to attend a picnic instead of returning for dinner. He told her that he would be home between 7 and 8 o'clock.

At about 9 o'clock that night, Larry called home once again to ask his mother to turn the filter on in the pool, that he and his friend had decided to go swimming. There was no answer. He remembered that his mother was going to see Mrs. Newman that night, to look over some divorce papers, so he called the Newman house. Margaret Newman had not seen his mother and was very annoyed at her failure to keep the appointment.

Larry, accompanied by his girlfriend and her father, returned to his home. The front door was open, but the screen door was closed. The dog was barking and the hall light, which was rarely left on, was on. Larry found the screen door had been locked. He walked around to the back porch and went in and unlocked the back door leading to the kitchen. He made no observations at this time. He walked through the house and then went upstairs but found no one. When he returned to the back porch, his girlfriend was standing just inside the porch door. Larry glanced down at the floor and to his horror saw what looked like teeth. He quickly picked them up and hid them from his friend's view. He realized that it was his mother's upper dental plate which he had seen on prior occasions.

Larry then looked to the floor where his girlfriend was standing and saw a pool of blood. He had not yet turned on the porch light, but he knelt down and felt the sticky substance that was all around them. Larry went back into the house, frantically searching for his mother. He was now in a state of panic and his mind was conjuring up dreadful thoughts. His girlfriend and her father were not aware of what was transpiring. At that moment, Geraldine, his sister, had returned home with her friend Nancy, and he tried to tell her what he had found, but she brushed by him and went into the bathroom. His girlfriend and her father left, unaware of anything.

Larry went to the bathroom door and yelled to his sister, "Gerri, what does Mom's plate look like?"

Geraldine came out of the bathroom. "What do you mean?" she screamed, herself becoming panicky.

Barry Grennan had permitted the young man to go on with his testimony, without interruption. The quiet in the courtroom was deafening. The poise and articulate manner of the witness was startling. It had been a composure and calmness that he had sustained since the disappearance of his mother six months earlier. It was a quiet, reserved posture that many who had been in his company found almost unnatural.

Grennan continued his examination, which would now focus on the details.

"When your sister came out of the bathroom, Larry, what did you do then?"

"I went looking around the house again, and I had just started to go downstairs when I heard Gerri scream and Nancy scream right after her. . . . and I ran back into the porch area and the light was on. Gerri was on the floor and I saw that there was blood all over the porch and blood on this carpet rolled up and I turned around and underneath the chair there were keys and a globule of blood."

"When you say 'keys,' would you look at exhibit sixty-five for identification? Do you recognize those keys?"

"Yes. . . . they are my mother's keys," replied the youth, lowering his head, his expression intense, his words barely audible. Tom Busacca fussed with his necktie. He never took his eyes off his son, who seemed satisfied to ignore his father's presence.

The witness marked on the photograph shown him where he had found the teeth and the keys. As he viewed the vivid color photo, he turned briefly away.

"What did you observe about the keys?" asked Grennan.

"There was a little blob of what appeared to be blood, and it was on the floor."

"Now, Lawrence, what else did you observe, if anything?"

"Well, there was blood on the rolled up carpet that was on the porch and blood spattered all over the walls," he answered calmly.

"What did you do at this point?" continued Grennan.

Young Larry went on to tell how he tried to calm his sister, who had become hysterical; and then of receiving a telephone call from a very concerned Margaret Newman, who immediately returned to the Busacca home after learning what the children had found. The police were subsequently called and arrived at the house.

"When did you see your father?" Grennan asked.

"It was about three ten A.M."

"Where was he when you saw him?"

"He was in the driveway."

"Between the time of the arrival of the police and three ten in the morning, did anything occur in the house?"

"The detective came in and the police were looking around the house."

"Did anything else occur between five and ten before twelve?"

"My father's car went by the house."

"What did you do or see?"

"I heard my father's car go by."

"What you thought was your father's car," corrected Grennan. "What did you hear?"

"The noise that my father's car makes. It's got a bad muffler."

"What occurred?"

"I heard the car and Gerri said, 'There goes Dad's car,' because she saw it and I had gotten up to take a look, but the car was already gone."

"Now, did you have any conversation with your father at three ten?"

"I couldn't. I was in the house and he was outside."

"When did you next see your father?"

"The next night at police headquarters."

The witness then related that at that time he had a brief conversation with his father. He did not speak to or see his father again until the visit to the jail in early October with his sister.

Lawrence reiterated what Mrs. Newman had testified to earlier in the trial concerning his mother's trip to Paris and her arrangements to have Margaret Newman check on their welfare while she was away.

"Lawrence," asked the District Attorney, "who was present at the time you had the conversation with your father at the jail?"

"My sister."

"Had anyone, specifically any police officer, D.A., or any law enforcement official requested you to go to the jail and visit your father?"

"No, . . . no one said anything."

The question and answer were important. It would be the defense's position that the visit was made at the behest of the police and, therefore, make the children agents of the police department. That being the case, Zevin would contend it made any conversation by the defendant inadmissible, because he had already obtained counsel and could not be questioned.

". . . . tell us what conversation took place between your father, your sister and yourself on that date."

"We got to the jail and we said 'hello' and the first thing my father said was, 'Has there been any word from Mom yet?' and I told him, 'Of course not,' and he said to Gerri, 'Did you have to call the cops on me? All I needed was a simple apology.' He wanted to know where we were staying and I told him a friend's house. . . ."

His sister pressed him for information concerning the fate of their mother. He simply stated that they had finished a meal and were carrying on a conversation, when an argument ensued after he had suggested that his mother and father move in with them. After the altercation, his wife left the house, and he alleged seeing her in the embrace of a person standing in the driveway of their home. At that point, Tom asked his daughter if it could have been her whom he saw with her mother. "He said he saw her embracing somebody, and he tried to go outside, but my mother was holding the door closed; and he said my mother came in and she hit him first; and then he hit her; and she fell down; and he backed up and tripped over something. When he got up he had a stick or something in his hand with a ball on the end of it; and he said that he beat his wife with it; and then put the body in the trunk. . . . of his car."

"Did he say 'body'?" interrupted Grennan.

"Yes."

"Go ahead," said the District Attorney, his eyes panning the jurors who adhered to every word of the young man's testimony.

Lawrence spoke with deliberation and clarity as he continued. ". . . . and he came back in to clean up the mess he had made in the porch, because he didn't want me to see it. We brought out Mrs. Newman to him and he said, yes, he remembered her coming; and he said if she would have come in right then, that it would have been over. I mean he would have taken her to the hospital, but he said he was getting changed and didn't say if she left or what. . . ."

The witness then recounted a story that had been repeated by his father over and over: The trip to Suffolk County and his father's hearing his mother kicking in the trunk. His father drove to Holbrook, where he stopped and assisted his wife from the trunk, whereupon she cursed him. He left her, drove back to the house, arriving there about midnight. He drove away without getting out of the car, and returned at about 3:10 A.M.

"That was the conversation as best you can recall on September first?" asked Grennan.

"Yes," replied the witness.

At this point in the young man's testimony, it was necessary for the prosecution to conduct a suppression hearing with regard to a photograph that had been obtained from the witness a week earlier. The photograph was of the missing woman, Florence Busacca, and it was Barry Grennan's desire to enter it into evidence at this time. The laws governing the admissibility of evidence once again had to be applied, and the prosecutor was obliged to show that the photograph was legally obtained, and in this instance, voluntarily surrendered to the law enforcement officials by the youth not acting at their behest or as their agent, since a search warrant had not been obtained. It would be argued by the defense that Lawrence Busacca had no legal right in his father's darkroom, where the young man reproduced the negative.

The jury was then led from the courtroom, unaware of the nature of the delay; and the suppression hearing on the one issue began with Lawrence Busacca still on the witness stand. Grennan showed Lawrence the photograph of his mother and had the youth identify it. Lawrence went on to testify that on March 2, he delivered the photo to Mr. Grennan. He had made up the negative in the darkroom that he had been permitted to use.

"Does your father use the darkroom as well?" Grennan was to ask.

"Not any more," Lawrence replied, staring for a moment at the abject figure of his father, whose demeanor now reflected the uneasiness and pain of having to suffer the condemnation of his son's testimony.

"Is that where you obtained the negative?"

"Yes."

"Were you doing anything in connection with that and other negatives?"

"Yes. I was trying to make prints from this negative."

"Prints of your mother?" Grennan qualified. "And you yourself, at that time, were working with regard to this?"

"Yes."

The prosecutor then turned the questioning over to Marvin Zevin. Zevin's strong objection to the introduction of the photograph would be evidenced in his intense questioning of the witness.

"On August twenty-nine or August thirty, was the darkroom locked?" he began.

"I don't know!" replied Lawrence. "I don't remember."

"Did the police have to break the door down to get into it to see if there was anybody inside?"

"They didn't break the door down. . . . No, sir."

"What did you do to get in?"

"Objection!" shouted Grennan, before the witness was able to answer.

"Objection overruled," said Lockman. "If he knows."

"Judge, what they did on the twenty-ninth has no connection with what they did on March second," complained Grennan.

"But it is relevant to the issue," corrected Lockman. "If he knows how they got into the darkroom, he can tell us. I didn't hear his answer, incidentally. Was it locked on the twenty-ninth?"

"I don't know whether it was or not," repeated Lawrence.

"Does it have a lock on it?" asked Lockman.

"No. . . . as far as I know," replied the witness.

"Are there any nails to secure the door?" asked Zevin.

"I think there was. . . . but. . . . I don't know if that was used or not."

"What do you mean you 'don't know if it was used,' " asked Zevin.

"I remember seeing the hole and the nail sticking out of it."

"And that was the method your father used to keep the darkroom secure, right?" asked Marvin Zevin, matter-of-factly.

"I don't know . . . I guess so . . . I never knew about it because it wasn't there in the beginning when we first started living there. We were living in the house about ten years, and we. . . . I was down there with him before and I never knew it was there."

"I see," said Zevin understandingly, "Somewhere, whenever you were down there with him before. . . . then. . . . whenever you were down there in the darkroom before August thirty, nineteen seventy-six, your father was always there with you?"

"Yes. . . . that's if I was doing work," replied the witness.

"He'd never let you go down there to work alone in the darkroom without his being there?" pressed Zevin.

"Usually not . . . no."

" 'Usually' or always 'not'?" asked Zevin; seeking to solicit a more positive response.

"I was never down there alone, but he said that I could eventually," explained the young man, a bit more anxious and seemingly uncomfortable with the questions that were now being raised.

"He said you could eventually?"

"Yes."

"And by eventually, he meant that when he had taught you the use of the equipment and chemicals?" suggested Zevin.

"When I had learned, yes."

"And as of August twenty-ninth or thirtieth of nineteen seventy-six, he had never permitted you to go down there alone to use the darkroom?"

"No."

"And he kept the door secured, though you never saw how, and he had it secured?"

"I never knew it was secured because I was in there a few times and he did not know about it because it was not locked," replied Lawrence, not knowing how to explain the situation and having it understood in the proper vein.

"You were in there without his permission?" queried the defense counselor.

"Yes."

"But he never gave you permission to use it without his being there?"

"Well, I never asked for permission. . . . so. . . . he never gave it to me," explained Lawrence.

"But you said before that he said that he would permit you to use it eventually when you learned how to use it?"

"Yes."

"But he never got to the point where he said, 'Well, now "eventually" has come. You have now learned and you can use it without me!' He never said that to you?"

"No."

"Did he ever authorize your sister to go into the darkroom?"

"I don't know."

"You just weren't there and you don't know?"

"Right. . . . he might have when I wasn't around, but as far as I know, I don't know," said the witness, his uneasiness yielding to calm, his voice crisp and his confidence regained.

"When you went down to the darkroom after August thirtieth, who asked you to go down there?"

"When are you talking about?"

"After August thirty, nineteen seventy-six, did anybody ask you to go down to the darkroom to look around?"

"No, I was down there on my own," replied the witness.

"Had the police already been there?"

"I think so."

"And they had opened the door to get in?"

"I guess so. I don't know."

"But you do know the police had been there before?"

"Yes."

"Somewhere between August twenty-ninth through the early part of September, as far as you know, the police had been there, and when you came back to the house near the end of September you had access to the darkroom?" persisted Zevin.

"Right."

"But that access . . . your father never told you, while he was in jail, that you could go into the darkroom, correct?"

"Right," answered Lawrence. "He had told me at one time that I should sell his equipment."

"When had he said that to you?" asked Zevin.

"I don't remember exactly."

"Was it in nineteen seventy-four."

"No, it was while he was in jail."

"And is that in one of your statements?" pressed Zevin.

"I don't think so."

"No, but you did write the statements right after you spoke to him, right?" asked Zevin doggedly.

"Yes."

"Now, when he told you to sell the equipment, did he specifically mention the Pentax camera?"

"Well, he did not tell me specifically to sell it. I got. . . ."

"Oh! He didn't tell you?" interrupted Zevin.

"Not me . . . I don't know who he told; but I got it through Gerri. I think he did it through my grandfather, to tell me."

"So you don't know what equipment he was talking about?"

"The message I received was to sell his photograph equipment," said Lawrence.

"Were there cameras upstairs?" asked Marvin Zevin.

"Yes."

"And was one of them a Pentax camera?"

"Yes."

"But you never received any direct word from your father to sell the equipment?" Zevin continued.

"I think that the topic was brought up on one of the visits to the jail. But, we didn't go into it."

"I have no further questions, Your Honor," Zevin said.

Judge Lockman leaned across the bench toward the witness. He had some questions of his own to ask the young witness. His voice was soft and kindly.

"Do I understand this is your father's darkroom?" he asked.

"Uh huh!"

"And do I understand he kept it nailed shut when he wasn't using it?"

"Now, I learned. . . . I guess he did, but I didn't know it . . . but. . . ."

"In other words, the only time you were allowed in

there, as far as he was concerned, was when he was with you?"

"That's right," replied Lawrence.

"All right. The motion to suppress is granted," declared Lockman turning to meet the challenge of Barry Grennan who was already on his feet.

"May I have the courtesy of being heard?" petitioned the prosecutor.

"You certainly may," permitted the judge.

"Even if a civilian were to illegally seize an item, the exclusionary rule would not keep it out," explained Grennan. "This was not a seizure by the police department."

"But, he was doing it as your agent. You told him to get it," countered Judge Lockman.

"No, sir!" argued Grennan, his voice reflecting annoyance. "I asked him for a picture. His testimony. . . ."

"I had been in the darkroom a while," interrupted Lawrence Busacca.

"When he was already in the area working on it?" questioned the prosecutor.

"There was a case on the front page of yesterday's law journal where they criticized the very procedure of the police using civilian agents to do what they're not allowed to do themselves. This falls right into that category," declared Lockman.

"Judge, I didn't ask him to enter any premises. He was already in it. I merely asked him for a photo," pleaded Grennan. ". . . I believe that this is so basic that I have to be heard on it."

"Proceed," allowed Lockman.

"In no way can any of what we've heard today indicate he was constituted an agent. He made no. . . ."

"You called him up and you told him. . . ." started the judge.

"No! . . . I went to him," challenged Grennan.

"And you told him to get you a picture of his mother, and he did."

"No! I asked him if he could get me a picture of his mother!" declared Grennan.

"And at the same time you knew that his father was represented by a lawyer, and you knew his father had been removed from the house by the police. So his father was no longer available to protect his property. And you knew all these things," chided Judge Lockman, his arms stretched outward across the bench and his hands clasped firmly, gently massaging the palms.

"The boy, Judge, told us that he was already in the darkroom working on this matter," contested Grennan. "Let's assume that illegally he was there. That would not result in a suppression of any exhibit he turned over to me at my request."

"As *you* say," remarked Lockman sardonically.

"I didn't ask him to enter the room. He was already there. And further, Judge. . . ."

"As you say, Mr. Grennan, it's basic; the ruling is basic," interposed Lockman.

". . . and furthermore, Judge, the boy has not said at any time he found it to be locked. He doesn't know anything about this nail."

"Whether it was locked or whether it was an area he had no permission to go to, this was in the exclusive control of his father," said the judge.

"And he disobeyed his father," added Grennan.

"At your request!" snapped Lockman.

"No, sir!" protested Grennan vehemently, his arms flailing towards the heavens, his frustration more evident. "He had already done that, Judge, according to his testimony."

"I was already in there!" declared the witness, almost shyly, surprising Grennan and Judge Lockman with his impromptu remark.

"Well, let's find out about that," conceded Lockman. "When was it that you obtained the negative?"

"I don't know when I got the negative, but I had had it for a while because I was trying to work on it; but I had been busy in school, and I'd been trying to find time for about a month. I had worked every now and then. I had started to learn how to use the darkroom and use the enlarger and the chemicals, so I knew what I was doing. And I went downstairs and I was practicing with negatives, and I got a hold of these negatives."

"Where were you keeping the negatives?" asked Lockman.

"Well, at the time they were. . . . I brought them downstairs. I don't know. When I got them they were upstairs. They were in a big photo album we had," said the witness.

"The negative with your mother's picture?" asked Lockman, an expression of surprise on his face.

"Yes."

"Was it upstairs when you got it?" asked Lockman curiously.

"Yes. Upstairs when I got it."

"Where was it upstairs when you got it? Where was it upstairs when you got it, Larry?" asked Lockman.

"In the dining room," Lawrence said.

"That changes the whole picture," declared Lockman.

Lockman then determined that the location of the picture, from which Lawrence had made the negatives, was not in an area solely under the control of his father, and, therefore, could not have been illegally seized by the witness. Lawrence Busacca obtained it from an area he was entitled to go to.

Marvin Zevin was visibly upset with the turn of events.

"Do you want to question him, Mr. Zevin?" offered Judge Lockman.

"Why not? We'll get *another* story!" snarled Zevin derisively.

"Judge, I wouldn't make a comment about that comment, but I don't believe it belongs in the record," protested the prosecutor.

"That comment will be stricken," agreed Lockman.

"Where was the negative, Larry?" asked Zevin, glaring intensely at the witness, his head slightly back, an air of arrogance.

"In the dining room," replied the young witness calmly.

"Where in the dining room?"

"On a cabinet in a photo album."

Marvin Zevin turned to the bench and addressed the court.

"I call for the production of the photo album," he declared.

"That's a reasonable request. Your request is granted," replied Lockman.

"Well, except, Judge, that we go back to my basic argument. . . ."

"Look, I'm not going to go over that again, Mr. Grennan. You have my ruling and you have an exception. That's what we have Appellate Courts for. To me, it's fundamental. It's about as basic as a thing can be," scolded the judge.

"Well, I have to assume from your ruling, Judge, that we constituted him as an agent?"

"That's right," replied Lockman.

"And I just. . . ."

Judge Lockman leaned forward, pointing a very long finger in the direction of the prosecutor. "I say when you call up a civilian and tell him to get information that you don't have the right to send a policeman in to get, you do that at your peril. If he goes into an area that he had no right to go into, then you run that risk. The article I read, which was on yesterday's front page . . . It was this very same issue, a Court of Appeals decision."

"Then we will have to delay the trial to get this object. I don't know what it will prove . . ."

"I don't know either," interrupted Lockman, "but he certainly has the right to have it on the question of credibility."

"Are you directing me to go to the house to *seize* the photo album?" asked Grennan.

"No. I'm merely saying that he has the right to have the photo album produced," said Lockman.

"Well, are you directing me to go to the house to seize it?" insisted Grennan.

"No, I'm not directing you to seize it. I'm sure that he can get it any time he wants."

"Well, will that make him *your* agent?" asked Grennan. "You see, it's the same thing."

"He says it's in the living room. He has a right to go into the living room," countered Lockman.

"Is that where it is?" asked Grennan of the witness.

"Yes, the dining room. It's still there."

"Is that where the album was when you originally got the negative?" asked the prosecutor.

"Yes."

"And then you took it down to the darkroom?"

"Right."

"And when I asked you for it, you retrieved it from there and delivered it to me?" pressed Grennan.

"Yes."

"And he says, 'Let's see the album!' " interjected Lockman, referring to Zevin's request for its production. "There is another theory that you could go on, Mr. Grennan," suggested Lockman. "When the police broke in . . . I understand you have another picture. You told us the other day, when the police broke into the room. If they did break into it, then they were looking for a body. They had the right to do that. That was an emergency situation. If they picked up a picture of Mrs. Busacca at that time, they would be justified in doing that. Have you got the witness that did that?"

"That's not the photo I'm offering," protested Grennan.

"Well, that's different then. I thought it was the same negative. You told me it was the same negative," questioned the judge.

"That I would have to check with the officers about."

"That's what you told me the other day. Now are you changing your position," said Lockman.

"No, I'm not, Judge."

"That's my recollection," said Lockman resignedly.

"I said I believe at one time they had it," said Grennan.

"You probably did," conceded Lockman.

"But I have no actual knowledge that the same negative is involved."

"Your recollection is probably right," said Lockman.

"We'll have to delay and have him go get it," submitted Grennan.

Judge John Lockman had the jury brought into the courtroom. They had had a long respite from the trial testimony, and now they were dismissed for a lunch recess. Young Busacca was driven home by Detective Walker to retrieve the controversial album. Court would reconvene at 1 o'clock.

Afternoon
March 17, 1977

At the afternoon session, Marvin Zevin went right to the heart of the matter. He questioned young Lawrence with regard to the photographs in the album:

How many were actually taken by him? How many were taken by his father and other family members? Lawrence established that it was a family album, but Zevin went from page to page, picture to picture, identifying each one as to who took the picture. Grennan's attempt to expedite the proceedings was to no avail.

Zevin then asked the witness to go through the album and pull out all the negatives, to which young Lawrence replied, "There aren't any."

"There *aren't* any negatives?" bellowed Zevin, a facetious smirk contorting his face as he looked toward Barry Grennan.

"No," replied the young man nervously.

"Didn't you advise the court this morning that you *did* find a negative in that album?"

"Yes."

"That negative in the album was placed there by you . . . wasn't it?" asked Zevin.

"No."

"Didn't you get the negative out of the darkroom downstairs?" queried Zevin.

"No."

"Didn't you make three A, cross exhibit three A for identification?"

"Yes, I did."

"With the negative that you showed us here today . . . with the negative you used to make this photo?"

"Yes."

"Where did you get that paper?" demanded Zevin, his fingers pounding on the lectern as he spoke, his voice sharp and intimidating.

"This paper . . . I'm not too sure. I have my own
paper downstairs. . . . this might be a piece of it."

"You have your own paper downstairs? Where
downstairs?" asked Zevin relentlessly.

"In the darkroom," replied young Busacca almost
reluctantly.

"In the darkroom?" asked Zevin almost rhetorically.

The intensity of Marvin Zevin's interrogation of the
young witness with regard to the photographs was unrelenting, but so was Lawrence as steadfast and per-
severing in his responses.

At first it was enigmatical—to fully comprehend
what possible ignescent function the photograph could
possibly have on this trial or why Marvin Zevin was
so pertinaciously calling for its exclusion as evidential
matter. But it could be reasoned that since there had
been introduced into evidence numerous vivid photographs of the apparent carnage that had taken place
at 1442 Circle Drive West, this photo of a beautiful,
dark-haired, mature woman in a strikingly pious pose
would add a human element to the scene that heretofore had simply been a figment in the minds of the
jurors.

Should the photograph be allowed into evidence,
the distinction from inanimate to animate could be
made. The association of a human being, a living person, would be identified with the blood splatters, the
fatty tissue, the bone chips and the portion of the ear
lobe. The face of Florence Busacca would now be su-
perimposed over the entire brutal scene and could
possibly weigh heavily upon the minds of the twelve

members of the panel. Death, in and of itself, has no dramatic impact on a person after the fact. However, if that heinous death could be put in juxtaposition with the human beauty and elegance that it once represented, then the impact could be significantly more illustrative of what the prosecution was attempting to make evident during the trial.

Marvin Zevin was to subsequently lose his argument to have the photograph excluded. His attempt to have the young witness deemed an agent for the police department and the District Attorney's office failed. Judge John Lockman then asked a few questions of his own of the young witness.

"Other than Mr. Grennan, did anyone ask you for a picture of your mother, for you to make or get for them other than Mr. Grennan?" he asked.

"Yes, Mrs. Newman."

"When was that?"

"I don't remember exactly when, but I know she has been asking me for a long time," said Lawrence Busacca.

"Were these pictures obtained because of the request of Mrs. Newman or did you do this on your own?" asked Lockman, his voice deliberate and clear.

"I wanted the picture anyway," replied the witness.

"And this was before Mr. Grennan got in touch with you?"

"Yes."

"And no one other than Mrs. Newman and Mr. Grennan asked you for pictures?"

"No!"

"All right. Anybody want to be heard?" asked Lockman, addressing the barristers.

Their reply in unison was "No."

"The finding of facts are that the negative that was used to prepare People's Exhibit twenty-four was in possession of Larry Busacca three weeks ago, at which time he made a positive, using that and other negatives. The request by Mr. Grennan was after Larry Busacca already had the negative in his possession. Therefore, your motion to suppress must be denied," concluded Lockman.

An exception was made by Mr. Zevin for the record and the jury was brought back into the courtroom.

Barry Grennan now had the photograph of the missing woman to place into evidence before the jury. He had the witness identify the photo and the approximate time it was taken. It was then viewed by the jury.

Tom Busacca lowered his head for a brief moment and turned away from his son seated on the witness stand. Lawrence had tried hard to avoid direct eye contact with his father throughout his testimony, but for a brief moment he stared questioningly, pleadingly, his eyes demanding answers he knew would not come.

Marvin Zevin now had the opportunity to cross-examine the witness. For all intent and purpose, his questioning of the young man had begun during the mini-suppression hearing, but there were other areas on which Zevin would concentrate.

There was testimony from the young man with regard to the impromptu visits from his grandfather that

SILENT TESTIMONY 211

his mother resented. The grandparents usually spent
Christmas Eve with the family, but the tradition
ceased for reasons unknown to the witness. Young
Busacca described how his grandfather would bring
money and food over to the house for the family.

Lawrence had always witnessed most of the arguments between his parents, which now had become a
daily occurrence. However, he had never seen his father strike his mother, nor seen him physically violent
toward her. He knew that his mother was planning a
divorce from his father, but never let it be known to
him. It was a secret kept between Gerri, Mrs. Newman and Florence.

Over a period of time, young Lawrence began
speaking less and less to his father, who would now
"hide" in the basement a great deal more than usual,
spending long hours there.

Zevin was able to solicit from the witness of his
father's inability to get employment even though he
made genuine efforts to gain work. He did things
around the house and painted.

The young witness was impressive. His responses
were addressed only to the questions posed, and he
seldom volunteered information not asked of him. His
confidence and certainty manifested themselves in his
lucid testimony. Marvin Zevin could not shake the
young man's resolve.

"Lawrence," Zevin continued, "when there were
social gatherings at the house, would your father frequently leave or go into the basement?"

"Yes."

"Would you say that he was generally depressed?"

"What do you mean by depressed?" questioned the young man.

"I'll withdraw the question," conceded Zevin. "When he came down to the basement, would he say, 'Goodbye. I'm going to do something,' or just would he turn around and walk out?"

"Sometimes he would tell us he was going down; sometimes he wouldn't," replied young Lawrence.

". . . . What was the first thing he said to you at the jail when he saw you?" asked Zevin.

"Well, he said 'Hello . . . was there any word from Mom yet?"

"He said, quote, 'Was there any word from Mom yet?' closed quote."

"Yes."

"You found the partial plate?"

"Yes."

"And when you took them into your sister at a later time and asked her if she knew what the plates . . . she knew what Mom's teeth looked like . . . right?"

"Correct."

"Then you saw some blood. Is that correct?"

"That's correct."

"You saw blood on the rolled up carpet and on the walls. Is that correct?"

"Right."

"And that's about it, right?" pressed the defense counselor.

"Well, I saw. . . ."

"Is that it or not?" interrupted Zevin.

"No I ask that . . . I took an objection to the question we're now about to get an answer to, and he's being interrupted before he can get it," complained Grennan.

"I'll permit him to cross-examine later on, Your Honor," snapped Zevin.

"Well, no!" chided Lockman. "He has a right to insist that you have an answer unless you withdraw the question."

"Well. . . ." started Zevin.

"In other words, if you ask a question, you have to get an answer unless you withdraw the question. You can't interrupt the answer. Do you want the answer?" asked the judge.

"Yes, sir."

"All right. Answer the question," said Lockman, turning to the young witness.

"That was not all I saw. I also saw that pool that looked like . . . looked damp. It looked sticky, that whole thing," replied the young man calmly.

"You also saw that?" thundered Zevin.

"When I came in with Jill, I also noticed there was a spot on the floor—it appeared to be damp and when I felt it it was sticky and it looked like somebody had gone out of the pool but it wasn't wet like it usually would be if someone was drying off."

"Was the spot dry?" queried Zevin.

"I thought it was. . . . yes."

"You touched it and you knew it was dry, didn't you?"

"Yes!"

"It wasn't wet?"

"No."

"And the rug that was rolled up under the table had

been rolled up and left there before that time, right?"
continued Zevin.

"A month or so."

"Now, what time did you call home and get no answer?"

"About nine twenty."

"And you spoke with Mrs. Newman after that?"

"Yes, I did."

Marvin Zevin then digressed to the scene that had
been testified to so many times by previous witnesses.
The same questions from the police, the same responses from Thomas Busacca. What Zevin was establishing was simply that Thomas left his wife alive in
Suffolk County, and his story did not change from one
police officer to the next; nor when he related it to his
children.

Barry Grennan was able to get in a parting question. "Larry, you have been asked what you viewed
in the porch. Did there come a time in the early
morning hours of the thirtieth or the late evening of
the twenty-ninth when you looked at the driveway?"

"Yes."

"What did you see in the driveway?" asked the
prosecutor.

"There was a trail of blood!" replied Lawrence, his
soft voice beginning to tremble with emotion. The
young man who had stood up so well to the direct
and cross examinations of the attorneys, the young
man whose calm and lucid testimony had won the
praise and admiration of those present in the courtroom, was now emotionally drained. The nightmare

had been relived. The bad dreams would linger a bit longer.

"No further questions," said Grennan softly.

"No questions," said Zevin as he stood motionless and watched the young man leave the witness stand and walk briskly past the defense table and out of the courtroom, refusing to acknowledge the beseeching stare of his father.

But for young Lawrence, the ordeal was not over. His mother had not been found in the intervening seven months and now all he had to do was wait and try to rebuild his shattered young life. He was not even certain that his father would be convicted of anything, even of simple assault. There had never been a conviction in New York State without the body of the victim and only one such conviction on record in the United States and that occurred in California. His thoughts wandered as he tried to relax in the office of Assistant District Attorney Barry Grennan. His sister would now have to relive the same horror, the same nightmare. But that would be another day.

Chapter Eleven

GERALDINE BUSACCA, THE older of the two children, was a professional singer, composer, lyricist, and graduate of one of the nation's top music schools. She also gave music lessons and, with her mother, contributed toward the household expenses.

Geraldine loathed the ineptitude and oscitance of her father. His lack of responsibility and his complete dependence on the handouts from his father annoyed her. And now she was called upon to testify against him, as he stands accused of murdering her mother, who had yet to be found. There was so much that she had wanted to tell at this time, but it would not be allowed because of its inflammatory nature. Foremost in her mind was the note that her father had left for her mother. ". . . today I suffered the pangs of a killer. Don't leave her alone for me to get at her. Her arrogance, activities concerning you and I, or our friends have become part of you."

She was escorted into the courtroom by Detective Walker. Once again the room was crowded to capacity. As she walked past her father, she paused briefly and stared vengefully at the fawning figure. Tom Busacca looked away and Walker ushered her along, fearing a confrontation between the two.

She took the stand, a strikingly attractive young lady, her long dark-brown, waist-length hair hiding her mysteriously beautiful large brown eyes. She was sworn in by the clerk, and Barry Grennan began his direct examination of the witness.

"Miss Busacca, you are the daughter, are you not, of Thomas and Florence Busacca?"

"Yes."

"And that is your father, Thomas Busacca, seated here in court next to Mr. Zevin?"

"Yes, it is," she replied, her head slightly bowed, her voice soft but articulate.

Grennan then began to lay the foundation for the introduction of items belonging to Florence Busacca and putting them into evidence. There was a deposit slip dated August 27, 1976, showing a deposit made by Geraldine's mother two days before her disappearance. Then there was the bankbook, the passport, the wallet containing credit cards and driver's license. Florence Busacca's glasses and checkbook were introduced. As the items were introduced, the witness' voice began to fill with emotion and she lowered her head, her dark hair falling gently over her face.

Barry Grennan showed her an earring and she brushed away a tear as she identified it as belonging to her mother. The jury was solemn, sympathetic, themselves feeling the distress of the young woman.

"Geraldine, were you present in your home at fourteen forty-two Circle Drive West in Baldwin during the morning of August twenty-eighth, nineteen seventy-six?"

"Yes."

"Who also was home at the time?"

"Larry, my father and my mother."

"And was there any conversation going on that you heard?"

"That's how I woke up. They were arguing."

"Would you relate to us, as best you can, what conversation you heard between your mother and your father on the morning of August twenty-ninth?"

"They were arguing about bills and a Blue Cross insurance policy that was Larry's and my mother's, and one of my student loans from school. And how my father said, 'We should pay the bills,' and she said, 'What do you mean we pay the bills?' And it was a usual argument, so I went back to my room."

"Now, how long did you remain at the house that morning?" asked the prosecutor.

"I came downstairs a little after noon, I think."

"When you came downstairs a little after noon, was your mother home?"

"No."

"Did you remain at home?"

"For a while . . . yes."

Geraldine next saw her mother at about 5 o'clock that afternoon. Her father was also home at the time. At 6:30 her mother was eating dinner and her father was pacing the floor in the den; and it was at this time that she left the house to go to the beach. Before leaving, she looked for a beach umbrella in the back seat of her father's car, but saw nothing. She left for the beach with friends without it.

"Did there come a time when you returned home?" asked Grennan.

"Yeah, I came home at about nine forty-five."

"Who was home?"

"Well. . . . I didn't see Larry at first. Larry's girlfriend was there and her father," replied the witness. "They were in the doorway. As a matter of fact . . . and. . . ."

"Where did you go?" interrupted Grennan.

"I was going right into the bathroom. Larry was coming down the steps when I was going into the house."

"Did you go directly into the bathroom?"

"Yes, I did. Larry was talking to me . . ."

"You had a conversation at that point with Larry?"

"Yes."

"I'm not asking you any conversation . . . Did you come out of the bathroom?"

"Yes. . . . because he said something."

"He said something to you?" pressed Grennan.

"Yes."

"What did you see or observe when you came out of the bathroom?"

"Well. . . . through the door he said, 'What do Mom's plates look like?' like as if . . . you know . . . so I came out and he had her plates in his hands." Her voice began to tremble, and once again she lowered her head and then turned away as if to chase away the image in her mind.

"Would you look please at twenty-nine in evidence? Do you recognize it?"

"Yes." She began to sob as the upper plate was placed on the bar before her.

"My mother's plate." She paused, raised her head quickly, brushing her hair from her face as she did.

"At the time you observed them, Geraldine, were they in one piece?"

"Yes."

"Now, what happened after he showed you this plate?"

"The phone rang. It was Margaret . . . and she said something strange," replied the witness.

"Did you speak to Margaret?"

"Yes," she paused, placed her forefinger on her lips. "All I remember though. . . ."

Grennan interrupted, not wanting the witness to reflect the mechanics of her mind. "I don't want to know what she said to you, but did you speak to Margaret?"

"Yes. Then I went into the porch and turned the lights on, and I looked directly ahead. Here is the door to the kitchen," she gestured with her hands, "and straight over here underneath we have a slatter bench and there was a rug rolled up, and the whole thing was bloodstained and I was down on the floor at that point." The young woman was suddenly silent. She stared directly down at the floor as though seeing what she was describing, a strange expression etched in her face. The courtroom was silent, the jurors now leaning forward in their seats. "There was blood all over the place." Her voice trembling with emotion she continued, "And then I turned around and underneath. . . . we have a chair with two arms. . . . and I saw my mother's keys first, and I moved the chair out of the way and next to the keys was a clot. It looked like the inside of someone's mouth. It looked like skin from the inside."

The silence in the courtroom was deafening. Marvin Zevin sat motionless, an air of resignation infiltrating a once confident posture. It was the most intense testimony to date.

Barry Grennan paused, allowing the witness to regain her composure. He then continued. "Did you say or do anything at that point?"

"Well, besides screaming, Margaret came in and I was outside the driveway before the time she came in the door."

"Did you look at the driveway?" asked Grennan.

"With a flashlight. I had a flashlight."

"What did you see?"

"There was blood coming out of the door of the porch, down the steps and around to where the passenger side of the car is. . . . since the car was backed in when I left the house and. . . ."

"What did you do?" Grennan interjected.

"There was hair. . . ." started the witness.

"What did you do at that point?" asked Grennan.

"Well, Margaret came at that point and then we went into the house and we called some hospitals."

"At any time did you go back to the bathroom?"

"Yes. I went back into the bathroom and at this time there was blood in the bathroom, too, that I didn't notice the first time."

"Mrs. Newman was on the telephone at this point?"

"As far as I can remember, yes. And then we called the police."

After the arrival of the police, the witness described the circumstances when, at about midnight, she saw her father's car drive past the house. She had heard the motor and recognized it. The car drove slowly past. She and Larry ran outside but the car drove off. The witness continued her testimony, reiterating what had been testified to so many times before.

She then was asked about her visit to the jail with her brother to see her father. He described to them the scene he remembers—seeing his wife in the embrace of a person whom he did recognize. He was yelling at her and trying to open the door but she was holding it closed. When the door was finally opened, they exchanged blows and he fell back. When he got up, he struck her with an object about the head several times and then put her in the trunk of the car; he then changed his clothes and cleaned up the blood with a green towel. It was at that point that Margaret came to the door. She banged on the door and asked for "Floria," but he told her that she was on her way to "your house." Then he left the house.

"When he left, did he say where your mother was?" asked the prosecutor.

"In the trunk."

"What did he say specifically?"

"Before he cleaned up the blood, he said he put her in the trunk. He went east on Southern State Parkway. He said the first thing he was going to do was dump her in Lindenhurst Bay but he heard her kicking in the trunk and he decided, 'I'll go to the hospital.' Then he made a wrong turn off Wellwood Avenue and went south . . . I think. I think it's south to Sunrise Highway, and he went east on Sunrise near some bright yellow lights, he said, near a model home, and helped her out of the trunk and left her against a fence and went to a gas station in Holbrook and then back around the house at midnight. Went to Long Beach after that and then came back."

Grennan asked several more questions, establishing the fact that all of her mother's clothes were still at home after the 29th of August and that her mother had never left Larry alone for any extended period of time.

Grennan ended his direct examination and a recess was called by Judge Lockman. The testimony had left everyone emotionally drained. Marvin Zevin's cross-examination would not be as compassionate or as understanding. He had his job to do, however displeasing it may be.

When the court was called back into session and before the jury was brought in, Judge John Lockman sought a clarification of a point that he had noted during the testimony of Geraldine Busacca.

"Once again, I'm confused," he said. "The people have the burden of proving the voluntariness of what was told, she alleges, by her father. There has been no testimony on that issue."

"You're absolutely right, Judge," conceded Grennan. "I just omitted it."

"I don't mean it as criticism," Lockman qualified.

"No, but you're absolutely right," said Grennan.

"I feel that you have one hundred seventy-three exhibits and I really don't see how anyone could expect you not to overlook some things. I thought you had a theory that I was missing. That's why I brought it up."

"I went right into the conversation that I had preliminary questions about which to ask and omitted that portion and I ask to reopen my direct examination."

It was granted by Lockman and the jury. Then the witness was brought into the courtroom.

Barry Grennan reopened his direct examination. "Geraldine, just a couple of more questions. The conversation on September first at Nassau County jail . . . Did any police officer, any police authority or enforcement authority or the District Attorney request in any way that you have that conversation with your father?"

"No."

"Now, since August twenty-ninth, nineteen seventy-six, have you seen your mother or had any contact with her?" asked Grennan.

"No."

"You may examine," said Grennan turning to Marvin Zevin.

"Good afternoon, Gerri. Gerri, did you ever see your father strike your mother?"

"No."

"In the last five years, have you ever seen your father act violently?" he asked.

"Verbally or physically?" questioned the witness.

"Physically," said Zevin.

"No."

"By the way, Gerri, do you always wear your hair that way?" he asked.

"This way? Yes!"

"So that it covers up the side of your face, your ears and everything?"

"Usually."

This question by Marvin Zevin was designed to show that a woman, missing part of her ear lobe and scarred by a beating could easily hide the anatomical defects by merely fashioning her hair in a particular manner. Certainly he had laid a foundation to incorporate in his closing arguments at the end of the trial.

"Now, your father somewhat prior to August twenty-ninth had been acting irrationally. Is that right?"

"Yeah, sort of," replied the witness.

"Do you want to tell us what he did that was irrational?"

"He picked an awful lot of fights."

"Verbal fights?" asked Zevin.

"Verbal fights," said the witness.

"As a matter of fact, didn't he say at one time that you and your mother had become one person?" Zevin asked.

"Yes."

"And you told him that he needed mental help, right?"

"Yes, I did!" she replied, her voice raised slightly and her eyes fixed on the slumped figure of her father—conveying a message by her actions.

"And his reaction was to say that everybody else was crazy?"

"Right."

Zevin then questioned her with respect to his employment record. The witness pointed out that for the short time he was with a particular company he was good at what he did. Her belief was that he was one those employees that was laid off after the space program. She knew little of his military career, and he never told her any war stories.

Zevin continued, "Did your father want your grandfather to come and live with you?"

"Yes, he did."

"And that was so that your grandfather could help pick up the payments on the mortgage?"

"Yes . . . he wanted to pay off the mortgage."

"Now, your grandmother and grandfather, did they ever come over for Christmas Eve?"

"Yes."

"Except that stopped the Christmas of seventy-five, correct?" asked Zevin.

"I think they were there . . . I think so, I don't remember," replied the witness.

"Did there come a time when they no longer came over Christmas Eve?" pressed Zevin.

"No. The year before this one they were there."

"Are you sure? Perhaps it will help you to refresh your recollection that when Larry testified, he did remember a time when they stopped coming," suggested Zevin.

"Christmas Day," replied Gerri matter-of-factly.

"Would they come over on Christmas Day?"

"We would go to my cousin's in Englewood on Christmas Day."

"What did that have to do with your grandmother and grandfather?"

"They were invited and they chose not to come," replied the witness.

Zevin pursued the issues concerning the family's relationship with the grandparents and then he went into the relationship that Thomas had with his family. Geraldine acknowledged that there was little or no conversation with her father at the dinner table except for simple requests to "pass the salt." Thomas would sit at the opposite end of the table facing away from everyone and watching television. His only conversations were with Larry.

After family arguments, Thomas would withdraw to the basement and his darkroom and lock the door. During the month of August, 1976, the arguments continued as aggressively as they ever had. Geraldine contributed to the household to help her mother. She was asked by Zevin if she had ever set any conditions before she would contribute to the household. The young woman answered that she thought it was unfair that she and her mother always put in for food and extra things but never made any demands of her father.

Zevin continued. "Did anyone ever tell your father about the divorce papers being prepared by Mr. Newman that you know of?"

"Not that I know of," she replied.

"It was supposed to be a secret, right?"

"Right. . . . for a reason . . ."

"But it was supposed to be a secret?"

"Yes."

The witness described her father as a good photographer but as far as she knew, he found it difficult to get a job in that field.

Marvin Zevin then returned to the conversations she had at the jail with her father with Larry present.

"At one point," Zevin asked, "he said he put his hand on her throat and couldn't do it because she was a singer?"

"Yes."

"Then he said that while he was hitting your mother he thought he was seeing you. Is that correct?"

"Right."

"Who is Aida?" pressed Zevin.

"My aunt."

"Is that the woman your mother went to Paris with?"

"Yes, it is."

"He indicated that if Margaret or someone would have come, they would have gone immediately to the hospital. Is that correct?"

"Yes."

Geraldine was not permitted to testify to the fact that her father had also indicated that Aida "was next," a threat that Thomas Busacca had made while he was confined in the Nassau County Jail and not a threat that had been taken lightly by the family—considering his obvious capacity toward violent behavior.

"Was your family ever on public assistance?" Zevin asked.

"Not until now!" Gerri snapped, her large, dark eyes fixed menacingly on her father.

"Well. . . . before?" qualified Zevin, taken aback by the answer.

"No."

"Now, when he spoke to you on October fourth, the first thing he said to you on that occasion was also 'Is there any word yet?' "

"Right."

"As a matter of fact, in the conversation of October fourth, you told your father that he was hallucinating, right?"

"Yeah. He said that when Margaret came to the house, that someone was with her and he said it was Margaret's husband," responded Geraldine.

"And you told him he was hallucinating?" repeated Zevin.

"Yes."

"Your father has been described as non-violent, non-aggressive, non-ambitious and a vegetable. Is that a fair description?"

The question was objected to by Grennan before Geraldine could respond and sustained by Judge Lockman. Zevin ended his cross-examination at that point. But, Barry Grennan had a few more for the witness.

"Geraldine, when your father said to you that he was going to take your mother to a hospital, was your mother in the trunk at that point?" asked Barry.

"Yes."

"Was he going to take her to the hospital in the

trunk?" he asked, a mocked expression of astonishment on his face as he turned to face the jury.

"Objection," cried Zevin.

The objection was sustained but the point had been
made by Mr. Grennan.

"You can ask her if her father told her how he was
going to take her to the hospital," suggested Judge
Lockman.

"Did he tell you?" asked Grennan.

"He didn't say."

"And when Margaret Newman came to the house,
he said he was going to take her to the hospital?"

"He said if Margaret would have come in," answered Geraldine.

"At that time, had he told you where your mother
was, at the time Margaret Newman came to the
house?" asked Grennan.

"No, because he had already said. . . . I'm not
sure. . . . right after Margaret left he left, so he also
had said. . . ."

"Objection to any conclusion," said Zevin. "All
right. That's not a conclusion," yielded Zevin.

"All right. Miss Busacca, as long as you are telling
us what your father said, it's all right," instructed
Lockman.

"The order in which he told me what happened
was: he came in after he put her in the trunk of the
car; he cleaned up blood with the green towel so Larry
wouldn't see it. Then Margaret came to the door while
he was changing," continued the witness.

"He didn't want Larry to see it?" asked Grennan.

"Yes."

"Did he tell you why?"

"I just assumed because Larry is young," she replied.

"He didn't want. . . ."

"Did he say that to you, Miss Busacca?" interrupted Judge Lockman, turning to the witness.

"No."

"All right. Please don't. I understand but please don't do that." Lockman turned to the jury. "The jury will disregard that answer."

"But he didn't want Larry to see it?" pressed Grennan, making his point clear.

"Yes!"

"He said that?" asked Grennan, forcefully.

"He said that!"

"And, what did he say about why he didn't touch her throat? I believe you said something. Didn't he say anything as to why he didn't?"

"He said she was a singer. He was originally going for her throat," answered Gerri.

"And he knew that a singer used her voice and her throat, right?" suggested Grennan.

"Yes."

"You've been asked several times now about different jobs that your father had. How long did he hold these different jobs?"

"Let's see. . . . when I was little he was freelancing. When we moved to Long Island he worked at Fortunoff's."

"How long ago was that?" asked Grennan.

"Sixty-seven I think was the closest time between

Fortunoff and Aeroflex that he worked successively,"
said the witness.

"How long?"

"Two years at Aeroflex; then there was a break in
between, then to Tech-Matten."

"What was the next job?"

"I think it was my senior year in high school."

"Well, in time, how long was that?" asked the prosecutor.

"Well, it ended in my freshman year of college, so
it's somewhere in a year," answered Geraldine. "I
don't know."

"And since that job, since your freshman year at
college?" Grennan asked.

"Something to do with printing. That's all I know.
It was a. . . ."

"Was it a regular basis? By that I mean a nine-to-
five type job?" interjected Grennan.

"No."

"What was it?"

"He just went in one night a week for a couple of
hours. That's all. He never went in in the morning
and came back at five," responded Geraldine.

"Any other job other than what you have related to
us?" asked the prosecutor.

"He did some theatrical head shots."

Grennan's questioning then went back to the conversation in the jail. There was more information that
had not been brought out in testimony and the D.A.
felt that the opportunity to raise the issue was now.

"Judge, before I go into the next questions, I would

like to approach the bench and make an offer," said Grennan.

Zevin and Grennan approached the bench out of the hearing of the jury.

"We went into, on cross-examination with this witness, the question of rationality. I believe in that area I now intend to go into the conversation relative to his statement with regard to his being blamed for what had occurred," said Grennan. "I believe that is admissible on the question of criminal responsibility."

"What do you say, Mr. Zevin?" asked Lockman, leaning back in the large reclining chair.

"Your Honor, with regard to October fourth, I only asked her two questions. One of them was the question of the first thing that was said to her by her father on October fourth," defended Zevin. "And the other question and answer involved Mr. Newman and that she said it couldn't have been Mr. Newman and that he was hallucinating. Now he was hallucinating seeing Mr. Newman there when it was only Margaret.

"I haven't gone into anything else or any of his feelings as of October fourth. Now he wants to elicit testimony as to how he felt on October fourth."

"Well, I think that you are misinterpreting what I am saying," suggested Grennan.

"Perhaps I am," admitted Zevin.

"What I am saying is that on cross-examination he went into the question of rationality of his witness. For that reason, I am going into this," suggested Grennan. The issue had been raised by the defense and thus opened the door to an area that otherwise would not have been legally possible for Grennan to explore. But since it was the defense that initiated the line of questioning, now Grennan could explore the issue himself.

"Yes," agreed Lockman, turning to Zevin. "You cross-examined her about the fact that he was acting irrationally and that he had many verbal fights."

"Prior to August twenty-ninth, yes," protested Zevin.

"Right. Now what are you going to attempt to establish, Mr. Grennan?" asked Lockman.

"Judge, where he discusses blame for the occurrence, he's obviously discussing the question of right and wrong of the incident," answered Grennan.

"What did he say?" asked Lockman.

"Here it is, Judge . . ." started Zevin.

"He said he can no longer be blamed for what happened," interrupted Grennan, "He said he 'cried enough and that enough was enough.' "

"I would feel that the people are entitled to that. What is your objection?" asked Lockman.

"That's October fourth. It has nothing to do with the twenty-ninth or thirtieth," declared Zevin.

"No, but it shows his state of mind," hinted John Lockman.

"As of October fourth!" moaned Zevin.

"Oh, no. . . . He's referring to the incident," prompted the prosecutor.

"Yes. I'll permit it. While you are here, Mr. Grennan, you have not established, as I recollect, that she wasn't sent by the police on October fourth," warned Lockman.

"No, because I haven't had a chance or re-direct. He went into this area," agreed Grennan.

"I understand. I didn't know if you were aware of that. I didn't want to have the same problem," said Lockman. "Now, Mr. Zevin, you asked the last question . . . was something about a vegetable?"

"Yes," said Marvin Zevin. "Mrs. Newman had testified that in her opinion, Mr. Busacca was non-violent, non-aggressive and had no ambition and was a vegetable, and I asked if that was a fair description and that was objected to, and you sustained the objection."

"The statute says you can ask whether he conducted himself in a rational way. You can also ask her to describe whatever he had done," advised Lockman. "It would be allowed to ask specifically on cross examination in particular instances. But, these conclusions do not come within the rational definition. That's why I sustained the objection.

"So, I tell you that in case you want to be guided by that in any way," he concluded.

"Also, in the course of the conversation, she said to him, 'What are you going to do, plead insanity?' and he said, 'I'm not insane. They'll get psychiatrists for that.' "

"Well, I would feel that was admissible, of course. He's the last one in the world to make that decision," said Judge Lockman.

"Your Honor, we are again dealing with October fourth. We're not dealing. . . ."

"Yes," interjected Lockman.

"I'm sorry. We're dealing with a conversation on

October fourth, number one. Number two, he's not an expert. The fact that he says he's not insane is not determinative. It's prejudicial, particularly when she says, 'What are you going to do, plead insanity?' She was leading him right down that path. Now, there might not have been any police there to tell her to do it, and I don't know that there were, but it's quite clear from that conversation her entire attempt was to go in there and elicit conversation. Also, 'My lawyer told me not to talk to anyone.' "

"Well, everything you say goes to the weight. It doesn't go to the admissibility," said the judge.

Marvin Zevin was angry. "Oh. . . . I think it's tremendously prejudicial. The only questions. . . ."

"I agree with you," interrupted the judge. "It is tremendously prejudicial. But in my view, it's also admissible. This is an argument Mr. Grennan has been making."

"Not only that, Judge," said Grennan, seeing an opening, "but I think it is significant. I left it alone. I knew I could use this; we had a hearing on this. The point is he went into the question of rationality and then he goes head-on into the conversation of October fourth. Now, that being the case, he now wants to have his cake and eat it too, so to speak, in that he doesn't want us to go into the very same issues in the very same conversation."

"I restricted myself to two specific areas in that conversation," said Zevin defensively. "I don't think that restricting myself to two specific areas opens up that entire conversation to the District Attorney."

"Once you raise the issue of your client's sanity,"

admonished Lockman, "you really are putting in issue this kind of evidence. Now, technically, the People might be required to bring her back. I'm not inclined to bring this young lady back for obvious reasons. She has suffered a great deal. It must have been a terrible thing, a terrible experience for her to have to come in and testify, and I'm very grateful to her for not breaking down. As far as I can see, she has never cried or broken down on the witness stand. She has shown great strength. And if that happened, it would have been very difficult to deal with. So, I'm anxious not to make her come back.

"You've indicated that you're going to raise the issue of insanity. You've indicated that you are going to bring in a psychiatrist on that issue, and so rather than make her come back, I'm going to permit Mr. Grennan to bring out this information at this time."

"If you do, Your Honor, then you're opening up that entire October fourth conversation for me to go in. . . . for me to go at her with," cautioned Zevin.

"I understand that. But that's got to be the People's choice," said the judge.

"You know, you're going to have a breakdown, and you're going to have her cry and you're going to have all the hysterics in the courtroom," pleaded Zevin.

"Mr. Grennan," said Lockman sternly, "I'm going to permit you to go into this area. However, because of the hour, whenever you agree to conclude, we will conclude for tonight; and I'm going to request that you speak to this witness and tell her how important it is that she continue to maintain her equilibrium. I know you can't be responsible for her equilibrium, but she has been magnificent up to now. I want her to show the same strength she's shown up to now."

"Judge . . . ," started Grennan.

"My point is. . . ."

"No, I'll save us all some time," interjected Grennan. "I'll do this. Rather than involve ourselves in a whole new area, which I believe will take considerable time, I'm going to ask her relative to communications back and forth between herself and her father, if they both understood each other. They were rational type conversations, and that's it."

"Well, you're certainly entitled to that," said Lockman, a sigh of relief beaming forth from a once pained expression.

"All right?" asked Grennan.

"Yes," replied Zevin, himself somewhat relieved.

Barry Grennan withdrew his last question and started over. "Geraldine, you had several conversations following August twenty-ninth with your father, correct?"

"Yes."

"And in some of those conversations did you discuss business matters such as what was to be done with the house, what was to be done with Larry and so forth, with your father?"

"Yes."

"Now, did you communicate back and forth with him, and did you both respond to the questions you asked each other?"

"Yes."

"And was the conversation rational?"

"Yes."

"And prior to August twenty-ninth, did you have conversations back and forth with your father, where you both communicated, exchanged ideas, although you might have been in disagreement?" asked Grennan.

"Yes."

"And was that rational?"

"I always understood him," she replied.

"But you always didn't agree with him, did you?"

"Always!"

"I have no other questions," said Grennan.

"No further questions, Your Honor," relented Zevin.

The trial was adjourned until two o'clock, March 18, 1977.

Chapter Twelve

ON MARCH 18, 1977, the trial of Thomas F. Busacca was continued. Upon completion of the testimony of Geraldine Busacca, the People rested its case. The afternoon began. The defendant was brought into the courtroom and the jury was seated.

"Your Honor," Zevin began, "at this time the defendant moves for a trial order of dismissal based upon essentially two positions. Initially I recognized that there is no law as to New York authorizing a trial and a conviction upon circumstantial evidence of death as opposed to direct evidence of death. Recognizing that, I recognize that when the law was revised, that particular section was left out . . . and I submit to the court that I would revert to the old common law and in the old common law there was a requirement of direct proof of death. In this case, there being no direct proof of death, I move for a trial order of dismissal.

"My second ground of moving for a trial order of dismissal, Your Honor, is the failure of the evidence to show an intentional act. The testimony is replete with testimony concerning the defendant's nonviolence, particularly toward his wife. I don't think that any interpretation of the evidence can show an intentional act to intentionally cause the death of Mrs. Florence Busacca."

"Denied!" said Judge John Lockman, firmly.

"Judge," said Grennan, "before the jury comes in, I had a discussion with Mr. Zevin and I've also had a discussion with an attorney representing an inmate named Occhipinto, and Mr. Zevin advises me he intends to call Mr. Occhipinto as a witness. I had a brief discussion with Mr. Zevin relative to the nature of the testimony to be expected from Mr. Occhipinto. From my discussion with Mr. Zevin, it's my belief and certainly I would ask for an offer of proof prior to that witness as to the nature and extent of his testimony. In any event, from my discussion with Mr. Zevin, I anticipate that the area he would be called upon to testify about would quite clearly be not direct and positive evidence, but rather would be collateral matter which Mr. Zevin brought out on cross-examination of one of our witnesses and which now he intends to introduce extrinsic evidence.

"Perhaps before the jury comes in, we could dispose of that matter now. I asked Mr. Zevin if he cared to go into it now and he said he would. I would have pretrial advised you of it, but I didn't know the nature of his, or of the proffered testimony."

"Your Honor," said Zevin, moving closer to the bench and gesturing with a pencil, as though writing on an invisible board, "part of the testimony Walter Smith referred to the relationship he had established with Mr. Busacca and it was based on that relation-

ship that he said Mr. Busacca had this conversation
with him. I want to call the inmate who was at the
jail at the time that Mr. Busacca and Mr. Smith were
there, to testify as to his observations of the common
relationship that was. . . . that existed between Mr.
Smith and Mr. Busacca. I don't think it is collateral.
It goes to the very heart of the basis for Mr. Smith's
testimony. I'm not asking whether or not when Mr.
Smith, for instance, indicated he had one child, if I
brought someone who'll say he didn't have one child,
he had three children, that certainly would be extrinsic evidence on a collateral matter which would be
inadmissible. That is not the kind of evidence we're
bringing.

"We're bringing one that goes to the very heart of
the issue. Was there any relationship between Walter
Smith and Mr. Busacca which was of such a nature
that would lead Mr. Busacca to make a statement to
Mr. Smith."

"Well, Occhipinto . . . is it Occi Pinto, two words?"
asked Lockman.

"It's Joseph, which is the first name, Occhipinto,
which I believe is. . . ."

"O-C-C-H-I-P-I-N-T-O," volunteered Grennan.
"Joseph A." Barry had done his own research on the
inmate's background.

"It seems to me, Mr. Grennan, that Smith is a crucial witness here. If Mr. Zevin were going to question
him on collateral matters such as used in his illustra-
tion, that would be one thing. But if this man can say
that Smith was . . ."

"How could he say it though?" protested Grennan.

"For example, first of all, can you give me an offer of proof of what he would say? That would help me a great deal."

"For instance, Mr. Smith testified that he dined with Mr. Busacca. Mr. Occhipinto will testify that *he* dined with Mr. Busacca. Mr. Smith never dined with Mr. Busacca and indeed at the jail the whites and the blacks don't eat at the same table," explained Zevin.

Judge Lockman leaned forward. "Well, how would Occhipinto know whether on some particular occasions he may have dined with him."

"Because Occhipinto dined with him during that entire period," said Zevin.

"All of the time?" asked Lockman.

"Well, all I can say is what I believe him to testify to," replied the defense attorney.

"Of course. But what I would need to know is were there any times that Occhipinto was not there?" argued Lockman.

"I don't know. But you know what Mr. Smith indicated was that he dined with Mr. Busacca frequently. Not every day, but frequently."

"Yes," replied Lockman. "Mr. Grennan?"

"Judge, actually Ms. Boklan will argue it but my discussion with Mr. Zevin had considerably more detail to it, to wit: the phrase, the expression 'Hamster.' Whether this witness knows what hamster involves itself with. I don't believe that. I certainly believe that it is extrinsic matter. Also, as to whether blacks and whites eat together in the jail. I don't believe this is a proper matter to be brought in amongst other areas.

"But the question will be argued by Ms. Boklan.

But the disclosure he made to me went into more detail than what he is relating to the court now."

"I've been saved by the bell," announced Judge Lockman mockingly. "They tell me the jury is here. We'll argue it after we conclude. All right. Bring the jury in please," he directed.

The jury was seated and defense called its first witness. A prominent psychiatrist, Dr. Henry Joseph, was called to testify.

Zevin waded through the perfunctory examination of the witness. His qualifications, his medical expertise, his practice and all the thrasonical deeds, real or imagined, were revealed in response.

Dr. Joseph's specialty was neuropsychiatry. He met Thomas Busacca on February 21, 1977, and interviewed the defendant and found him to be suffering from paranoia-schizophrenia, which has had a duration of at least thirty years. The examination of the defendant took approximately one hour and the doctor's diagnosis was made within five or ten minutes of the commencement of the interview. His diagnosis was based, he claimed, on Thomas Busacca's behavior, his responses to questions and the fair content of his ideas, which simply put, meant the way in which the individual answered questions, whether the subject had any delusions or hallucinations, specifically his emotional reaction to various questions or even without questions.

He went on to explain that a delusion in the case of Thomas Busacca was a fixed, false idea not in keeping with reality. Joseph explained that the defendant had a specific delusion that dated back to the day President John Kennedy was assassinated, at which time his wife's former boyfriend who had seduced her prior to their marriage, began to chase them in a white car. He saw only the shadow of the man, but said that the woman was blonde.

Joseph testified that Thomas talked in circles, never getting to the point. Joseph was asked to describe the mechanics of schizophrenia, which he set forth as being a progressive disease, starting late teens and early twenties and usually associated with a prolonged history. Some people have remissions and recover from it. "But where you have a history of a man who has been unable to work, unable to keep a job for all these years, and unable to relate to people, a recluse, isolated unto himself, everybody picking on him, one would assume that it came on twenty-five or thirty years ago."

Marvin Zevin listened as the doctor remonstrated his study, his examination of the defendant. Then he asked, "And is it normal for this type of disease to get progressively worse?"

"Yes, it is. But as with prisoners, they say they burn out, that is, they do not react to their symptoms except on occasions, and they may be just harmless individuals remaining in their homes. However, they could also have acute relapses and acute agitated states. The one thing that is predictable is that it is unpredictable."

"Now, during this conversation you had with him, would you describe him as coherent or rambling, or logical or illogical?" asked Zevin. "How would you describe it?"

"He rambled through every question but a specific factual question. For example, if you say what day is today, he would say March eighteenth, I believe, because yesterday was the seventeenth. However, if you asked him how do you feel about your wife or why did you have a fight with your daughter, it's impossible to get a coherent answer."

"Doctor, was there made available to you a transcript of another interview with Mr. Busacca by another psychiatrist?" asked Zevin.

"Yes, I have a copy of the interview."

"And have you read that interview?"

"Yes, sir, I have. It is very difficult to read," responded Dr. Joseph.

"Well, would it in any way affect your opinion?"

"It confirms it. Not only does he ramble incoherently on the night of this. . . ."

"Objection," shouted Grennan. "The doctor wasn't there. I object."

"Is the report of the People's doctor?" asked Lockman, facing the witness.

"Yes, sir."

"Overruled," said Lockman, settling back in his chair once again.

"It is a transcript of a conversation," protested Grennan. "He was not present at the conversation. I object."

"And you have my ruling," chided Lockman firmly.

"May I have a voir dire?" asked Grennan.

"Yes," replied the judge.

"Doctor, you were asked upon what do you base your opinion, and you related it to us. In any way, do you base your opinion on that transcript?" asked Grennan.

"I did not say that. I said it confirmed my opinion. There is a difference," explained Joseph.

"My question is," said Grennan unyieldingly, "do you base your opinion on that transcript?"

"No, sir. My report was sent to you or to whomever it was sent to before I ever knew about this report," answered the witness.

"So that transcript is in no way involved in the opinion that you formulated?" pressed Grennan.

"That is correct. My opinion was formulated prior to my receipt of this. But I read one hundred forty pages. I assume it was sent for some reason," said Joseph.

"I renew my objection," said Grennan, turning to Lockman.

"Same ruling!"

"Exception!" snarled Grennan.

"Shall I read some of these?" asked the witness, showing an eagerness to continue.

"Yes, sir," answered Lockman, still looking at the District Attorney who had not yet taken his seat, seemingly pondering a next move but then conceding.

Dr. Joseph then expounded upon the document in question.

"On page fourteen," he began, " 'You say the reserve? In the wartime they call it reserve. Not like the reserve you go in on the week time. In the peace time. Weekly involvement now. Now they call it reserve because they didn't want the regular men to feel that they were taking the inferior off the street. They gave it to your United States Marine Corps. That means the guy who was in it for life, USMC Reserve. In war

time meaning selective service men.' Now, not only is
it incoherent. . . ."

"I most respectfully object again and ask for an opportunity to be heard," interrupted Grennan, annoyed over his prior objection having been overruled
and now by this kind of testimony he felt strongly was
improper.

The jury was removed from the courtroom as was
the witness.

"I have to object, Judge," began Grennan. "Because reading of the transcript is of the rankest hearsay to start with. Number two, the doctor has clearly
testified that his opinion was formulated without the
transcript. The offer, as indicated by Mr. Zevin, is
buttressing by reading a transcript of a conversation
that he was *not* present at and he did not even consider at the time he formulated his opinion."

"Are those your grounds?" asked Lockman.

"Absolutely!" said Grennan uncompromisingly.

"What is hearsay?" asked Lockman rhetorically.
"This isn't offered as true. It is a conversation that
your doctor had with the defendant."

"Judge, absolutely. But he wasn't even at it. And
why read it?"

"Anyway, that is my ruling," responded Lockman.

"May I ask for what purpose you are reading it?"
asked Grennan.

"He is reading it to the jury to substantiate his opinion," answered Lockman. "He says 'I found this man
lacks substantial capacity to be criminally responsible
and I base it on my conversation with him and then

it was confirmed when I read the People's doctor's report,' and he wants to explain this to the jury."

"He is buttressing his own opinion," argued Grennan.

"Of course he is," acknowledged Lockman.

"That he formulated even before the occurrence of this conversation that he is reading into the record?" asked Grennan incredulously.

"Precisely," said the judge rapping his open hand gently against the top of the bench, his point being made.

"All right. As long as I am clear in my objection. I can't argue any further," conceded the prosecutor.

"Bring in the jury," said Lockman.

But Grennan was far from satisfied. He turned suddenly toward the bench, a quizzical expression masking his face. "Besides foundation, Judge, I assume that is considered in my argument?"

"What foundation?" asked a puzzled judge.

"For whatever he is reading?" answered Grennan.

"Are you saying it is not accurate, that this is not the report your doctor submitted?"

"Is it not outright hearsay?" countered Grennan.

"No!"

"What foundation has been laid?" asked Grennan.

"It is not being offered for the truth of the matter asserted in there," explained the judge. "This is a conversation that your doctor says that he had."

"Then may I continue my voir dire?" asked Grennan.

"Yes," allowed Lockman.

"I will waive the jury's presence if I may."

"All right. Do you have any objection to the jury's not being here, Mr. Zevin?" asked Lockman.

"No, I guess they ought to be here, Judge," said Grennan, reversing himself. "That would be more proper."

The jury and witness were once again returned to the courtroom.

"You testified at your examination as part of your opinion was your observations of all the actions, conduct and so forth at the time of your interview?"

"Yes, sir," replied Joseph.

"And this entered into your opinion. Is that correct?"

"That's correct."

"That conversation that you read had not even been held at the time of your conversation?" said Grennan.

"Yes, sir, that's true."

"Now, at your interview, in addition to the actual questions and answers, you had the benefit of your observations, as you said, and the defendant, correct?"

"I did have them."

"His mannerisms?" asked Grennan.

"I don't know what you mean by the word 'benefit?' " questioned the witness.

"In arriving at your opinion. . . ."

"Of his behavior?" interrupted Joseph. "Yes, sir."

"His behavior, his mannerisms, and the way he appeared and looked at you and so forth?" said the D.A.

"May I change the 'benefit' by 'observing him'?" asked Joseph.

"Well, it entered into your opinion, your observations?"

"Yes . . . by observing him," replied the witness.

Marvin Zevin rose quickly from his chair. "I don't know what this voir dire applies to as to this specific issue that was raised," he said.

"I'll get to the point right now," retorted Grennan. "Were you *not* present at the other doctor's interview?"

"No, sir, I was not."

"So, you didn't in any way have the opportunity to make those observations?" pressed Grennan.

"Obviously, yes. I was not there."

"You don't even know of your own knowledge that such a conversation was held?"

"Well, I assumed it was held . . . otherwise it would not have been sent."

"Somebody told you it was held and somebody gave you a paper," said Grennan.

"The paper was sent to me. Yes, sir."

"No other questions and I renew my objection," said Grennan.

"Same ruling," answered Lockman. Then he turned to the witness. "Would that affect the fact that you say reading this report confirmed your opinion, Doctor?"

"Yes, because. . . ."

"Wait now, did you hear my question?" asked Lockman.

"It confirmed my opinion," said Joseph.

"No! My question was the fact that you didn't see him answering the question affecting your statement that it confirmed your opinion. You said you weren't present when this other doctor examined Mr. Busacca. The fact that you weren't there and did not see him, would that affect your opinion that your original opinion was confirmed by what was contained in the doctor's report?"

"May I state it differently?" asked Joseph; and then continuing without a response from the bench. "My examination of him yielded the same answers to the same questions. However, there was one statement in the other document which says. . . ."

"Wait . . . that *isn't* my question, Doctor. My question is a very simple one. You have a report that you received from another psychiatrist?" said Lockman.

"Yes, sir."

"You were not present when the other psychiatrist conducted his examination?"

"Yes, sir."

"You have read the other psychiatrist's report?"

"Yes, sir."

"You have testified that having read that report, it confirms your original opinion?"

"Not his report, sir. . . . this is a transcript. The report I disagree with entirely," answered the witness.

"This is *not* the report?" asked an astonished judge.

"No, this is a transcript of the interview and we did not have a secretary when I was there."

"The question I am asking is a very simple one," said a rather perplexed judge. "Do you have to be present and observe him to have confirmed your opinion by reading this report?"

"No, sir. I do not have to be present."

"Continue, Mr. Zevin," said Lockman, apparently satisfied with the doctor's response, or really not understanding the answer himself.

Zevin turned back to the witness and continued his questioning. Doctor Joseph began reciting the questions he had asked the defendant and Busacca's responses:

"What was your position in the Marines?"

"At the end, I came out a corporal but they called me non-com because they gave me a Chinese pagoda; a park with electrified barbed wire and we feed our men and some of the Japanese prisoners in China. And I was called the NCO because of involvement and may be becoming a sergeant etc. etc. . . . But I had held that thing for about four months."

"What is your memory of your impression of these years that you were growing up?"

"Well . . . the outstanding thing is if you will. . . . was I think the one that gave me a feeling about. Maybe the work that I do even now. Not the last seven months, but I remember the largess of my Dad at one particular time in our life—nineteen thirty-three."

Marvin Zevin then interrupted with a question. "Now, Doctor, from your own interview, are there similar examples you can give?"

"Yes, sir."

"Would you give us some, sir?"

"Is there a transcript?" asked Grennan, springing to his feet. He did not recall any such record being received by him.

"Was there a transcript, Doctor, of your interview?" asked Lockman.

"Yes, sir. I sent a report to Mr. Zevin," replied the witness.

"You are confusing him," said Zevin. "The doctor sent me a report which I gave to Mr. Grennan. We did not have a stenographer to transcribe."

"Can we just establish that through the witness?" asked Judge Lockman. "Was there a stenographer like the gentleman sitting to your left?"

"No, sir."

"Now, you know what a stenographer is, I'm sure," asked Lockman almost mockingly.

"Yes, sir."

"Was there a stenographer present for your interview with Mr. Busacca?" the judge continued.

"No, sir."

Doctor Joseph was permitted to continue his testimony relating to his own interview with Thomas Busacca:

"Why did you quarrel with your daughter Christmas Eve," Joseph had asked.

"She said, 'you philosophize too much,' and besides, she's a babysitter. She is very good . . . but not my son Larry, with an 'L'."

"Doctor," Zevin asked, "are these incoherents, this surrounding, is this a typical symptom of schizophrenia?"

"Yes, sir. It is a very precise symptom of schizophrenia."

Doctor Joseph's testimony painted a rather pathetic picture of a man whose mind was, in Walker's view, in advanced stages of deterioration. During the long investigation, the same depraved, inarticulate ramblings of the defendant had been described. "Tell me about your son Larry," Joseph had asked. "Larry is 'L'. Larry is a good kid. I'm going to send him up to Canada. No. . . . I'm going to keep him with me." Then he was asked about his father, how he felt toward him. "Well. . . . Pop was great, but Pop didn't. . . . he was a Papa as a Pop."

Joseph was unable to get anything from the defendant with regard to the night of his wife's disappearance. Unless a specific factual question was asked, the answers would be merely ramblings.

Joseph described him as a man with no anxieties, no worries about anything, who smiled and giggled inappropriately, regardless of the nature of the question. At times, his responses had little or nothing to do with the questions asked.

Joseph concluded that the inappropriate emotional reaction was characteristic of schizophrenia, especially so in the hebephrenic type which he diagnosed as silliness and dilapidation of function. He saw no change in the emotions of his client except to smile cooperatively. He found Thomas to be paranoid or feel persecuted.

"With regard to a delusional system," asked Zevin, "is jealousy one of those symptoms?"

"Jealousy is perhaps the most common, or one of the more common symptoms of schizophrenia. 'They're after my wife' or an 'individual wants to take my wife.' Any variation of the theme to the extent where they had their wives paralyzed so frequently, they can't move out of the house to go shopping."

"Did he indicate any other delusional symptoms or were there any other examples?" asked Zevin.

"Well, the insurance man who was after him, the neighbors, a Mr. Newman—I couldn't figure that out very well—His wife taught piano and sent students to him. But, ah, Mr. Newman was out after him. That about covers it, I believe."

Joseph found no organic problems relating to the defendant but described a disease called general paresis, a tertiary syphilis, which was very common thirty years ago, and for which Joseph would have had him examined under the circumstances.

Asked about the problem of malingering, Joseph concluded that the "malingerer always has some fixed definitive point around which he goes, about his history of the past thirty years, he could not have been a malingerer for so long a duration including the delusional symptom that he had."

"And your diagnosis again of Mr. Busacca?" asked Zevin.

"My diagnosis would be chronic schizophrenia, with heberphrenic and paranoid threads," answered the doctor.

"Doctor, could you give us a conclusion as to Mr. Busacca's capability to understand or to have criminal responsibility for his actions at the time of this incident?"

"I would say that not only at the time of the incident but for many years previously that he just does not have the rational capacity to understand and behave in accordance with elementary conduct and elementary principles of the law."

Barry Grennan began his cross-examination of the witness. It would prove to be a very taxing and frustrating experience.

"Doctor, did you make any other notes or any other documents you've referred to in formulating your opinion?"

"Your Honor, I've given the District Attorney a copy of the report of Dr. Joseph. These are Dr. Joseph's notes taken at the interview. I know of no other notes," protested Zevin.

"Well, is there any objection to my question?" asked Grennan with indignation.

"But can't the District Attorney ascertain that from the witness?" asked Lockman, turning toward Marvin.

"Certainly," relented Zevin.

"My question is, Doctor, you formulated an opinion on February twenty-first, right?" continued Grennan. "I want to know if there were any writings that you made or any documents you referred to in formulating your opinion of February twenty-first."

"I'm sorry, I don't know. Do you mean did I read any books on the subject?" asked a rather confused witness.

"No. I know you draw on your entire medical background but what I mean is anything specific, any hospital records or anything of that sort?" urged Grennan.

"No, sir."

"You had no hospital records that you. . . ."

"No, sir," interrupted the witness.

"By the way, did you ascertain if this defendant had been treated at any time psychiatrically?"

"He said he had never been under treatment," replied the witness.

Grennan's subsequent question explored the witness' medical experience. Joseph had testified as an expert in twenty-five to thirty cases. Out of that number, the majority were criminal cases, two involving murder. The defendants in those cases were examined by Joseph and he was called as a witness for the defense, a point that Barry Grennan placed emphasis on while soliciting the answer.

"Have you ever testified in a criminal case that a defendant was sane?" asked Grennan.

"I would not testify in a case if the person were sane, as I told Mr. Zevin before I examined this man. There are of course. . . ."

"That's not my question," argued Grennan. He repeated the question, his voice raised slightly, forceful. "Have you ever testified in a criminal case that a defendant was sane?"

"No, sir. I would not."

Joseph indicated that he has interviewed hundreds of prisoners in jails throughout the area.

"When you examined—by the way, your examination of Mr. Busacca was on February twenty-first?"

"Yes, sir."

"And on February twenty-fifth, based upon your report, the defendant entered the plea of lack of criminal responsibility due to mental disease or defect. Did you know that?" snarled Grennan.

"I don't know anything about that," replied the witness.

"Now, Judge, that's not the way it happened, and the District Attorney knows it," protested Zevin, his face flushed with anger.

"I ask the court to take judicial notice of the record," offered Grennan, staring directly at Marvin, his lips puckered rigidly, hands characteristically on his hips.

"He's saying that because of the report something was done," said Zevin.

"Oh, no . . . ! I'm saying that that's the sequence," explained Grennan. He then turned back to the witness. "You examined him, did you not, on the twenty-first?"

"Yes, I did."

"Now, Doctor, at the time of your examination, you consulted with no other person, other than the defendant prior to formulating your opinion?" asked Grennan.

"That's true . . . oh, I did speak with Mr. Zevin, of course," the witness corrected.

"And what did he tell you?"

"Not very much."

"Did anything he tell you assist you in arriving at your opinion?" continued the District Attorney.

"No, sir. We did not discuss the case at all. What I said to him was that I would examine the man, but if. . . ."

"All right. You've answered my question," said Grennan, raising his hands in a halting manner to stop any further comment from the witness.

"No, I want him to finish, Your Honor," urged Zevin.

"Mr. Grennan?" said Lockman, motioning in askance.

"No!" replied Grennan firmly.

"He wants to finish that answer and I want him to," demanded Marvin Zevin.

"I move to strike it," declared Grennan.

"You move to strike his answer?" asked Lockman.

"As not responsive," explained Grennan.

Lockman had the answer read back and after hearing it a second time, directed that it be stricken from the record.

"So that your opinion then is based solely on your one hour interview with Mr. Busacca?" asked Grennan.

"Yes, sir."

"Now, at the time you were examining, Doctor, you were examining him, were you not, in order to arrive at an opinion as to the defendant's criminal responsibility?"

"No, sir."

"Oh! You *didn't*?" asked Grennan, surprised by the answer.

"No, sir. That is not my responsibility," declared Joseph.

"You were examining him for what purpose, a diagnosis?"

"A diagnosis," replied Joseph.

"And you arrived at a diagnosis of schizophrenia?"

"Yes, sir."

"Doctor, do you have any further opinion other

than your diagnosis of schizophrenia?" pressed Grennan.

"I'm sorry. I don't know what you mean by 'any further.' "

"Is it your opinion that this defendant has schizophrenia? You testified to that," said Grennan. "Paranoia-schizophrenia, as a matter of fact. Did you render any other opinion in connection with Mr. Busacca?" asked Grennan, becoming agitated by the witness' inability to understand the simple questions put to him.

"I'm sorry. Do you mean by that any other diagnosis?" asked the witness.

"OPINION!" shouted Grennan, startling the courtroom and awakening those who had long before chosen to sleep this one out. "With a reasonable degree of medical certainty."

"Do you mean diagnosis, sir?"

Grennan turned toward the jury, a frown on his face, annoyed and tired. Here's a doctor, a psychiatrist, whose time is spent analyzing people and cannot answer the most elementary question put before him.

"No!" barked Grennan. "I mean *opinion*."

"Well, when I made. . . . well then. . . . may I define the difference between what we're saying? If I go in to examine a man with pneumonia or an ingrown toenail, that's all I have, a diagnosis, not an opinion."

"I understand," said a beleaguered Grennan. "Do you have an opinion, and I'm not asking you what it is at this time, but do you have an opinion at this time, the crime allegedly involving Mr. Busacca, that Mr. Busacca as a result of mental disease or defect, lacks substantial capacity to know and appreciate either the nature or consequence of his conduct, or that that conduct was wrong? Do you have an opinion on that?"

"Yes, sir, I do," said Joseph.

"Isn't that why you examined him?"

"No, sir."

"When did you formulate the opinion I just asked you about?" asked Grennan.

"After I examined him."

"When?" asked Grennan, wanting a more precise answer.

"Oh. . . . within an hour or so driving home," replied the witness.

"But on the twenty-first?" corrected Grennan.

"The twenty-first. Yes, sir."

"And that opinion was formulated solely on your one hour interview with Mr. Busacca?"

"I would say entirely on the one hour interview."

"Entirely, no question about it?" asked the District Attorney, pinning the witness down.

"Entirely, no question about it," replied Joseph.

"And that opinion is based solely on what he said to you?" continued Grennan, pressing his attack.

"No, sir. I defined that earlier."

"Well, all right. I'll withdraw that. On what he said to you and how he acted at the time of your interview?"

"And also his mental association and mental trends, not history," said Joseph.

"What I am getting at, Doctor, was there any input

in arriving at your opinion other than what Thomas Busacca either did or said?"

"Will you repeat that, please?" asked the witness.

Grennan was now beside himself. He looked at Judge Lockman for help. There was none forthcoming. "I withdraw the question and I'll try to rephrase it. What I'm getting at . . . WAS THERE INPUT INTO YOUR OPINION, OTHER THAN YOUR OWN OBSERVATIONS OF THE DEFENDANT, AND YOUR OWN CONVERSATIONS WITH HIM, DID ANYBODY TELL YOU ANYTHING ABOUT HIM OR ANYTHING OF THAT SORT THAT ASSISTED YOU IN ARRIVING AT YOUR OPINION?" Grennan enunciated it as clearly as he could and waited for the reply.

"In terms of diagnosis?"

"Yes!" Great Scott, thought Grennan, what do I have to do?

"By opinion, you mean diagnosis?"

"Yes!" This is ludicrous thought Grennan. This man is an expert witness?

"I'm too old to have other people influence my diagnosis and certainly nobody discussed diagnosis with me. As a matter of fact, I didn't speak with Mr. Zevin or anybody else from the day I left the jail to the day I sent a report," said Joseph, himself becoming perturbed.

"At this time, I would like an opportunity to look at the notes and then I'll go further," suggested Grennan, directing his remarks at the bench.

Barry returned to the prosecution's table, shook his head in bewilderment at Walker and sat down. He scanned the doctor's notes closely, jotting down a question or two as he went along.

The testimony of Dr. Joseph had strengthened Detective Walker's long standing belief that the only thing a good psychiatrist was deserving of was another psychiatrist. Their opinions and conclusions were based on who was paying the tab.

Barry reluctantly continued his cross-examination. "Doctor, with regard to schizophrenia, there are many people in the world with mental disease or schizophrenia. Is that correct?"

"Yes, sir."

"Is it your position, Doctor, that they all lack criminal responsibility?"

"No, sir, I used the word 'arrested' before. There are many 'arrested' schizophrenics, who behave in a normal fashion and carry on excellent work records and scientific records and whatever you wish," replied Joseph.

"May schizophrenics know right from wrong?" asked Grennan.

"There are many who know right from wrong except where it is associated with a delusional symptom at times, from which they can break down."

"Schizophrenics can distinguish right from wrong, right?"

"No, sir. I did not say that."

"No schizophrenic can distinguish right from wrong?" shot back Grennan.

"Many may distinguish right from wrong," said the doctor.

"There is an organization of Schizophrenics Anonymous, is there not? And they're not all hospitalized and not all in jail, are they?" said Barry scornfully. "You have heard of that organization, Schizophrenics Anonymous?" he asked.

"Yes."

"They are not all hospitalized or in jail?"

"That's true."

"They can distinguish right from wrong in most cases?"

"They are arrested schizophrenics," countered the witness. "They can distinguish right from wrong."

"They actively have the disease?" Barry asked.

"No, sir, once they . . . we use the word arrested as in cancer, as in pernicious anemia, as in diabetics . . . and by arrested we mean that at that point in time, they have no symptoms of the disease mentioned."

Barry Grennan's cross-examination went on and it did not become any easier to extract an answer that even slightly resembled the question put forth to the psychiatrist. The doctor found Grennan's question confusing and seemed embarrassed at his own performance on the witness stand.

"Doctor, in your report you made reference to malingering, that it must be seriously considered, correct?"

"Correct."

"Now, with regard to your opinion, in any way did you do anything to double-check Mr. Busacca's story that he related to you, prior to formulating your opinion?" asked the District Attorney.

"Would you repeat the question, please? It is not clear," asked the witness.

The question was reread by the Court Reporter at the behest of the judge.

"I don't understand the question. What do you mean by double-check?"

Grennan was astounded. He couldn't believe this was going on. "You don't understand the question?" he asked in amazement.

"No, sir, I don't," answered Joseph, feeling very uncomfortable before the whole courtroom, and trying desperately to get some help from Marvin Zevin in any form.

"I will ask it again, perhaps in another way," said Grennan scornfully.

"Would you define 'double-check?' I don't understand." The witness was now apparently completely in turmoil.

"Your Honor," Zevin quipped, "while he is defining, would he also define the word 'story'?"

Judge Lockman turned abruptly to Zevin, and with displeasure evident in his voice, instructed that the jury disregard the remark. Zevin then asked to approach the bench but John Lockman's longanimity was wearing thin, and the defense counselor's sarcasm had no place in his courtroom at this point in time.

"Please, Mr. Zevin, if you want to make an objection, make your objection," he said with disdain.

Marvin Zevin sat down. It had been a spontaneous remark that would have been better left unsaid.

Barry Grennan continued his questioning of the

psychiatrist. "By double-check, Doctor, did you do anything that verified what he was telling you?"

"I still don't understand with whom would I double-check? I'm not sure I understand what you mean," responded Joseph.

"*Verify* anything he related to you in any way before you formulated your opinion? Did you seek to *verify* it?"

"As a physician, if I make a diagnosis of pneumonia, I don't seek others to verify the diagnosis. If I make a diagnosis of schizophrenia, I don't know with whom I would verify. My diagnosis stands as does every psychiatrist's."

"You accept then what the defendant tells you at face value?"

"No, sir. I said originally that the diagnosis is based upon, number one, what he tells me; two, his behavior during the interview; three, his mental trends; and four, emotional reaction to the situation. Not what he told me."

"When he told you about his wife, for instance, being seduced, did you make any effort to find out whether she actually had been seduced?" asked Grennan.

"It doesn't matter to me, whatsoever, in the diagnosis of pneumonia, whether a man's wife was seduced, nor in a diagnosis of schizophrenia. It has nothing to do with the diagnosis," maintained the doctor.

Grennan's cross-examination was now becoming intense. The witness was becoming more and more unglued as the relentless district attorney applied pressure.

"When he said that he hit his wife," Grennan shouted, his arms flailing about, "did he know that he hit his wife or did he think he was turning on a light bulb?"

"Or did he think what? I'm sorry. . . ."

"Did he know when he hit his wife, did he know he was hitting something with his hand?" continued Grennan.

"Frankly, I don't think he knows what he did."

"Did you not accept his words at face value in that area?"

"No, sir. I didn't accept any words of his because the next sentence, 'she was on the first step, I was on the third step, I went to the second step,' became irrational, incoherent. I stopped the questioning on that area since the questions themselves do not make the diagnosis."

The agony continued. Grennan held fast and bombarded the doctor with a brutal salvo of unrelenting questions. It was beginning to appear that Dr. Joseph himself would be seeking help after this was all over. His was the most preposterous performance by an expert witness that Walker had ever seen. When Grennan concluded his cross-examination, Dr. Joseph walked from the stand a bruised and distressed man, his air of confidence peeled away by the blistering attack of the District Attorney.

Chapter Thirteen

March 22, 1977

Marvin Zevin called Detective Charles Fraas of the Scientific Investigation Bureau to the stand. Fraas was a seven-year member of the force with five years assigned to S.I.B.

Zevin established the witness' qualifications and other perfunctory information and began his examination.

"Did there come a time when you received various hair samples with regard to this case?" asked Zevin.

"Yes, sir."

"Now, did you receive hair samples which were identified as being from Mrs. Busacca's hair curlers?"

"Yes, sir, I did."

"Were you able, from that hair curler, to identify Mrs. Busacca's hair?"

"Based on information received from the homicide squad, I considered hair samples from her hair curlers and from various hair brushes that also were submitted. I did consider that to be a standard hair sample of Florence Busacca."

"When you say various hair brushes, you mean brown, yellow and a broken yellow hair brush?"

"Yes."

"You examined all of those and came to a conclusion as to which were Mrs. Busacca's hair samples?" asked Zevin.

"Yes, sir," replied Fraas.

"Now, on those hair brushes and hair curlers, with regard to the hair curlers and the hairs on the three brushes, was there a second set of hairs found?"

"There were two classes of hair found, yes, sir."

"And the second class was not Mrs. Busacca's hair, correct?"

"I would venture to say, yes, they were her hairs. I had to consider the evidence, and looking at it, I postulate that the two sets, based on the fact that one particular group of hairs was more darkly stained or dyed than the other, and thus I could not identify enough microscopic characteristics in the hair to positively identify it," reasoned the witness. His voice spoke with authority and confidence.

"So, therefore, there might have been a second group of hairs on these curlers and brushes?" asked Zevin.

"There was a second group of hairs, yes," replied the witness.

"And you don't know from whom that second group of hairs comes or came?"

"Again, I would assume they came from the same person being that they were dyed as were the other groups of hairs; but more deeply dyed, and as a result,

I could not identify enough individual characteristics," countered the detective.

"They could have come from a second person?" asked Zevin.

"There is a possibility, yes."

"Now, with regard to the initial set of hairs that you identified as Mrs. Busacca's, you were not absolutely certain that Mrs. Busacca's hairs were found on the other samples that were given to you and by other objects . . . the quilt, in the driveway . . . the pocketbook hairs, etcetera?"

"What I'm certain of. . . ."

"No!" barked Zevin abruptly. "Are you absolutely certain?"

"I cannot say with one hundred per cent certainty. No," conceded the witness.

"But isn't it a fact that the hairs found on the quilt and the hairs found in the driveway were similar, correct?"

"They were microscopically similar, yes."

"And the possibility that they came from the same person is what?" pressed Marvin Zevin.

"Based on studies?"

"Just give me the figure!" snapped Zevin.

"The chance of an error is approximately one out of forty-five hundred."

"Now, with regard to the second group of hairs that you found in the curlers and brushes, you found those hairs on other objects, correct?"

"Yes."

"With regard to the secondary type of hairs found on the curlers and hair brushes, the hairs you could not positively identify, those hairs were found on the pocketbook correct?"

"They were found on the vent, inside the porch, pocketbook and front seat."

"The vent, pocketbook and front seat and also weren't they found on the samples from the inside of the porch?"

"Yes, sir."

"Now, it's your testimony that the secondary hairs found on curlers and brushes were similar to the secondary kinds of hair found in the various items we just discussed?" asked Zevin.

"Yes, sir."

"You, also, I believe, testified that they may have come from another person?"

"Yes, there is a possibility. Yes, sir," replied Fraas.

"Thank you. No other questions, Your Honor." Marvin turned to Grennan and motioned toward the witness.

Barry Grennan rose slowly from his seat and walked to the lectern, studying the assortment of papers he had been going over during Fraas' direct examination, one hand characteristically at his hip, his lips pursed.

"Detective, you had a known sample, did you not, or what you could call a known sample, of hair from Geraldine Busacca?"

"Yes, sir."

"Did you compare that with all the other items of hair you had?"

"Yes, sir."

"What did that comparison reveal?"

"Geraldine's hairs were dissimilar from those hairs on the other items."

"All right. Likewise, you had what would be called a known sample of hair from Lawrence Busacca, right?"

"Yes, sir."

"Did you compare that with all those other samples that you had?" asked Grennan.

"Yes, I did."

"What did that comparison reveal?"

"They were dissimilar, also."

"Now, you had what you called a known hair sample from Thomas Busacca, correct?"

"Yes, sir."

"Did you compare that with all the other known samples?"

"Yes, sir, I did," replied Fraas.

"And what did that reveal?"

"They were dissimilar."

"All right. Now, Officer, you testified you had some curlers and some brushes that had been identified to you as having been used by Florence Busacca, correct?"

"Yes, sir."

"Now, did all of those items have two types of hair on them?"

"Yes, sir."

"All right. Now, microscopically but for the staining or dying or whatever you said, are they identical to each other?"

"Aside from the staining and the particular characteristics that I could identify, yes, they were similar," said Fraas.

"All right. Now, those items that you examined from brushes, curlers, et cetera, that Florence Busacca had been known to use, did you compare those first of all with the pocketbook, the hairs from the pocketbook?" asked Grennan.

"Yes."

"From the hair curlers and the brushes?"

"Yes."

"That were identified to you as having come from Mrs. Busacca. Did you compare those hairs, first of all with the hairs found in the pocketbook, on the pocketbook?"

"Yes, sir, I did."

"What did that comparison reveal?"

"The more deeply dyed samples were similar to the more deeply dyed samples that I found on the pocketbook."

"All right. Now, Officer, you mentioned the chance of your error as forty-five hundred to one."

"Yes, sir."

"Officer, if injected into that, you were to become aware of the blood type in connection with that hair, would it change these percentages that you made references to?"

"Objection!" shouted Zevin.

"Overruled," replied the judge.

"I don't think he had indicated that he is an expert in that area," protested Zevin.

Lockman agreed. "All right. I'll sustain it. Lay a foundation, Mr. Grennan."

"He's not my witness," declared Grennan.

"I know, but on cross-examination you have to lay a foundation. You can't have a person testify as an expert," admonished Judge Lockman.

"Would it affect his opinion?" asked Grennan.

"Don't argue with me. . . . ask your question," scolded Lockman. "You have to lay a foundation."

"Are you a blood expert?" asked Grennan.

"Yes, sir."

"You've had some training in connection with blood?"

"Yes, sir."

Charles Fraas iterated his qualifications for the court; his four year degree from Hofstra, six months of training in the examination and analysis of blood, and training at the John Jay College for examination and techniques in the examination of blood.

"Now, Detective, in connection with your expertise in the field of hair identification, if you became aware of the blood type in connection with the hair, would it change your chance of error from forty-five hundred to one to another figure?"

"What it would do is introduce another factor, another independent factor. You would have two independent factors, your hair results and your blood results. If one's probability of error is one in forty-five hundred, such as it is in the hair examination, you have a hair sample then that would represent approximately two one-hundredths of a percent of the population. Now, if you introduce a blood factor such as in this case, I believe where we're talking about an AB blood factor, which represents approximately four percent of the population statistically, you could multiply these two independent factors together, and in doing so, you reach a conclusion that the hair-blood combination is representative of approximately one one-hundredth of a percent of the population in the United States," replied Fraas in a very smooth and impressive dissertation.

"One thousandth of one percent," qualified Grennan.

"Yes, sir."

"Now, what did your microscopic examination reveal with regard to the hair sample from the pocketbook with those identified as coming from Florence Busacca?" asked Grennan.

"The comparison of my known hair samples, and I would have to say the two standards that we're talking about, the dyed and less-dyed samples, I could only identify the more-dyed hair as being similar."

"Now, with regard to the quilt. Did you obtain hair from the quilt?"

"Yes, sir."

"What did your microscopic comparison with regard to the known sample of Florence Busacca with the hair from the quilt indicate to you?"

"Those two samples were microscopically similar."

"And, with regard to the hair in the driveway or that which was identified as coming from the driveway, did you compare those microscopically?"

"Yes, sir."

"What did that comparison reveal?"

"They were microscopically similar."

"And the hairs from the front seat, were they microscopically similar with those known samples of Mrs. Busacca?"

"I don't believe they were. No, sir," replied the witness, checking his report.

"All right. I have no other questions," said Grennan.

"No redirect," said Zevin, now wondering why he had called the witness in the first place. It did more damage than good to his defense.

Marvin Zevin then called Joseph Occhipinto to the stand. Occhipinto was present with his attorney and would endeavor to refute the testimony of Walter Smith, who had testified that Thomas Busacca and he had become close friends while in the Nassau County Jail.

Joseph Occhipinto met Thomas Busacca at the jail during the latter part of 1976. It was there that he also met Walter Smith and was still on the tier when Smith left. Occhipinto testified that he ate at the same table with Thomas Busacca every day, three times a day. Walter Smith was never at the same table and Occhipinto never saw him eat at the same table as Busacca.

Marvin Zevin then asked for a conference at the bench out of the hearing of the jury.

"Your Honor, I was going to ask a few more questions, but before I do, may I approach the bench?"

Both attorneys approached Judge Lockman.

"Before we get into that," interjected Grennan, "everyone of these questions is leading. I object to leading the witness."

"I don't blame you," agreed Lockman. "You were allowed to, but you didn't object."

"I just want to point it out," replied Grennan.

"I agree," said the judge.

"He is asking too many leading questions of the witness."

"We made an offer of proof before; so far the questions I have asked are within that offer of proof," explained Zevin. "I am now going to ask him some additional questions which were not covered, and rather than do it and have it objected to, I would like a ruling from the bench. I'm going to ask him, 'Have you had conversation with Thomas Busacca regarding Florence Busacca' and if he says yes, which I think he would, then I would say, 'What are those conversations?' "

"Unless they are admissions, they are hearsay and selfserving," declared Grennan.

"They would be selfserving," acknowledged John Lockman. "I don't understand your theory."

"Judge, we have left in every statement so far, forgetting about the one to Marjoribanks for a moment, not because they were admissions or confessions to a death or to a murder, but simply because the statements and admissions, whether they were inconsistent or whether they are consistent. And I submit that the statements made to Mr. Occhipinto may be inconsistent but are admissible statements."

"The People have a right to introduce statements of your client. They also have a right to object to anything that may be selfserving that you may attempt to introduce. I assume there will be an objection," cautioned Lockman.

"I assume the statements are not admissions but are selfserving declarations," said Grennan. "I don't imagine the defense would offer admissions."

"Is that a fair assumption?" asked Lockman, focusing his attention on Zevin.

"I do not believe they are admissions, but certainly may be inconsistent in some respects with previous statements, however corroborative of other statements offered with regard to what Mr. Busacca told the detectives," replied Marvin Zevin.

"But, a defendant can't engage in conversations and then bring in people to put his case before the jury and what he told other people because it's hearsay. The reason that the People are allowed to put it in is an exception to the hearsay rule and there were no objections to the statements. If you had said they don't constitute admissions when they were offered, there might have been a different ruling. There has to be an admission in order to be admissible. It isn't *any* statement that the defendant makes that is admissible," defined Judge Lockman.

"I agree with you. That's the law," said Zevin. "However, I thought that these statements were admissible or were admitted as admissions or confessions."

"What is he going to say now?" asked Lockman.

"No. . . . I'm sorry. All the other statements made by other people, I assume, were admitted as to the exception."

"Exactly. They were admitted because they bore on whether he was guilty or innocent and therefore, they were an exception to the hearsay rule," explained Lockman. "Now, the People have objected. There is one possible thing you may do and that is make an offer of proof at this time, and tell me what he's going to say. I can't believe that if it is a true admission, that Mr. Grennan would object to it."

"I know of no true admission that he would testify to," said Zevin, "so we have Your Honor's ruling."

"Yes, my ruling is that based on the record before me, the objection to any statement that the defendant made to this witness is sustained," declared Lockman.

"Based on Your Honor's ruling, I certainly will not ask the question."

"And I thank you for the way you handled it," said Lockman.

Marvin Zevin asked no further questions and Barry Grennan was given his opportunity to cross-examine the witness.

"Mr. Occhipinto, do you have a tatoo of a star on your left hand?" asked Grennan.

"Yes."

"Mr. Occhipinto, do you own a blue and white Pontiac?"

"Yes."

"Does that have the registration four three three XPG?"

"I don't remember. I don't recall," replied the witness nervously, not anticipating this line of questioning and wondering what else the District Attorney had learned in doing his homework.

"Mr. Occhipinto, when you are not in jail, you make your living selling cocaine and heroin, sir?"

Zevin was on his feet in a flash, objecting to the question which was promptly overruled.

"Does that mean I have to answer?" asked a perplexed witness.

"Your lawyer is here. You instruct him," advised Lockman, pointing toward Mr. Mainella, the attorney for the witness.

"Your Honor, I'm going to object to that question," he declared.

"You are instructing him to refuse to answer on the grounds that his answer may tend to incriminate him?" asked the judge.

"That's exactly correct, Your Honor," said the attorney.

"I'm sustaining the objection. His answer might tend to incriminate him, his lawyer says," said Lockman.

"Well, is it an objection or is he exercising his right not to answer because the answer might incriminate him?" asked Grennan.

"Well, the lawyer objected to give him a chance to rule. And then he, as I understand the procedure, he just instructed his client not to answer on grounds his answer may tend to incriminate him. You said, 'Does he make his living selling drugs?' That's a crime," cautioned Lockman.

"Well, let me direct your attention to March five, nineteen seventy-six, at approximately eleven forty-five, Mr. Occhipinto. On that occasion did you sell some cocaine to an undercover agent for a sum of four hundred dollars?" asked Grennan firmly.

The witness seemed to go into immediate shock. His face turned ashen white and he loosened his tie.

"Don't answer that question," instructed Mr. Mainella, looking ruefully at his client.

"I refuse to answer," said the witness.

"On that occasion, did you make the following statement. . . ." started Grennan.

"Your Honor, I'm going to object to this whole line of questioning on behalf of the District Attorney," declared Mainella.

"Your Honor. . . ." Grennan began, but was interrupted by Zevin.

"I, too, would object, Your Honor. The District Attorney now knows that the witness is going to take the Fifth Amendment to any continued questioning in this area would simply prejudice the defendant," he said.

"The District Attorney can ask the witness about any crime that the witness has been convicted of. He can also ask him about any prior immoral act of the witness which the jury may find bears on his credibility. He has to establish good faith for those questions, and since the lawyer for the defendant is here, if there is going to be a refusal to answer on the grounds that his answer may incriminate him, I have to know that before I can rule on how we're going to proceed," declared the judge.

Judge Lockman then excused the jury until the issue could be resolved and a ruling made from the bench.

"Before we proceed, Judge," started Barry Grennan, "I would object to the attorney taking objections. It's not his position to take objections. He may instruct his client and the client can exercise his privilege, but I believe the exercise of that privilege must be exercised by the client, not by the attorney."

"You are stating the rule accurately," agreed Lockman.

"In addition, I am ready, willing and able to make

an offer of my good faith in the area of asking these questions. However, I don't believe that the attorney should be privy to the information that I am about to give the court. It comes from a Federal document in which Nassau County detectives participated in its preparation. I'll be very happy, however, to make presentation to the court and defense counsel, but not for Mr. Mainella. He represents the witness. I don't believe it's necessary that he be privy to this information, so long as I can establish my good faith."

"I agree," said Judge Lockman, accepting the District Attorney's argument. "As long as the defense attorney can hear it, there is no reason why the attorney for the witness would have to hear it. Would you come up?"

"My objection goes beyond that," interjected Zevin. "We know that there are pending matters involving Mr. Occhipinto in this court as well as other courts. So does the District Attorney. The District Attorney knows that when he asks these questions with regard to these pending matters, that Mr. Occhipinto is going to take the Fifth Amendment right to refuse to answer. Now, we could have fifty-five or a hundred questions, each of which Mr. Occhipinto says he'll refuse to answer on the grounds it may tend to incriminate him. And I submit that the conduct of asking those questions results in answers that are prejudicial to my client. Because Mr. Grennan, at this point, first of all knows there are pending matters and knows he hasn't been convicted of them and knows that he is awaiting trial."

"Judge, and I might point out that the defense counselor was fully aware before they put this witness on the stand, of his intentions to exercise the privilege," chided Grennan. "That being the case, we could do one of several things. We could move to strike the testimony if the court deems it appropriate. The other alternative is to allow the People to bring it out and treat it, of course, in their summation."

"Well, let's find out the good faith first," said Judge Lockman.

But after a long discussion between the attorneys, an agreement was reached that precluded the examination of good faith. The jury was returned to the courtroom and the testimony of Occhipinto resumed.

Barry Grennan then addressed the witness. "Did you make the following statement in response to a question as to how much cocaine you could supply: 'As much as you want—this is my business. This is how I make my living. I sell about one ounce a day at about a thousand dollars an ounce.' Did you make that statement on March fifteen, nineteen seventy-six, to an undercover agent?"

"I refuse to answer on the grounds it might tend to incriminate me," answered the witness.

Grennan continued a scathing attack upon the criminal record of Joseph Occhipinto. Before an appalled courtroom, Barry Grennan outlined the drug dealing activity of the witness, who invoked the Fifth Amendment each time. "Did you have an occasion, on April two, nineteen seventy-six, at that time to be present at the Melville Diner in Melville, Long Island, Huntington?" he was asked. "On that occasion, did you sell cocaine and receive twenty-five hundred dollars from an undercover agent? On that occasion did you agree to sell two and one-eighth kilos of cocaine?"

As the questioning went on, Marvin Zevin sank deeper into his seat. Occhipinto was beginning to panic. It was quite obvious that neither he nor his attorney had expected this kind of grilling from the District Attorney. Zevin and Mainella stood by helpless to do anything, their witness crippled, his credibility destroyed.

After having effectively nullified Mr. Occhipinto's potential value as a credible witness, Grennan began questioning him with respect to his association with Thomas Busacca while incarcerated at the Nassau County Jail. It had also been established that Occhipinto had spent some of his time in Suffolk County Jail.

"Tell us, what days were you in jail in Suffolk County?" asked Grennan.

"I don't recall," replied a badly shaken witness.

"But it was in this period, wasn't it?"

"It wasn't when Walter Smith was on the tier."

"Were you there?" asked Grennan, the staccato of his questions unrelenting.

"I don't understand," replied the witness.

"Were you there? Can you say Walter Smith wasn't there?" pressed Grennan.

"Because he left and I was still there," declared the witness.

"Didn't you go to Suffolk County on January tenth," asked Grennan.

"I don't remember the dates."

Zevin was on his feet in a flash. "Now, I do consider that to be bad faith," he snarled, "because Walter Smith testified as to when he left that tier, and it had nothing to do with January tenth."

"I'm not finished, counselor," Grennan shot back, his lips pursed, his eyes squinting like two piss holes in the snow. "And I will make this statement, Judge, that I have never, ever in my career acted in bad faith, in response to what Mr. Zevin had to say."

"You shouldn't have been saying that in front of the jury, either of you," scolded Judge John Lockman.

"I understand," said Grennan, apologetically, "but that's the second time I have been accused of bad faith, and I have never been accused of it before."

"In four weeks of trial we have had very good co-operation from both of you," said Lockman, calmly, "and I don't want any more of these outbreaks in front of the jury. This is material you don't discuss in front of the jury, either of you. And, members of the jury, you will disregard it. The only evidence in this case is from that witness stand and the exhibits. But, what anybody else says, including myself, doesn't mean anything as evidence in this case. They put their witness on and they have to prove it through witnesses."

It had indeed been a long, exhausting four weeks of trial. It was now winding down, and heretofore subjugated feelings and emotions of both attorneys were being vented at the very slightest provocation. Both men exchanged glances and turned away. Zevin returned to the defense table and Barry Grennan continued his cross-examination of the witness. After only a few questions, Grennan concluded his cross. Zevin had no further questions. He had had enough.

Marvin Zevin's next witness was Mr. Robert Berg from Pennsylvania, a forty-four year old advertising manager for McCall magazine in New York City. It was this man who testified that he was seventy-five percent sure he had seen Florence Busacca in a restaurant in the Pan Am Building. Berg testified that he sat down next to the woman and they carried on a conversation, during which the woman expressed a desire to return to Italy and Europe and to sing at La Scala. This conversation, according to the witness, took place in either September, October or November of 1976.

Berg described her dark hair, olive skin and Italian features. He didn't recall much else about her features and had not noticed her ears.

Barry Grennan could not believe the boldness of this witness. Giving him the benefit of the doubt, it would appear he did everything wrong as Grennan would establish during his cross-examination.

"You are a busy man?" said Grennan.

"I delude myself to think so. I think I am, yes," replied Robert Berg.

"You had a casual conversation with a woman in September, October or November?" asked Grennan.

"I don't know if the word is 'casual.' It was a chance conversation where you, sir, and I, may go to a luncheon and have a conversation with a stranger," replied Berg confidently.

"Was it less than casual?"

"It was a chance . . . and I term it casual conversation. I guess that's the best description I could use."

"And you recall this woman?" Grennan asked.

"Yes."

"In connection with this case?"

"Well, I can tell you how I came to sit here," offered the witness. "I commute to Pennsylvania, and I saw an article in the New York Post, and the more I read the article, the more I said to myself 'that has to be the woman I spoke with.' "

"When did you see the article?" asked the District Attorney with curiosity.

"About three weeks ago."

"The article in the Post, did it have that picture in it?" Grennan asked, referring to the photograph that had been given the witness by Marvin Zevin.

"No, there was no photograph."

"So, you read the article in the Post three weeks ago?"

"Right."

"And you recall the conversation that you had in September, October or November?" continued Grennan, in a voice rising in disbelief.

"As a matter of fact, the details. . . ."

"That calls for a *yes* or *no*. You can answer that?" said Grennan satirically.

"The answer is yes."

"And then you went to somebody with that information?"

"I'll tell you what. I tried to call a Mr. Capazolli or somebody who wrote the article. I discussed it with my family at dinner and. . . ."

Grennan interrupted. "My question is, did you come forward to somebody in connection with the information that you read?" he asked.

"I did," answered the witness.

"Who did you come forward to?" pressed Grennan.

"To Mr. Zevin. I had my secretary locate him.

"Did you know from the article that a massive manhunt was going on in connection with this woman?"

"I wouldn't say. It didn't imply a massive manhunt," insisted Berg. "The article in the Post simply said that the headlines were, the claim was that this murder victim was alive and from the gist of the article, I was of the mind that I had spoken to this woman. I had remembered having a conversation with a woman that described some of the experiences that were related in that article. I don't know if it makes any sense."

"Did it make any reference at all to the fact that the police had looked high and low for this woman?" asked the District Attorney.

"I have the article in my wallet."

"May I see it?"

"Yes. My daughter tore it out, and I believe this occurred about three months ago," answered Berg, handing Grennan a folded news clipping.

Grennan was permitted a few moments to scrutinize the article, and then continued his questioning.

"This article reminded you of the conversation you had, this casual conversation you had with a lady?" asked Grennan, his fists characteristically buried into his hips.

"Only because you have a chance meeting with somebody who talks about singing in La Scala, and having been in Paris. I put two and two together and I remembered a conversation that dealt with those facts," replied the witness rather prudently.

"The article opens, 'Florence Busacca isn't dead, the lawyer said at her husband's murder trial. She simply tired of family life and took off for a more rewarding existence as an opera singer. For all anyone knows, she could be in Milan and waiting in the wings of La Scala for a call to center stage, he said.' And *that* reminded you of the conversation?" asked Grennan disbelievingly.

"Certainly."

"How old was the lady you were speaking to?"

"I thought her to be in her forties."

"Did she smile?" asked Grennan quickly.

"Yes. It was a relatively pleasant conversation."

"Did she smile?" repeated Grennan.

"Yes!"

"Describe her teeth, if you will," asked the District Attorney.

"I don't recall her teeth," conceded Berg.

"Did she have false teeth?" pressed Grennan.

"I could not tell you that, sir."

"Did she have *no* teeth?"

"I doubt it, but again I can't answer it," relented the witness.

"Is it possible she had no teeth?" queried the D.A.

"Sure."

"How long did this conversation last?"

"I would estimate fifteen–twenty minutes. She left before I did and we bid each other good day."

"Now, you're under oath and you have been asked if that is the woman, referring to exhibit twenty-four, and you say you're seventy-five percent sure."

"That's the best I can do. That's the best of my recollection," answered Berg.

"Are you twenty-five percent not sure?" asked Grennan.

"Right."

"Have you ever seen the woman again?"

"No, I have not."

"You knew, did you not, from the same article, at least it stated in the article that Busacca beat his wife to death and dragged her out of the house and stuffed her in the trunk of the car and drove twenty miles to Holbrook and dumped her against a fence? Did you *read* the article?" asked Grennan, showing his contempt for Robert Berg's entire testimony.

"I read the whole article," answered the witness, hesitatingly.

"Did *that* remind you of the conversation?" pressed Grennan.

"No . . . the details of the fact about La Scala and about being in Paris stuck in my memory."

"Is La Scala in Paris?" asked Grennan, mockingly.

"No, but the woman had told me. . . ."

"It is not even in Milan as it is in the article?" interrupted Grennan.

"I don't know. It could be in Turin. I don't know where it is, but I think it's in Milan," answered a rather nervous witness.

"So it was the content with regard to the singing and so forth that reminded you of this particular person?"

"Well, it would . . . only because how many times do you have a conversation with a woman who talks about singing opera? I mean it is a very unusual avocation I imagine," explained Berg.

"But, no pictures in the paper?" said Grennan curiously.

"Exactly, that's true."

"But when did you see the picture for the first time? You saw it before today, didn't you?"

"Yes, I did."

"When?" asked Grennan.

"I saw it approximately two weeks ago when an aide to Mr. Zevin came to my office and asked me to identify a photograph and I told him the same thing I told you."

"Did he show you a group of photographs and ask you to pick one out, or were you only shown one picture?" asked Grennan.

"I was shown one picture."

"And you are seventy-five percent sure and twenty-five percent not sure."

"Yes."

"No other questions," intoned Grennan, gesturing his arms towards the heavens.

Where'd he come from, thought Walker. At the very least he should be charged with audacious social misconduct for impersonating a witness.

Grennan sat down and looked over at the detective. "Where'd they get him?" he asked rhetorically.

"Asked myself the same question," replied Walker.

Chapter Fourteen

Dr. Daniel W. Schwartz, a forensic psychiatrist, was called as a rebuttal witness for the prosecution. Schwartz had been used by the District Attorney's office in the past, but quickly pointed out that he had, on occasion, testified on behalf of the defense. His findings were not necessarily limited to determining a defendant's incompetence but his competence as well, irrespective of for whom he was testifying.

On February 25, 1977, Dr. Schwartz examined the defendant Thomas Busacca. Prior to that examination, Schwartz stated that he had conferred with the District Attorney, Detective Walker, Lieutenant Dolan and the defendant's daughter. He had also conferred with Dr. Joseph.

His examination of Thomas had lasted a little more than three hours and his subsequent conclusion was that Thomas Busacca did not—as a result of mental disease or defect—lack substantial capacity to know or appreciate either the nature or consequences of his conduct or that such conduct was wrong.

Schwartz found the defendant to be "alert, pleasant, polite and cooperative. He would often smile and occasionally laugh, but in a rather mirthless, hollow way." Such a reaction was, in Schwartz's opinion, a nervous response. Schwartz was quite struck by Busacca's lack of emotional display which did not vary, regardless of some of the subject matter discussed, which was quite emotionally laden at times. Schwartz drew the conclusion that Thomas had difficulty dealing with emotionally laden subjects. Such conversations would cause him to ramble on until he was brought back to the original subject.

Schwartz found the same rambling in his speech that others had spoken of during the initial investigation and so often testified to by police officers and other witnesses.

Thomas Busacca grew up as an only child in Bensonhurst and spoke about his father at length, but had very little to say about his mother. He became a marine and was discharged in 1946 with the rank of corporal. He described his own work history as a "checker board existence." Photography was his main interest but he found few jobs to accommodate him.

He had known his wife since he was 17 and they were married in 1950. At first she worked as a typist and singer but then, because of the children, gave up both positions to become a housewife.

Friction between Thomas and his daughter began when she went away to school, and in 1974, "she cursed me down in front of my whole family." This conflict with his daughter and what he considers her "lack of respect" for him is very much on his mind.

Their marriage began to deteriorate in 1976 when he was not permitted to sleep with his wife any longer. After a while he was permitted to sleep in the bed, but not to have sex.

When his wife went to Paris in July of 1976 with her sister, he feared that she was going purposely to have extra-marital sex. It was also in July that he had a tremendous argument with his daughter. The next day, Thomas Busacca claimed that he and his wife had a tremendous "sexual" reunion together, but was told after that he would never be allowed to touch her again sexually. He admitted to himself a few days later that it was over with. When asked how he felt about the prospect of his wife leaving him, he responded "empty."

The rift between Tom and his daughter widened and reached the point where verbal communications ceased and notes to one another were written on pieces of paper or the blackboard. He was financially broke, unable to obtain a bank loan and detested the way in which his daughter would spend her money on such things as a bicycle for Larry and an air conditioner for the house.

His account to Schwartz about the night of the occurrence, August 29, 1976, was difficult to follow because of his rambling. The gist of it was that he was "factually innocent of causing her death." He had suggested to her on that night "a last ditch possibility of saving us all," namely that his father take over the mortgage to the house and move in with them. It was an idea that was totally unacceptable to his wife. Thomas then told of the incident outside of the house, the other person embracing his wife, the fight with his wife, the arrival of Margaret Newman and his subsequent journey to Suffolk County.

"Now, Doctor, from your examination, did you determine whether or not Mr. Busacca, in your opinion, had mental disease or defect?" asked Grennan.

"Yes."

"And that disease, sir?"

"I believe he was suffering from schizophrenia and that it had been a case of latent schizophrenia for many, many years," replied Schwartz.

"Now, Doctor, do you have an opinion with a reasonable degree of medical certainty whether as a result of that disease this defendant lacked the substantial capacity to know or appreciate either the nature and the consequence of the conduct or that it was wrong?" asked Grennan.

"No. I do not believe that the existence of the schizophrenia prevented him from knowing or appreciating the nature or consequence of his conduct or that it was wrong," concluded Schwartz.

In explaining his opinion, Schwartz pointed out that schizophrenia is "an illness that primarily affects the thinking, the reasoning capabilities of an individual. There is a type of reasoning, a type of thinking called primary process thinking, in which conclusions are reached on a rather illogical basis or in which ideas follow one after the other on other than logical grounds. It is the type of thinking seen in little children, but is the type of thinking we usually outgrow and replace with what is called secondary process thinking. However, it also exists in our dreams. The type of reasoning, the type of thinking that makes things happen where one would follow another in a rather strange way in dreams is precisely this kind of thinking. But, merely because a person is subject to this type of thinking does not mean that they cannot function in a reasonably normal manner. The vast majority are functioning in a reasonable manner these days outside mental hospitals. Nor would this type of thinking in and of itself necessarily deprive someone of the capacity to know the nature and consequences of his act or that they were wrong, if they were in fact wrongful acts.

"We would have a situation where a person was in an acute schizophrenic episode, something that came on suddenly, and in which he was totally disorganized, and then behaved in a rather berserk, wild, rampant manner. But that is not the picture in this case at all. This case involves a man who for many years was probably functioning at a marginal level; rather a reclusive man; no personal contact; hiding himself to a great extent in his basement with his photography, not working. He probably was functioning on this level for many, many years. There is no picture here of a suddenly berserk, totally disorganized action. In fact, the present offense, if he in fact committed it, involved a whole series of connected acts.

"The thing that was directing all his thinking at the time was the fact that his wife was leaving him and wanted him out of the house. And, I believe that there were indications from others that this was not a delusion, that this was in fact true, that she did want to leave him. She did deny him the marital bed and she did tell him to get out. So, he was responding to reality, not to a delusion, and in this reality-stress situation, he did, if it is so, he did react in a way that indicates a rational or at least realistic reason for behaving the way he did. . . . if he did behave that way.

"If there is evidence that he struck her repeatedly with a blunt instrument, and if there is evidence that the amount of blood that she lost would have been enough to cause her death, this would argue that he knew the nature and consequence of what he was doing, if and when he was hitting her and there is evidence that he tried to clean up."

Dr. Schwartz had been asked by the District Attorney to explain the inconsistency in some of Thomas Busacca's revelations to him as opposed to what he had consistently told the police some months before, citing as an example Busacca's claim of being struck from behind and knocked unconscious, a story told to Schwartz, but not the police.

"It's not unusual for me to see situations in which months after a particular event a person tells a somewhat different story. It's my opinion that in a case like this, what has probably happened is what I would call retrospective falsification. If the facts are so, if they are true and on the night of August twenty-ninth Mr. Busacca did in fact bludgeon his wife and then did take her away and deposit her in Suffolk County, it's not the most pleasant memory for a non-criminal person, for a person who is not a professional killer. It's not the most pleasant memory to live with. It's quite possible, as the saying goes, that the mind plays tricks and what he remembers now is a more acceptable story, a story that psychologically is easier for him to live with and still maintain some self-respect, a story in which he is struck from behind by someone else and is unconscious, he doesn't know how long, but that during that time someone else is bludgeoning, and thereby killing, his wife," explained Dr. Schwartz.

"Did you find or elicit any evidence in your conversation with Mr. Busacca, indicating schizophrenic thinking with regard to his conduct of August twenty-nine, nineteen seventy-six?" asked Grennan.

"Well, there was a lot of schizophrenic thinking throughout the entire three hours of conversation that we had, but at no time did I get any kind of schizophrenic explanation of what happened that night, schizophrenic justification for what happened that night," responded the doctor.

"All right. Now, Doctor, you had, I believe you testified, a discussion with Mr. Busacca relative to a change of clothing?"

"Yes, sir."

"Would you tell us what that conversation was?"

"He had been telling me about heading home after he had left his wife out on the Island. He had stopped for gas and then he said, 'I remember going down the road toward Ronkonkoma. In other words, in that direction. Anyhow, I can't pinpoint exactly where I stopped, but right there on the road, on the tar, because of the pain, and I changed shirts.' I then asked him why, and his answer was, 'I was all wet, the neck . . .' I asked him from what and he responded, 'my blood and water, too, no doubt. I had a freaking towel on my neck—thrown under my collar. I was trying to feel myself. . . . sticky here and at least the shirt went out there. . . . I threw the shirt on the floor. I didn't try to hide it or anything like that or go into the woods.'

"We had a few questions after that in which I asked him 'on the floor of what' and he said, 'on the tar, I think right there on the side of my car. I took off that blue shirt.' I asked, 'You left it on the road, on the ground?' and he responded, 'Right.' "

"Now, Doctor, did you have a discussion with him relative to the disposal of clothing?" asked Grennan.

"Yes, sir."

"What was the discussion, Doctor?"

"He told me later about having driven to the Scharf Hotel in Long Beach, and parking across the street from it, and then he said, 'I changed my clothes,' at which point I interrupted him and asked him what clothes he was changing. He said, 'The clothes that I came home with. I had a pair of blue pants and red shirt.' I asked him why he changed his shirt and pants and he said, 'I had a pair of shorts on, a pair of old ripped off shorts. I had gotten that out of a box from the car. I had put those things on and I don't know . . . cold. . . . I don't know. I packed up whatever I had on my passenger's side on the floor. I tried putting them together and getting rid of it at that point. . . . get out of the car. If I remember, I put it in a plastic bag. I threw it under the car. I was oozie. I remember seeing a little dog and a man. The man fell down across the street. Anyhow, I don't remember how I turned from there. I think I saw a dairy barn, and I managed to get back home. That's more or less the evening.' "

At this point Judge John Lockman charged the jury as to how they were to treat the testimony of Dr. Daniel Schwartz.

"Members of the jury, I am permitting the doctor to tell you conversations he had with the defendant. Now, these conversations are in violation of the defendant's right not to incriminate himself. However, it is necessary where there is a defense of criminal responsibility that if the defendant wishes to introduce his medical testimony, he submit to medical testimony by a doctor selected by the District Attorney. However, nothing that is said to the doctor can be used on the issue of the defendant's guilt. You can't consider anything that was said to this doctor on the issue of the defendant's guilt. You may only consider it on the issue of criminal responsibility and the doctor's evaluation of the issues of whether you agree with the doctor or not, as an expert."

Lockman then turned to Barry Grennan and the District Attorney continued his examination of the witness.

"My question is, Dr. Schwartz, the discussions of the . . . ah, you covered my question, Your Honor. . . ." Grennan said in retrospect. "But, the change of clothing and the disposal of clothing wasn't pertinent to your conclusion with regard to the defendant's criminal responsibility."

"Yes, sir."

"In what area, Doctor?"

"Hypothetically certain actions had taken place that night, and if there were blood-stained clothing in the car, this would suggest, in my opinion, that the defendant appreciated the wrongfulness of what he had done," said Dr. Schwartz.

"Will you explain," pressed Grennan, "with respect to the change of clothing and the disposal of the clothing as pertinent to you in the area of whether the defendant was aware of the wrongfulness of his conduct as of the twenty-ninth of August, nineteen seventy-six?" explained Grennan.

"Yes. If someone had in fact committed a crime of violence resulting in a lot of bloodshed, and he appreciated that this was wrong, it would be consistent with some knowledge and appreciation to want to dispose of such bloody clothes, which might, if this had all happened, be evidence against him," said Schwartz.

"Now, your opinion, with a reasonable degree of medical certainty, would you state it for us?"

"Yes, sir. It is my professional opinion that at the time of the present offense, the defendant did not, as a result of mental disease or defect, lack substantial capacity to know or appreciate either the nature and consequences of his conduct, and that such conduct was wrong," concluded Schwartz.

"And you are referring to the conduct of August twenty-nine, nineteen seventy-six?"

"Yes, sir."

Grennan turned to Marvin Zevin. "You may examine," he said politely, pleased with the doctor's testimony and his professional and confident appearance that he had maintained throughout. Grennan was confident that the same calm and lucid manner would hold up under Marvin Zevin's cross-examination.

Daniel Schwartz handled Marvin Zevin's questions deftly. He was authoritative and confident with his answers and Marvin Zevin was unable to unsettle or shake his testimony.

During redirect examination, Barry Grennan was able to elicit from the witness certain facts that Marvin Zevin failed to bring out during his cross-examination. When Tom Busacca had spoken of the man in the white car, chasing him and the Kennedy assassination, it was Marvin Zevin who brought the subject up.

"Did Mr. Zevin remind him of it?" asked Grennan.

"Yes."

"And this was after you had gone through the details with respect to the events of August twenty-ninth?" pressed the District Attorney.

"Yes, sir."

"Was it in any way connected with the occurrences of the twenty-ninth?" asked Grennan.

"Not that I could see. No, sir."

"Doctor, were there questions in the course of your interview which the defendant did not answer?"

"There were times when the answer he gave never really got to the question I posed. Yes, I guess it is fair to say he didn't answer, but by that I don't mean that he remained silent. He said something, but it wasn't in answer to my question."

"Well, did you ask, for instance, with regard to his

wife, as to why he didn't take her to somebody else?" asked Grennan.

"Yes, he had told me that after he left her, his feeling was in effect that somebody else could take care of her. So, I asked him that question and his answer was, 'I don't know, I just. . . . my pain. . . . my own pain must have been doing it to me, whatever. I just couldn't stomach the whole thing anymore. It was just something . . . we don't live this way. We haven't been involved this way.' I said to him. . . . 'You've had enough of it, is that what you are saying?' and he said, 'Oh, yeah. . . . yeah, somebody else take care of her. That's really. . . .' and then he went off onto a tangent. But he never really answered the question. If he thought that somebody else should take care of her, why didn't he take her to somebody else?"

"Did you ask him, Doctor, as to what his wife's physical condition was when he left her?"

"Yes."

"How did he answer it?" asked Grennan.

"I will read it to you: 'What do you think your wife's physical condition was when you left her?' His answer was, 'Well, that voice was pretty strong, ah-ha.' 'The voice saying what?' He said, 'Fuck you. Ah ha, okay. You know I'd say something, it sounds way out, maybe, but I had no idea about this teeth. . . . in my ear now I can hear her talking when she is say ph-ph-ph . . . the breathing, the ridiculousness, that kind of. . . . this is it.' So I said, 'So you thought her voice was strong?' 'Yes.' 'What did that mean to you as far as her physical condition?' 'Doc, I was pretty looped myself, you know, I don't think I was trying to calculate that so much as just this was a breakup. This is it.' 'And just trying to make sure I understand, if what I say is wrong, correct me, please. It sounds as though you are saying you were so angry at her, that took priority over everything else. You weren't concerned about her physical condition because you were so angry at her?' He answered, 'That sounds reasonable. I mean that's about no answers. . . . and this past history, you know, I call it past history . . . last two years or whatever it is and they'll treat it as dirt, you know that's. . . . well, it shouldn't happen to anybody.' "

"Was he referring to the two years previous to the rejection by the family and so forth?" asked Grennan.

"The two years of mistreatment by his wife, yes," answered Schwartz.

After lengthy redirect and recross by both attorneys, the testimony of Daniel Schwartz was concluded. Both sides rested their cases. It was now down to final summations, the judge's charge to the jury, and the jury's deliberation.

Thursday
March 24, 1977   The Summations

Martin Zevin began his summation. His argument would be divided into three categories. The first question would be with respect to reasonable doubt, the second question relative to an alternative theory as to what happened that night, and the third he would argue the question of insanity. Zevin placed great emphasis on Dr. Schwartz' report, imploring them to take it with them into the deliberation room and read it, study it and think seriously of what it said. He capsuled the various testimonies of the trial, highlighting the issue of reasonable doubt as to whether or not Florence Busacca was in fact dead. "Where is Mrs. Busacca's body, if she is dead?" he asked the jury members. A man who is considered an incompetent, a man who could not hold a job, who could not get a job, who could not socialize, who hid in the basement, has not outwitted the entire police department's K-9 Corps, the helicopters of both Nassau and Suffolk Counties.

But in reality, Zevin maintained Florence Busacca had gone away. She tired of the whole situation at home and decided that she would start a new life someplace else.

Marvin Zevin challenged the People's case in proving that Florence Busacca was, beyond a reasonable doubt, dead, that the blows administered to her by Thomas Busacca, beyond a reasonable doubt, killed her. That all the blood found in the house and in the trunk was, beyond a reasonable doubt, that of Florence Busacca.

Zevin concluded his remarks by pleading with the jury to deliberate well. "The fate of this man is in your hands."

Barry Grennan then summed up on behalf of the People. His summation highlighted those points, made during the course of the trial, that he felt were important and necessary for the jury to consider in reaching a verdict, one that would find the defendant guilty.

After a lengthy and detailed summation, he concluded his remarks by asking, "Where is Florence Busacca?" He held aloft before the jury a vial containing a piece of bone. "She is here," he said. "She is here," as he raised aloft the passport of Florence Busacca. "She is here," as he raised aloft her car keys and house keys. "She is here," as he waved before them her bankbooks. "She is here," he said as he raised aloft her wallet and blood-stained pocketbook. "She is here in her credit cards, in her bloody eyeglasses, her teeth, and so forth. That's what we have of Florence Busacca," he concluded, the solemnity of his remarks provoking a deafening quiet in the courtroom.

For Marvin Zevin and Barry Grennan, the trial was now over. It would soon be in the hands of the jury and the wait for the verdict would begin.

At the afternoon session, Judge John S. Lockman charged the jury. He proceeded to expound upon the laws applicable to the present case. The verdict of the jury must be unanimous and based on individual convictions obtained from the evidence put before them, he explained. They were instructed that they could find the defendant guilty as charged, Murder Second Degree, or one of the lesser crimes outlined by the court.

The guilt of the defendant must be beyond a reasonable doubt, and each and every element of the crime he is found guilty of must be present to sustain that guilt.

It had been a long and exhausting trial. The combatants had executed their assigned duties with minimal damage to either's ego. Fatigue and strain were evident. They shook hands and wished each other good luck. The battle was over; they could go back to being friends, no longer antagonists. Walker and Abby Boklan gathered up the volumes of documents that had accumulated during the testimony, over a thousand pages of testimony.

And now the fate of Thomas Busacca was in the hands of the jury—eleven men and one woman. It was 4:30 P.M.

Grennan looked at Boklan and Walker, "How do you two feel?"

"Confident!" replied Walker, beaming.

"You did a beautiful job on your closing," urged Abby Boklan. "How do you feel about it?"

"I don't know," replied Grennan. "Zevin did a good job with what he had. . . . I just wish we had had a body." He smiled and walked away.

At 8:30 P.M. on that same evening, the jury returned with its verdict. After only four hours of deliberation, Thomas Busacca was found guilty of Manslaughter in the Second Degree. He was subsequently sentenced to not less than eight and one-third years and no more than twenty-five years in a state prison.

New York State now had a precedent case that would make its way into the law journals. Only one other case exists in the United States where a conviction had been obtained with out a corpus delecti and that occurred in the state of California.

IT ENDS. . . .

Epilogue

ON FRIDAY, NOVEMBER 21, 1980 at about 3:55 P.M., Detective Walker walked to his car that was parked in the employees lot at police headquarters. He had decided that he would drive out to the Hamptons and do some goose hunting over the weekend. As he maneuvered his 1972 red Torino through the rush-hour east-bound traffic, he was unaware of a drama that was unfolding in the town of Southampton. In fact it would not be until 8:15 A.M. the following morning that his intended itinerary would be shelved and some four years, two months and twenty-one days later, the Busacca case would once again come to the attention of the detective.

On Friday afternoon, at about 2 P.M. an off-duty Long Island Railroad Police Officer was enjoying the unseasonably mild weather of the day. As he walked the beach off Dune Road in Hampton Bays, with his dog playfully at his side, he saw a white sandal protruding from the sand. He casually walked over to it and kicked at it with his foot. To his horror the skeletal remains of a foot sprang forth, neatly in place in the sandal.

It was that newscast on the local news station that excited Walker. Since August 29, 1976, he had monitored most reports that he was aware of when they concerned the discovery of a female corpse. This was Florence Busacca. He was certain of it.

Hardly able to contain his glee, he telephoned the Homicide Office in Mineola. As coincidence would have it, Mike O'Connor was on duty.

"Mike! I think they've found Florence," said Walker, his buoyed mood translated in his voice.

"That right?" said O'Connor.

"Yeah. . . . I just heard a local station describing the discovery of a female body in the dunes in Hampton Bays, and by the description of what she was wearing, they're right on target."

"Where's the body now?" asked Mike.

"At the Suffolk County Medical Examiner's Morgue in Hauppauge," answered Walker. "They're carrying it as a 'who done it,' but I hope we have news for them."

"I'll get the case folder and a copy of that flier that we had sent out a long time ago. That'll describe what she was wearing. I'll call the morgue and get back to you."

"Okay, Mike, don't leave me hanging. I'll dress and be ready when you call. I'll meet you in Hauppauge."

Moments later, which seemed like an eternity, Mike called back. "It looks good, Roger, even to the rings on her finger. The body is missing an upper plate."

Walker had hardly put the phone back on the cradle before he was out the door and on his way to Hauppauge, some fifty miles away. His body was full of excitement and goose bumps. He hoped that Mike had remembered to sign him on duty since this was his day off.

Walker walked into the Medical Examiner's room where he spotted O'Connor and a couple of Suffolk County detectives and a white-smocked man whom he assumed to be the Medical Examiner. They were standing over a trundle that contained the skeletal remains of a human body. Walker approached cautiously, his excitement multiplying with each advancing step. There, as she had been so accurately described as to dress, was Florence Busacca with the black and white striped blouse, white slacks, white sandals and black hair, now matted with sand. Two rings, found in place on the skeletal finger matched exactly.

O'Connor and Walker now had to secure the dentures of Florence Busacca from the evidence locker in Mineola, and O'Connor would drive in and pick them up. Walker, in the meantime, notified Doctor Lowell Levine, the forensic expert who had testified at the trial and asked that he respond and make the identification.

At 3:30 P.M. the body of Florence Busacca was positively identified through dentures and X-rays. At 3:40 P.M. the children of Florence Busacca were notified that their mother's body had been found. To Geraldine and Larry it was as though a tremendous weight had been lifted from their shoulders. Now their mother could be given a Christian burial and family members and friends could pay their respects to the woman whom they had admired, loved and enjoyed.

Geraldine smiled as the long procession of limousines and private automobiles stretched as far as the eyes could see as they made their way toward St. Johns cemetery in Queens. Riding in the family car with Geraldine was her brother Larry, her grandfather, step-grandmother and Mr. John Sandhaas, the funeral director who was the father of young Larry's girlfriend.

Before the motorcade had reached the cemetery, Mr. Sandhaas removed a small box from his coat pocket and slowly handed it to the elder Busacca. He took it without a word and glanced furtively at it and nodded in the direction of the director. The elder Busacca had steadfastly wanted to believe that his son was innocent of the charges that had sent him to prison four years earlier. He slowly opened the small plain box and his body stiffened. His head lowered and the trace of a tear could be detected in the corner of his eye. He closed the box, clutched it for a long moment and peered out of the car window. He then placed it in the inside jacket and thanked the director. It was the wedding band and engagement ring that had been removed from his daughter-in-law's finger after her body was found.

When notified of the discovery of his wife's body Thomas Busacca simply said to the warden, "thank you," and walked away.

Thomas Busacca was released from prison in November 1986. He died in his father's home in Brooklyn of natural causes on February twenty-nine nineteen eighty-eight, the same date he killed his wife.